GAMES AND EMPIRES

MODERN SPORTS AND CULTURAL IMPERIALISM

"GAMES AND EMPIRES"

MODERN SPORTS AND CULTURAL IMPERIALISM

ALLEN GUTTMANN

COLUMBIA UNIVERSITY PRESS   NEW YORK

COLUMBIA UNIVERSITY PRESS

NEW YORK   CHICHESTER, WEST SUSSEX

COPYRIGHT © COLUMBIA UNIVERSITY PRESS

ALL RIGHTS RESERVED

Library of Congress Cataloging-in-Publication
Guttmann, Allen.
Games and empires : modern sports and cultural imperialism/Allen Guttmann.
p.   cm.
Includes bibliographical references (p.) and index.
ISBN 0-231-10042-6 (alk. paper)
1. Sports—Sociological aspects.
2. Sports—Cross-cultural studies.
3. Culture diffusion. I. Title
GV706.5.G88   1994   94-8868
306.4'83—dc20   CIP

Printed in the United States of America

C 10 9 8 7 6 5 4 3 2 1

TO HUGH HAWKINS AND WALTER RICHARD

CONTENTS

ACKNOWLEDGMENTS

My scholarly debts are many. Joseph L. Arbena, John Bale, Richard Cashman, Wolfgang Decker, Bernadette Deville-Dan-thu, Rolf Husmann, Wolf Krämer-Mandeau, Roland Renson, and Bart van Reusel have been especially generous in providing me with hard-to-find materials or information. John Bale, Maarten van Bottenburg, Wolfgang Decker, Dietrich Kurz, Tony Mason, Norbert Müller, Gerdtrud Pfister, Ruud Stokvis, and Victoria Saker Woeste invited me to speak on ludic diffusion and provided opportunities for stimulating discussion.

In the often frustrating quest for good illustrations, I have been helped by Vincent Casey, John A. Daly, George Kirsch,

Michael Krüger, Manfred Lämmer, Nicholas Priestnall, McDonald Sullivan, J.A. Mangan, Don Morrow, Marion Stell, Horst Überhorst, Gillian Unicomb, Erik de Vroede, Alfred Wahl, and Amanda Weaver.

Dean Ronald Rosbottom of Amherst College stretched the limits of budgetary discretion to contribute to the costs of research and photoreproduction. The interlibrary specialists of the college performed their usual miracles to borrow books for me and to obtain photocopies of articles from magazines of whose existence I was uncertain.

Der grösste Dank gehört der liebsten Helferin.

GAMES AND EMPIRES

MODERN SPORTS AND CULTURAL IMPERIALISM

INTRODUCTION:

THE INVENTION AND DIFFUSION OF MODERN SPORTS

Language provides a handy clue to cultural history. The frequent occurrence of French words in military parlance (*lieutenant, reconnaissance*) and of Italian terms in music (*aria, allegro*) are the linguistic residue of bygone political or artistic hegemony. Ignoring for the moment such exceptions as tennis and judo, we can say, with a bit of exaggeration, that the language of modern sports is English. German soccer fans shout their admiration for *einen guten Kicker* and French sprinters wait nervously in *le starting-block*. Latin Americans are wild about *fútbol*. The Japanese, too, attest to their modernity by a devotion to *supôtsu*. The peoples of the world have borrowed these and other sports terms from the English language because modern sports are to a large degree a British invention.[1] From the British Isles, modern sports went forth to conquer the world.

These introductory assertions about the British origins of modern sports are admittedly somewhat hyperbolic. After all, baseball, basketball, and volleyball were invented in the United States and disseminated by Americans rather than by Britons. The French also played an important part; the *Tour de France*, international cycling's premier event, created in 1903 by Henri Desgrange to boost the circulation of *L'Auto*, inspired the *Giro d'Italia* (1909) and a number of other grueling races.[2] (Linguistic evidence of French influence appears in the currency of terms like *vélodrome, peloton*, and *dérailleur*.) Nonetheless, from the eighteenth century until the middle of the twentieth, Great Britain's role in the development of modern sports was more important than that of any other nation. Not until after World War II did Americans finally supplant the British as the primary agents in the diffusion of modern sports.

The key phrase—"modern sports"—needs clarification. It does not refer merely to recent innovations like soccer and basketball. As I have argued in earlier books,[3] modern sports are best defined not by some specific chronology but rather by the presence or absence of a distinctive set of systematically interrelated formal-structural characteristics. These characteristics, which appear most clearly when modern sports are analyzed in schematic contrast to traditional physical contests, can be summarized as follows:

1. SECULARISM: despite their tendency to become ritualized and to arouse strong emotions, modern sports are not related—as premodern sports often were—to some transcendent realm of the numinous or sacred;
2. EQUALITY: modern sports require, at least in theory, that no one be excluded from participation on the basis of

ascriptive traits (such as race or ethnicity) and that the rules of the game be the same for all participants;

3. BUREAUCRATIZATION: modern sports are typically governed neither by priestly conclaves nor by ritual adepts but rather by national and transnational bureaucracies (of which the United States Olympic Committee and the *Fédération Internationale de Football Association* are examples);

4. SPECIALIZATION: many modern sports have evolved, like rugby, soccer, baseball, and American football, from earlier, less differentiated games, and many, like cricket, baseball, and football, have a gamut of specialized roles and playing positions;

5. RATIONALIZATION: the rules of modern sports are constantly scrutinized and undergo frequent revision from a means-ends point of view; athletes train scientifically, employ technologically advanced equipment, and strive for the most efficient employment of their skills;

6. QUANTIFICATION: in modern sports, as in almost every other aspect of our lives, we live in a world of numbers; the "stats" have become an apparently indispensable part of the game;

7. THE OBSESSION WITH RECORDS: the unsurpassed quantified achievement, which is what we mean by "record" in this uniquely modern usage, is a constant challenge to all who strive to surpass it and thereby to achieve a modern version of immortality.

Men, women, and children have always run races; the seven formal-structural characteristics presented here in simplified schematic form distinguish the 200-meter event contested at Barcelona in 1992 from the races run at ancient Olympia, in medieval London, or among the Timbira Indians of twentieth-century Brazil. When I refer to the diffusion of modern sports, I mean not only the worldwide adoption of a game like soccer but also the modernization of traditional sports, like Afghan buzkashi,[4] to bring them into conformity with these seven formal-structural characteristics.

The *reasons* given for the evolution of modern sports and for the primacy first of Great Britain and then of the United States are maddeningly complex and much disputed. Sports historians who agree quite amiably about the dominant role played by Britons and Americans disagree emphatically about the relative weight to be given to such factors as capitalist development,[5] industrialization,[6] urbanization,[7] and the scientific-technological revolution nurtured in seventeenth-century England by the Royal Society for the Advancement of Science and brought to maturity in the modern university.[8] It should be quite enough for my present purposes to insist that the formal-structural characteristics of modern sports distinguish them from earlier forms of physical competition, to observe that most modern sports did, in fact, originate in Britain and the United States, to examine the process of ludic[9] diffusion that distributed these sports across the entire globe, and—finally—to hazard some explanations and assessments.

Explanation and assessment are difficult tasks that I propose to delay until I complete my exploration of the historical data, but some preliminary remarks are in order. The ideological currents are treacherous and a glance at the map may allow a safer voyage through some choppy waters. In an important collection of essays entitled *Géopolitique du sport*, Claude Hurtebize has observed that the global diffusion of modern sports occurred at the same time as "the constitution of world markets and colonial empires."[10] Was it entirely a coincidence that Great Britain, the imperial power that seized the lion's share of colonial booty, was the foremost country in the development of modern sports? Surely not. Johan Galtung notes suggestively that the "massive export of [modern] sports" from developed to undeveloped areas followed "old colonial trade and control lines . . . into the last little corner of the world."[11] The cricket grounds in Bombay and Calcutta are as much the relics of British rule as the Red Fort in Delhi. What can be more obvious than to see not coincidence but causation and to conclude, therefore, that modern sports abetted the imperial expansion that carried them to the ends of the earth? The imperialists themselves insisted upon causal connections. An anonymous contributor to the *Cambridge University Magazine* for June of 1886 underscored the point:

> Politicians work out grand schemes with treaties and conventions to bind us and our colonies . . . but . . . we may also venture to say that a visit of a Canadian crew to Henley . . . will bind us and our cousins of the tongue far more closely than any amounts of diplomacy and trade convention."[12]

Similar sentiments came from the elite secondary schools. "In the history of the British Empire," proclaimed the Reverend J. E. C. Welldon, headmaster of Harrow School from 1881 to 1895, "it is written that England has owed her sovereignty to her sports."[13] Theirs were but two voices in the imperialist chorus.

Numerous scholars have taken Welldon and his jingoist peers at their word. Peter Rummelt, for instance, has characterized the spread of modern sports throughout Africa as nothing more or less than colonialism at work.[14] From the Marxist perspective that Rummelt shares with many other scholars, the Ibo tribesman who once wrestled to the beat of tribal drums and now harkens to the whistle of a soccer referee is as much a victim of colonialism as the Sudanese woman who gives her child the bottle instead of the breast. Other specialists in sports studies, influenced by the writings of André Gunder Frank and Fernando Henrique Cardoso[15] or by those of Immanuel Wallerstein[16], see the global expansion of modern sports as a hitherto neglected aspect of the "development of dependence" on the periphery of the "world system."[17] Still others, equally convinced that the displacement of traditional indigenous pastimes by modern sports has been a cultural disaster, have written in

Gramscian terms of the "hegemony" of Western sports.[18] The theoretical orchestration differs, the thematic lament for the actual or threatened extinction of traditional indigenous sports is the same.

Although the concept has become a little threadbare from overuse, hegemony is probably the most accurate term for the British and American dominance of the process of ludic diffusion because modern sports have always been "contested terrain." Antonio Gramsci—whose interest in sports was close to nil—revived the Greek word *egemonia* in his Prison Notebooks in order to emphasize the fact that political relationships between the rulers and the ruled cannot be characterized as simply the result of absolute domination by the former and absolute submission by the latter. The most stable form of rule is one in which the strong (who are never all-powerful) have their way only after the weak (who are never completely powerless) have their say.[19]

Despite the intellectual advantages of Gramsci's concept, which is as applicable in the realm of culture as in the world of politics, most discussions of ludic diffusion refer not to *cultural hegemony* but rather to *cultural imperialism*, which John Tomlinson usefully defines as "a form of domination . . . not just in the political and economic spheres but also over those practices by which collectivities make sense of their lives."[20] Although I intend briefly, in my conclusion, to return to the concept of cultural hegemony, I shall for the moment speak of cultural imperialism because it is the more frequently employed concept and because it enables me to formulate a complex question in relatively simple, relatively familiar terms: Can the diffusion of modern sports from Europe and the United States to the rest of the world be considered a form of cultural imperialism?

The concept of cultural imperialism is relatively familiar, but my question may nonetheless seem odd because mainstream scholarly discourse has seldom alluded to the domain of sports. One focus has been on artistic—especially literary—expression. Long before anyone coined the term "cultural imperialism," Romantic writers like Ralph Waldo Emerson complained about British influences on American habits. He boldly proclaimed that every nation needs its own language and literature. Although Emerson announced in "The American Scholar" that we had "listened too long to the courtly muses of Europe," he nonetheless thought that a distinctively *American* kind of English was an appropriate medium to express what he called—in *Nature*—"an original relation to the universe."[21] In our time, however, major postcolonial authors like Chinua Achebe and Léopold Senghor have been criticized by their countrymen for continuing to write and publish in English and French. Is the criticism valid? Does the continued use of the colonizer's language condemn the politically independent writer to cultural servitude? James Ngugi, concluding that it did, Africanized his name and repudiated the language in which he had written *The River Between* (1965) and a number of other vivid dramatizations of tribal life. As Ngugi wa Thiongo, he published *Decolonising the Mind* (1986), "which records his farewell to English as well as his attempt to further the cause of liberation by exploring African language and literature."[22]

It is not sufficient, however, for the formerly colonized writer to shun the colonizer's language. Literary forms developed in the West have shaped the work of writers everywhere. Modern Japanese novelists like Jun'ichirô Tanizaki and "postmodernist" Indian fabulists like Salmon Rushdie have allowed their imaginations to be shaped by the genres of European and American literature. Are these genres inappropriate for non-Western cultures? Have artists like Tanizaki and Rushdie betrayed their cultural birthright for a mess of verbiage? The question has been hotly but inconclusively debated.[23]

Language and literature have been one theme in the discourse about cultural imperialism; the mass media have been another. In the last twenty years, a great deal of theoretical and empirical work has emphasized Western control of the international system of information and communication.[24] Numerous mass-media studies have alleged that four Western news agencies—the Associated Press, United Press International, Reuters, and Agence France-Presse—determine the content and dominate the dissemination of what these agencies deem to be the world's news. The Associated Press and UPI, for instance, provide 50 percent of the international news published in Latin American newspapers. The information supplied is mostly news of the United States and Europe. How could it be otherwise when, in the seventies, the major agencies stationed 34 percent of their correspondents in the United States, 28 percent in Europe—and only 4 percent in Africa?[25] The radio spectrum, which has a limited number of frequencies, is dominated by Western stations. Tanzanians seeking information about events in neighboring Kenya listen to BBC broadcasts emanating from London. Empirical studies have also documented the percentage of American and European films in the world's movie theaters; in 1974, for example, 90 percent of all the films shown in Thailand came from the United States.[26] Laws limiting the number of American films screened in Europe are a source of friction between the United States and some of its closest allies. Many studies have demonstrated that New York's global hegemony *vis-à-vis* prime-time television has been almost as extensive as Hollywood's dominance of cinema screens.[27]

In reaction to this state of affairs, a majority of UNESCO, members, led by Amadur Mahta M'Bow of Senegal, called for a "New World Information and Communication Order" under which the dissemination of information was to be "balanced."[28] From a Marxist perspective, criticism of "imbalance" was too mild. Herbert Schiller condemned "cultural domination" and asked, rhetorically, "What does it matter if a national movement has struggled for years to achieve liberation if that condition, once gained, is undercut by values and aspirations derived from the apparently vanquished dominator?"[29] Anthony Smith, analyzing global disparities in the flow of information, was almost as pessimistic: "Those cultures," he concluded, "which are condemned to be the observed rather than the observers may in this, as in other matters, turn out to be not the beneficiaries of modernity, but rather the victims."[30]

Why should modern sports not be studied as intensely—under the rubric of cultural imperialism—as language, literature, and the mass media? Cricket tests are the passion of thousands of West Indians who have never read a line of Derek Walcott's poetry. Soccer football is played in venues still unreached by the Associated Press, UPI, Reuters, and Agence France-Presse. Basketball is popular even among people who prefer Indian films to American ones. If Marxist scholars can unmask Donald Duck as an agent of American imperialism[31], is it not high time that we ask some serious questions about Babe Ruth?

In asking serious questions, it is important that we emulate the best of the media studies and not lapse into ideologically fomented tirades about Donald Duck and "the imperial-patriarchal unconscious."[32] It is also important to realize at the outset that the colonized indigenes of Africa, Asia, and Latin America have not been the only peoples who have been induced to abandon their traditional forms of physical culture. In the industrialized "core" as well as in the agrarian "periphery," in Europe and in the United States as well as in the Third World, modern sports have displaced traditional ones. Consider, for instance, the careers of Flemish and Dutch cyclists like Eddy Merckx and Joop Zoetemelk. Spurning the communal pleasures of *klinkslaan* and *kolf* (games similar to croquet and ice hockey), Merckx and Zoetemelk sought and achieved international fame on the *Tour de France*, a contest invented in 1903 by the French journal *L'Auto* and sponsored today by a medley of multinational corporations. Were the cyclists any different, in principle, from the urban Zulu and the Papua New Guineans who have taken enthusiastically to soccer football?[33] Is the gradual disappearance of *maabza* among the Berbers of Morocco more deplorable than the fate of the nearly extinct Swiss game of *Hornuss*?

I propose to offer some answers to rhetorical questions such as these, but I am reluctant to do so before I have charted in some detail the course of ludic diffusion. Its twists and turns fascinate me; they may interest others. Since no scholar knows enough to narrate the story of every modern sport's reception in every part of the world, since few readers can be expected to have the patience to read through such an encyclopedic account if one were written, I have opted for selective narration—how *some* modern sports have been diffused to *some* more or less representative places. Having recently been faulted for saying too little about Gladys Palmer in a history of women's sports from Egypt's Queen Hatshepsut (15th century B.C.) to America's Florence Griffith-Joyner (20th century A.D.), I realize that some readers will be offended by my neglect of their favorite sports. To them I offer my proleptic apologies and a sad admission: I haven't traced the trajectory of my favorite sports either.

What, then, *have* I done? I have investigated and briefly described (1) the introduction of cricket into societies as different as the United States and India, (2) the arrival of soccer football in a number of European, Latin American, and African nations, (3) the export of baseball to Japan, the Caribbean, and Australia, (4) the spread of basketball to the Far East and to Western Europe, (5) the recent invasion of the European sports market by the National Football League, and (6) the global expansion of the Olympic Games from their European birthplace. These six chapters constitute part I: Diffusion. In them, I comment not only on geographical diffusion from nation to nation, which is my main focus, but also on the diffusion of modern sports from one social class to another. Where my sources permit, I also refer to some of the early attempts by women to gain access to what most people considered to be men's sports. In these chapters, my emphasis is on team games rather than individual sports because team games require more of a collective commitment than individual sports do, and they seem to evoke a more intense collective psychological identification.

Since the diffusion of modern sports has met prolonged resistance as well as quick acceptance, part II is a consideration of (1) the German and Slavic attempts to fashion nationalistic alternatives to the internationalism of modern sports and (2) the efforts of anthropologists, folklorists, historians, and political activists to preserve or revive traditional sports. In addition to what I hope is its intrinsic historical interest, the narration of parts I and II is intended to provide a data base—or less pretentiously expressed, a set of exemplary case studies—for the argument that follows in part III. My final chapter consists of what I believe are plausible generalizations (although I fear they may ruffle some ideological feathers). At any rate, part III is my best answer to the central question: Is the diffusion of modern sports from Great Britain and the United States an instance of cultural imperialism?

I

DIFFUSION

1

CRICKET

ORIGINS OF THE GAME

ENGLAND Cricket is a very old game whose origins are quite obscure. The earliest documentary evidence of the game derives from the late thirteenth century, during the reign of Edward I, when expenses for a prototype of cricket seem to have been responsible for a Latin notation in his son Prince Edward's wardrobe accounts for 1299–1300. What else can be meant by the amount disbursed for "*Creag et alios ludos*"? More certain is the mention of cricket—or *criquet*—in a French document from 1478. The reference was to a game played near the Flemish town of St. Omer.[1] (The town may have been linked to England by trade in cloth.) In 1598, John Derrick of Guildford, then fifty-nine years old, testified that "he and diverse of his fellowes [at school] did runne and play there at creckett and other plaies."[2] Allusions to cricket became frequent in the seventeenth century. When Oliver Cromwell sought to extend English power over Irish Catholics, he behaved in accordance with our stereotypes about Puritanism and pleasure; the invading army's depredations included the destruction of "all bats and balls in Dublin."[3] After the demise of Cromwell and the Puritan Commonwealth he ruled, the sports of "merry England" made their comeback. It confirms one's image of the Restoration to discover that members of the court amused themselves at "the cricket match at Dicker."[4]

About the details of the match at Dicker we know almost as little as about the medieval game of "creag." Specific information about the rules of cricket dates from the eighteenth century when, for instance, the dimensions of the bat and the pitch were determined and niceties like the leg-before-wicket prohibition were mentioned. The first complete set of rules appeared in 1744, which was also the first year from which we have records of a fully scored match. From southeastern England the game spread to the north and west.[5] In 1787, Thomas Lord and a number of other enthusiasts began an organization that became the Marylebone Cricket Club—the game's most authoritative institution.

Early in the nineteenth century, John Nyren, cricket's first great player-chronicler, reported crowds of 20,000 spectators. "Half the county would be present, and all their hearts with us."[6] Cricket was popular among rural Englishmen of every social class. The squire bowled, his tenants batted, the world was in order (at least until the last wicket was taken). The game was played not only on village greens but also at the "public schools" to which the nobility and the *haute bourgeoisie* sent their sons. The game became "a regular part of the life of Etonians, Wykehamists, and Westministers."[7]

Before the end of the eighteenth century, a number of village teams were formed for women to play the game. On Godsden Common, near Guilford in Surrey, on July 26, 1745, eleven maids of Bramley met a team from Hambleton

> dressed all in white. The Bramley maids had blue ribbons and the [Hambleton] maids red ribbons on their heads. The Bramley girls got 119 notches and the Hambleton girls 127. There was of both sexes the greatest number that ever was seen on such an occasion. The girls bowled, batted, ran and catched as well as most men could do in that game.

Only two years earlier, the *London General Advertiser* for July 14th referred to a kind of tournament at the Artillery Ground, Finnsbury, to which women's teams from several Sussex villages were invited. In the decades that followed, *The Times* and *The Sporting Magazine* reported a number of other cricket matches between the women of neighboring villages or between the married women and the maidens of a single country town. There seems to have been a hiatus in women's cricket during the early part of the nineteenth century, but there was a strong revival in the sixties and seventies when girls' schools and the newly founded women's colleges of Oxford and Cambridge adopted the game. Indeed, the spread of cricket among the women was rapid enough for *Punch* to speculate with weak humor that it was "all over with men. They had better make up their minds to rest contented with croquet, and afternoon tea, and sewing machines, and perhaps an occasional game at drawing-room billiards." *Cricket*, a magazine whose readership probably came from the same echelons of British society as *Punch*, managed to be more supportive: "The New Woman is taking up cricket, evidently with the same energy which has characterized her in other and more important spheres of life."[8] Toward the end of the century, women's cricket lost ground to field hockey, but the game continues to be played by at least a few women wherever English is spoken.

NORTH AMERICA In the eighteenth and nineteenth centuries, the British expelled the French from Canada and from India and extended their rule over much of the African continent. To the ends of the earth, cricket followed the flag. Early in the twentieth century, P. F. "Plum" Warner, president of the Marylebone Cricket Club, explained that the MCC's beloved sport

> has become more than a game. It is an institution, a passion, one might say a religion. It has got into the blood of the nation, and wherever British men and women are gathered together there will the stumps be pitched.[12]

Warner was right. From the remnants of wickets and bats, future archaeologists of material culture will be able to reconstruct the boundaries of the British Empire.

While the British colonists of North America certainly played cricket, we will never know the exact moment when the first ball was bowled to the first batter. By the eighteenth century, the game was quite popular among Southern aristocrats. William Byrd of Westover, the Virginian planter, recorded ruefully in his diary for February 20, 1710, that he "played at cricket" and sprained his "backside."[10] A generation later, Benjamin West painted *The Cricketers* (1763), a group portrait of five young aristocratic players: James Allen, Andrew Allen, and Ralph Wormley were Virginians; Ralph Izard and Arthur Middleton were South Carolinians. They pose proudly with their cricket bats (and Middleton's dog). Affluent New Yorkers also played the game. In the sixties, James Rivington's *Gazette* advertised cricket balls (along with battledores, shuttlecocks, and tennis rackets).[11]

The end of British rule over the thirteen colonies and the emigration of thousands of "Loyalists" hampered but did not halt the spread of cricket. A few years after the revolution, the game was played on the seaboard and as far west as Kentucky. There was a burst of cricketing activity in the Jacksonian period, but the action seems to have been concentrated in the Whiggish centers of commerce rather than among the frontiersmen who supported "Old Hickory" (who was, for his part, far keener about horse races and cockfights than about cricket matches). The St. George Cricket Club was founded in Manhattan in 1838 and Chicago had three clubs by 1840, when the town was less than a decade old. The Newark Cricket Club was organized in 1845; the British consul in San Francisco launched a club in 1852, in the midst of the gold rush, but Pennsylvanian fields proved the most receptive.[12]

Although English immigrants working in Philadelphia's textile industry played the game in the thirties, the "take-off" came a decade later when the city's mercantile upper class became involved. Robert Waller, an English merchant who had helped to found Manhattan's St. George Cricket Club, moved to Philadelphia and organized the Union Club (1843). At the banquet following an 1843 match between the two teams, Waller offered a toast: "Cricket, a sturdy plant indigenous to England; let us prove that it can be successfully transplanted to American soil."[13] Waller did more than swing a mean bat and lift a hopeful glass. He encouraged young William Rotch Wister, who had learned the rudiments of the game from James Thorp, another English immigrant, to organize a cricket club for his fellow students at the University of Pennsylvania. The students hired still another Englishman, William Bradshaw, to coach them. Both of these early clubs expired after Waller returned to New York and Wister left the university, but Wister filled the gap by organizing the prestigious Philadelphia Cricket Club in 1854. That same year, he encouraged the formation of a club in nearby Germantown. Younger boys, whom the older ones excluded from play, pelted the Germantown cricketers with apples and then, less aggressively, appealed for assistance to Wister's wealthy father and to "Sugar King" Thomas A. Newhall. "The two gentlemen supported the youngsters' desire to play cricket, and Newhall invited them to play on his property."[14] All went well and the Young America Cricket Club was born in 1855.

Most of the bowlers and batsmen on the greens of New York and Philadelphia were of British stock if they were not actually immigrants from the British Isles. Their enthusiasm peaked in 1859 when the All-England Eleven toured the United States, playing games in New York, Hoboken, Philadelphia, and Rochester. When the Pennsylvanians took the field against the All-England Eleven, thirteen of the twenty-one teammates were American born. In his 1860 publication, *The English Cricketers' Trip*, Frederick Lillywhite proclaimed optimistically that "cricket in Philadelphia has every prospect of becoming [the] national game,"[15] but it was obviously not to be. The best efforts of British merchants, aided by new tours in 1868 and 1872, were insufficient to woo Americans away from their love affair with baseball.

One reason for cricket's failure to hold its ground was the game's prominent ethnic identification. The English aura that made the game especially attractive to immigrants from East Anglia and Yorkshire and to the Anglophiles of Philadelphia sullied it in Irish-American (and German-American) eyes. The social pretensions of the mostly upper-middle-class cricket players also detracted from the game's popularity. Philadelphia's clubs, for instance, were dominated by merchants and professional men. "Very few club members worked in blue-collar occupations."[16] In 1870, 57.3% of the members lived in the posh Rittenhouse Square area and 17.6% in Germantown and Chestnut Hill. All four of the prestigious cricket clubs—the Philadelphia, the Germantown, the New Merion, and the Belmont—were located on the commuter railways that linked the affluent suburbs to the central city. After the bloody hiatus of the Civil War, baseball flourished and quickly came to be perceived as "the national game" while cricket, which had briefly rivaled baseball in popularity, languished in the relative obscurity of its Pennsylvanian enclaves. The anglophile elite kept the game alive for another generation, but theirs was a lost cause.[17]

Cricket put down deeper roots in Canada than it did south of the 49th parallel. "The game of the English landed aristocracy," wrote Alan Metcalfe, was "transmitted to the 'colonial' elite."[18] British soldiers had played the game in the eighteenth century and continued to take wickets and score runs throughout the nineteenth. Military men introduced the game in Toronto and they were an especially important factor in establishing it in Montreal, "the birthplace of Canadian sport."[19] In 1829, soldiers from the Montreal garrison, whose presence was required to convince the recently vanquished *Canadiens* of the permanence of British rule, joined the city's ethnically British civilian upper class to form the Montreal Cricket Club. It may well be that consciousness of their minority status in the midst of the French Canadians intensified the anglophones' desire to flaunt their ethnic identity with an unmistakably British game. (The French Canadians were, in general, much less enthusiastic about modern sports. A few of them were active in organizations like the Montreal Snow Shoe Club, but the century's most famous *athlète canadien* was Louis Cyr, the prodigious sideshow strongman.[20])

Montreal may have been the birthplace of Canadian sports, but Toronto and the other culturally British cities of Ontario brought modern sports to their maturity. In the later phases of cricket's development, soldiers played a smaller part than educators. Elite schools like Toronto's Upper Canada College, which officially adopted cricket in 1836, made sure that the boys were—in the words of their collegiate newspaper—"taught to play what, as British subjects, we regard as our national game!"[21] The boys must have been taught to play reasonably well; the year the college's team was formed it defeated eleven adults representing the Toronto Cricket Club (which had been founded two years earlier). In 1847, the school's team, which now included a number of alumni, vanquished an eleven composed of "gentlemen" from the entire Province of Upper Canada.[22]

The Victorian schoolmaster's attitude toward his pupils' involvement in cricket was expressed with exemplary clarity by Edward Thring, the games-mad headmaster of England's Uppingham School, in a letter to his equally games-mad Canadian counterpart, George Parkin. Cricket, he opined, was "the greatest bond of the English-speaking race."[23] The bond was strengthened in 1859 when an English team toured Canada. By that time, nearly three score cricket clubs dotted the vast expanse of British Canada.

As a summer pastime, cricket began to lose ground to lacrosse, a game derived from Native American stickball. In an 1867 article propagandistically entitled "The National Game" and published in the year of Canada's confederation, George Beers touted the advantages of lacrosse: "As cricket, wherever played by Britons, is a link of loyalty to bind them to their home so may Lacrosse be to Canadians. We may yet find it will do as much for our young Dominion as the Olympian games did for Greece or cricket for our Motherland."[24] Lacrosse, incorporated into Canada's Dominion Day celebrations, was promoted by an appropriately nationalistic motto: "Our country and our game." The campaign to popularize lacrosse was so successful that it became, for a time, "Canada's most popular team sport."[25]

Baseball, too, made inroads, especially among the Canadian working class. The first team, the Hamilton (Ontario) Young Canadians, appeared in 1854 when the Great Western Railway opened its main line from Niagara Falls to Hamilton, London, and Windsor. The railroad made it relatively easy to stage interurban contests. Within a few years, Hamilton alone had seventeen baseball teams. A short-lived Canadian Association of Baseball Players was formed in 1864.[26] The association expired, but the game it promoted continued to spread. On August 19, 1869, the Montreal *Gazette* reported that baseball "is gradually getting to be very popular amongst our young men."[27] In the Seventies and Eighties, Canadian teams like the London Tecumseh Redmen and the Guelph Maple Leafs joined with their American counterparts as members of the International Base Ball Association. The impetus for these minor-league forerunners of the Montreal Expos and the Toronto Blue Jays came less from expansionist American dreams of "manifest destiny" than from "mutual consent and Canadian solicitation."[28]

While proponents of cricket and lacrosse complained about unwanted Yankee intrusion, in the long run the cultural influence of the United States was too powerful to resist. Cricket survived, along with lacrosse and rugby, as one of the favorite sports of upper-class "empire loyalists." Governors-general, like Frederick Temple, Earl of Dufferin, supported the game as a means to preserve a sense of imperial unity, but baseball, which attracted the French as well as the British Canadians, became the only game played by all Canadian social classes.[29] By 1900 at the latest, it was "Canada's most popular sport."[30]

AUSTRALIA If ethnicity is one of the key factors in the process of ludic diffusion, then one might expect cricket to have flourished "down under," where a large majority of the entire population claims British ancestry. Cricket has, indeed, despite early challenges from Australian Rules Football and later ones from basketball and American baseball, not only flourished but also contributed importantly to the Australian sense of national identity. Reciprocally, conceptions of national character influenced the ethos of the Australian version of the game. Priding themselves on "outback" egalitarianism, the Australians abandoned the gentleman-player distinction that divided English cricket teams along class lines. It would in any event have been difficult to concoct dignified visions of strict social hierarchy when farmers and their cows shared the rustic atmosphere of the Australian cricket pitch.[31]

The game was played in Sydney in the first years of the nineteenth century, some fifteen years after the settlement of New

South Wales. The town's first clubs—the Military Cricket Club and the Australian Cricket Club—were both founded, in 1826, "in consequence of pressure from the army and navy garrison."[32] In 1838, clubs were founded in both Melbourne and Adelaide.[33] Rivalry among these three cities contributed to the diffusion of the game throughout New South Wales, Victoria, and South Australia. When the novelist Anthony Trollope published *British Sports and Pastimes* (1868), he commented approvingly on the Australian's passion for cricket.

In Adelaide, settled in 1836 as a model middle-class community and not as a penal colony, sports were a daily reminder that South Australia was "a new Britannia in the Antipodes." Francis Dutton reported, in 1846, that "All the British sports are kept up with much spirit in the colony; hunting, [horse] racing and in a less degree cricket are, in the proper seasons much patronized."[34] When Adelaide's St. Peter's College opened its doors in 1847 to the sons of the colonial gentry, it was cricket—not hunting and certainly not horse racing—that was emphasized. Interest in scholastic sports became a mania after 1854, when Cambridge-educated George Farr took the helm as headmaster. At St. Peter's as at the other colonial counterparts to Great Britain's "public schools," cricket seemed the ideal means to inculcate the rugged doctrines of "muscular Christianity." "When the 'All England Eleven' visited Adelaide in 1877 the whole school received two half-holidays to witness the game."[35] By the end of the century, Adelaide's girls' schools—Unley Park (1855), Hardwicke (1882), St. Peter's Collegiate School for Girls (1894), Tormore House (1898)—had cricket teams. Upper-class girls in Sydney and Melbourne were also instructed in bowling, batting, fielding, and instinctively discriminating between what was and what was *not* cricket. At Melbourne's Methodist Ladies' College, for instance, the young women were divided in 1891 into two teams, the "Kangaroos" and the "Possums," for intramural cricket.[36]

Adult women played the game as early as 1886, when Nellie Gregory led the Siroccos in a match against the Fernleas, captained by her sister Lily. Although the encounter was staged to raise money for charity, which "presumably reduced the potential for criticism," the *Sydney Mail* lamented the indecent spectacle and deprecated the possibility of a repetition. There were other matches, but female "cricketers could not be taken seriously."[37] The reason, of course, was the conviction, then current and still with us, that *serious* sports are a masculine domain. Cricket, which many Americans consider to be a rather effete upper-class tea-and-crumpets pastime, was celebrated "down under" as a symbol of egalitarian male vigor.

If the ability unflinchingly to defend one's wicket was indeed indicative of one's virility, all the more reason to challenge the English, who were not above condescending comments on the physical decadence of colonial populations. International matches began when an English team led by H. H. Stephenson docked at Melbourne on December 24, 1861. The visitors vanquished their hosts and left them with renewed determination to master the sport. The Australians received another lesson and the game another boost in 1873–74 when W. G. Grace toured Australia with a group of English cricketers. Large crowds gathered to see the man who was, then as now, the most famous cricket player of all time. When Grace returned home, two members of his team—Charles Lawrence and William Caffyn—stayed in Australia to coach clubs in Sydney and Melbourne. They must have done their work well. In 1877, Charles Bannerman led the Australian team to its first victory in a Test against a visiting English side. A year later, a team of Australians made the arduous voyage back to the home counties and managed to defeat the representatives of what was then (and still is) the very symbol of the English game—the Marylebone Cricket Club. The triumph occurred at Lord's, the MCC's home ground, despite the best efforts of the redoubtable Dr. Grace.[38]

The happy victors were not, however, the first cricket team to venture from Australia to the British Isles. Although their departure was illegal, thirteen aborigines left Lake Wallace in Western Victoria in the summer of 1868, evaded the colonial authorities, sailed to England, and challenged all comers. Playing against a variety of teams, but not against a representative national side, the aborigines won fourteen games, lost fourteen, and drew seventeen. (While abroad, the natives also gave exhibitions of prowess with spears and boomerangs.) Had they been better informed about life in the colonies, the British hosts might not have been as surprised as they were by their visitors' remarkable cricketing skills. Ten years earlier, a team of aborigines had easily defeated the best of Port Lincoln's white players.[39]

While the aboriginal cricketers have been forgotten by most Australians, collective memory has enshrined another antipodean team. Four years after Bannerman's team defeated the English at home, another group of Australian invaders duplicated the feat and stimulated the *Sporting Times* (London) to add a legend to the history of sport. The newspaper printed a mock obituary:

> In Affectionate Remembrance of English Cricket
> Which died at the Oval on 29th August, 1882,
> Deeply lamented by a large circle of sorrowing
> friends and acquaintances.
> R.I.P.
> N.B. The body will be cremated and the ashes
> taken to Australia.[40]

Since then, the "Ashes," physically represented by a large silver urn, have symbolized victory in a Test between England and Australia.

"Beating them at their own game" became a tradition, and great players able to accomplish the feat—like Victor Trumper and Donald Bradman—became heroic figures in the history of

Australian sports. As William Mandle has astutely noted, cricketing victories over the English were prized above other triumphs because they simultaneously affirmed Australia's membership in the British Empire ("we play the same game you do") and flaunted Australia's superior prowess ("we're better at it than you are").[41] Quite a number of Australian players, men like J. J. Ferris and William Midwinter, played for England in some Tests and for Australia in others; they became living symbols of shared culture and world-class achievement.[42]

The emotional stakes involved in a Test Series were never more obvious than during the "bodyline controversy" of 1932–33. The team sent to Australia by the Marylebone Cricket Club was led by Douglas Robert Jardine, a graduate of Winchester School and New College (Oxford), a solicitor, and a regular player for Surrey. When Jardine was appointed captain, a British pundit commented lugubriously, "Well, we shall win the Ashes—but we may lose a Dominion."[43] The problem was that Jardine seemed to bowl *at* the opposing batsmen rather than *to* them in the approved manner. Pelham Warner, the manager of the MCC's team, complained of Jardine, "When he sees a cricket field with an Australian on it, he goes mad."[44] (Some have noted, in defense of Jardine, that he had been severely and in his mind unfairly heckled during an earlier tour of Australia.) Despite the doubts about Jardine's fitness as captain, the tour proceeded. It did not go well. After the Australian batsmen had suffered a number of injuries, the Australian Cricket Board protested and received an imperially dismissive response from the MCC: "We the Marylebone Cricket Club deplore your cable message and deprecate the opinion that there has been unsportsmanlike play."[45] The controversy raged in the press of both countries and the Secretary of State for South Australia personally visited with the Secretary of State for the Dominions in an effort to calm the waters. Before the series was concluded, the prime minister was involved and "the relatively simple fact of two Australian batsmen being struck by an English bowler had grown into a major imperial problem at the highest political levels."[46] In retrospect, we can see that cricket, which had been a highly valued common bond between the "home counties" and "down under," eventually aroused fiercely nationalistic emotions that fortified the Australians' sense of a separate identity.[47]

THE CARIBBEAN Something similar can be said for the various islands that were once the British West Indies. Although political union foundered on the reef of insular nationalism, the former colonies were still able to field a unified cricket team, one that represented racial rather than national pride.

The British, who never constituted more than a small fraction of the islands' population, brought the game to the Caribbean for their own amusement. Among the first clubs were St. Ann's on the island of Barbados (1806) and the Trinidad Cricket Club (before 1842).[48] On Barbados, commonly referred to as "Little England," three "public schools" attended to the education of the white and black elites: Harrison College, The Lodge, and Combermere. The masters, no different from those in other outposts of empire, emphasized team sports in general and cricket in particular. As a result of their efforts, cricket became "not so much a game which inspires enthusiasm as a cultural institution, a way of life."[49] Schoolmasters like Edward B. Knapp were so successful in propagating the "games ethic" that, when the black lower classes took up the game in the twentieth century, "the codes and standards to which they aspired were those established and maintained by the culturally dominant cricketing products of the elite schools."[50]

At first, the adult members of the racially exclusive British clubs were annoyed rather than pleased that islanders of African and Asian ancestry were beginning to imitate "their betters," but the pressures of competition persuaded some clubs to recruit "colored" bowlers whose superior skills seemed indispensable when the outcome of a contest really mattered. When black and brown players began to surpass white ones at batting as well as bowling, pressure grew to include them in Tests against English, Australian, and Indian elevens. The selection committee bowed to necessity and began to name black West Indians like Learie Constantine to the representative eleven. When Constantine played in league cricket for the English town of Nelson, he enjoyed "the adulation of the local white population,"[51] but, back home, racially motivated resistance to the inclusion of non-whites lingered well beyond the middle of the twentieth century. Long after white players had become a minority on the West Indian cricket team, they insisted on reserving the captaincy for one of their own.[52] Black men, they felt, were good chaps with a bat but not quite up to demands of leadership.

The social tensions of the game can be studied in C. L. R. James's autobiographical account of West Indian cricket, *Beyond a Boundary* (1963). Born into Trinidad's black middle class, James claimed "Puritanism and cricket" as his twofold inheritance. By the time that he passed the entrance examination and was admitted to Government College, it had been drummed into him by his parents and teachers that hard study was the ladder to higher status, but the "first temptation was cricket and I succumbed without a struggle." Unlike John Bunyan, the seventeenth-century Puritan author of *Pilgrim's Progress*, who suffered pangs of guilt because he had been seduced by the pleasures of "a game at cat,"[53] James had no reason to regret his ardor for sports. By means of schoolboy cricket, he tells us, he was indoctrinated in the code of fair play. His subsequent discovery of Marxism made no difference. Orthodox Marxists ridiculed the liberal credo of "fairness and good sportsmanship," which they characterized as a typically liberal fixation on the rules of play when the true revolutionary's task was to change bourgeois society's inherently unfair game.

James felt differently. "I learnt [the code of fair play] as a boy, I have obeyed it as a man and now can no longer laugh at it." Visiting the United States, James was astonished and dismayed at the lack of sportsmanship he witnessed among baseball's unmannerly spectators:

> I didn't know how deeply the early attitudes had been ingrained in me and how foreign they were to other peoples until I sat at baseball matches with friends, some of them university men, and saw and heard the howls of anger and rage and denunciation which they hurled at the players as a matter of course.

James had a similar reaction when he learned how widespread bribery and fixed games were in American intercollegiate basketball: "These young people had no loyalties to school because they had no loyalties to anything."[54]

British adherence to the code of fair play did not, however, mean that the Queen's Park Cricket Club, which owned the island's best facilities and picked the Trinidadian team, was racially integrated. After leaving school, James had to choose between Maple, "the club of the brown-skinned middle class," and Shannon, which catered to lower-middle-class blacks. He joined Maple. At the time he felt that racial segregation "did very little harm and sharpened up the game," but he later came to realize that great black players—like Learie Constantine— were seldom given the credit due them. James was somewhat heartened in 1960 when Frank Worrell, after much controversy, became the first black captain of a West Indian team sent abroad to challenge the English and the Australians. When a quarter of a million Australians cheered Worrell through the streets of Melbourne, James glowed with optimism and evoked the names of Thomas Hughes and other English apostles of "muscular Christianity."[55]

Worrell's captaincy came ten years after a racially mixed West Indian team defeated the English in a Test (and a full twenty-four years before a Jamaican mulatto, Allen Rae, became the first nonwhite chairman of the West Indian Cricket Board of Control).[56] Considering the slow pace of racial justice, younger and more militant Marxist scholars have been less charitable than James about the progress of West Indian cricket. Commenting on crowd disturbances at Georgetown's Bourfda Ground, Port-of-Spain's Queen's Park Oval, and Kingston's Sabrina Park, Orlando Patterson noted that "only in matches against the English have riots taken place." The reason was obvious. "In the West Indies a test match is not so much a game as a collective ritual." It is not, however, the ritual of racial integration celebrated by James, but rather "a social drama in which almost all the basic conflicts of the society are played out symbolically." Test matches are one of the few occasions when West Indians can witness whites and blacks confronting one another on equal terms. They are, therefore, "one of the few exceptional occasions when the [black] West Indian lower classes feel solidarity."[57] Writing about Trinidadian ethnic politics in the Seventies, Kevin Yelvington came to a similar conclusion: "Caribbean cricket is rooted in the colonial past, and cricket matches in the modern era between England, the former masters, and the West Indies, the former slaves, have taken overt and covert themes of ethnic and national redemption."[58] The administrators of the game on the newly independent islands, acting on their conviction that cricket is a political institution, suspended Robin Jackman after he violated their ban on competing against racially segregated South African teams.[59]

Throughout what was once the British West Indies, basketball has begun to displace cricket, especially on the more prosperous islands where the ownership of television sets is widespread.[60] On the islands of Trinidad and Tobago, the black lower class has taken over basketball, a sport once popular among islanders of Asian descent, and made it into a vehicle for class and racial pride. Largely indifferent to the disorganized and inefficient Trinidad and Tobago Basketball Federation, black players follow

National Basketball Association games broadcast from the United States, adopt NBA team and player names, and mimic the moves of NBA stars. The point is less to express admiration for the United States than to mark the difference between basketball and cricket, a sport that has shed many of its British associations but maintained its upper-class aura. As played by the "Lakers" and "Celtics" of Trinidad and Tobago, basketball has become "an activity of empowerment."[61]

INDIA   "The Indian adoption of the English game of cricket," writes Richard Cashman, "was a paradox because, for the greater period of British rule, the sport was organized around exclusive clubs which were open only to Europeans. The cost of equipment together with the extensive capital required for the preparation of wickets and ovals made cricket the least appropriate game for India and the least likely to achieve the later status of a mass spectator sport."[62] And yet that is precisely what happened.

The paradox of cricket's popularity is underscored by the fact that precolonial Indian civilization had developed its own highly complex recreational forms, the most important of which were wrestling, hunting, and playing polo.[63] There was little reason to believe, at the time of the Great Mutiny (1857), that a game played on the verdant lawns of English country houses was destined to become the passion of Indian princes. Although seamen employed by the East India Company played at Cambay in 1721 and the Calcutta Cricket Club was in existence by 1792, the first indigenous Indian club, the Orient, was not founded until 1848. The founders were Parsees, and for decades this religious minority produced the most ardent and successful Indian cricketers. When a Parsee eleven toured England in 1886, the first Indian team to do so, *Cricket Chat* was quick to see the political utility of the game: "Anything which can tend to promote an assimilation of tastes and habits between the English and the native subjects of our Empress-Queen cannot fail to conduce to the solidity of the British Empire."[64] This seems not to have been the view of the average Anglo-Indian player, who hindered rather than abetted the spread of the game among the native peoples. It was considered quite "cricket" for him to ridicule native players.

How did this unlikely game become India's most popular spectator sport in the face of the ordinary Anglo-Indian's indifference or hostility to its diffusion? Largely, it seems, through the efforts of a series of British viceroys, two of whom subsequently became presidents of the Marylebone Cricket Club. Government policy, set in London, no more envisaged sports as a form of anglicization than did the average member of the officer's club in Madras or Calcutta, but Lord Harris, governor of Bombay, was from childhood an avid cricket player. Realizing the game's potential for promoting the "assimilation of tastes and habits" referred to in *Cricket Chat*, Harris encouraged the construction of cricket grounds and the organization of native teams. In 1892, he inaugurated an annual tournament between Bombay's resident Britons and the city's Parsee minority, a series that in time came to include Hindu (1907) and Muslim teams (1912). At an 1892 match in Poona, between an English and a Parsee side, Harris actually invited the Indians to lunch. This was considered by many to be a reckless act of excessive good will. When Harris retired in 1895, he assumed the presidency of the Marylebone Cricket Club and continued his efforts to foster Indian cricket. Thirty-one years later, as President of the Imperial Cricket Conference (the sport's highest administrative body), he disregarded the rules and insisted that the ICC accept two Indian representatives, named by him with his usual insouciance.[65]

Unlike the extreme conservatives, whose motto was "divide and conquer," Harris hoped that the game might bond together India's religiously, linguistically, and ethnically diverse population. "You do well to love [cricket]," he intoned on his eightieth birthday, "for it is more free from anything sordid, anything dishonourable, than any game in the world."[66] Fully sharing this idealism, Sir Stanley Jackson, governor of Bengal from 1927 to 1932, urged Hindus and Muslim to play on the same teams. Lord Bradbourne, who served as governor of Bombay (1933–37) and Bengal (1937–39), was another who imagined that cricket bats might knock down the barriers that separated Indians from each other. Bradbourne especially lamented the segregation of the spectators on the basis of religion. (In Bombay, for instance, the stands included officially designated sections for Hindus, Muslim, Parsees, and Roman Catholics.)[67]

The higher ranks of British officialdom encouraged the game by indirect as well as direct means. During his tenure as viceroy, Lord Curzon established Mayo College (1872) and four other "public schools" to educate the sons of the nobility. A principal aim of these schools was to transform physically timid higher-caste lads into manly equivalents of the Etonians and Harrovians who ruled the subcontinent. In his history of the college, Herbert Sherring wrote that "cricket played a very important part in the life of the Mayo College. . . . In fact, cricket . . . formed half the existence of the Mayo College boy. It was apparently . . . played every day of the week including Sundays."[68] A famous photograph shows the elegantly uniformed cricket team, complete with proudly worn turbans and a proudly held athletic trophy.

The teachers of these British schools were frequently missionaries in whose educational arsenal ball games were a powerful weapon. It was not easy to imbue "muscular Christianity" in the pampered sons of Indian princes, but the teachers' effort to wean their young charges from traditional recreations was eventually successful. T. L. Pennell exulted in 1901 that "the simpler native games are gradually giving place to the superior attractions of cricket and football."[69]

C. E. Tyndale-Biscoe quite agreed. He was an extraordinary person who deserves some brief attention. He was a blindly ethnocentric, ruthlessly stubborn dogmatist who was genuinely concerned to provide for what he conceived to be the welfare of the Kashmiri boys entrusted to his care. He was, in the words of James A. Mangan, "a cultural diffusionist of great interest and not a little importance. He took the physical activities of the English public school and ancient university, wrapped them in a packaging of moral certitude and introduced them successfully to a culture whose religious, social and sexual mores ran directly contrary to much of what he represented and advocated."[70]

His desire to imbue the lads with a belief in "muscular Christianity" was initially thwarted not only by their theological objections but also by their Brahmin conviction that muscular development was a sure sign of membership in a lower caste. Tyndale-Biscoe persevered. At one point he thrust two of his native assistants into a boat and forced them to row. In this manner, proudly recalled in *Character-Building in Kashmir,* he "made a beginning in making that low-caste stuff commonly called muscle."[71]

His efforts to introduce his reluctant pupils to the game of football met especially stiff resistance. In fact, the Hindus among the pupils were horrified when Tyndale-Biscoe showed them a football and informed them that it was made of leather. In a panic, they shouted to him that he should take it away because it was *jutha* ("unholy"). His response to their objections is perhaps the best example ever of self-righteous cultural imperialism. In his *Autobiography*, he recalled that

> I called the teachers together and explained to them my plans for the afternoon. They were to arm themselves with single-sticks, picket the streets leading from the school to the playground, and prevent any boys from escaping en route. Everything was ready, so at 3 o'clock the porter had orders to open the school gate. The boys poured forth, and

I brought up the rear with a hunting-crop. . . . We shooed them down the streets like sheep on their way to the butchers. Such a dirty, smelling, cowardly crew you never saw. All were clothed in the long nightgown sort of garment I have described before, each boy carrying a fire-pot under his garment. . . . This heating apparatus has from time immemorial taken the place of healthy exercise. We dared not drive them too fast for fear of their tripping up (as several of them were wearing clogs) and falling with their fire-pots, which would have prevented their playing football for many days to come.[72]

When the herded boys refused to begin the game, the teachers menaced them with their sticks and forced them to commence. A "player" who had become polluted when struck in the face by the ball was rushed to a nearby canal where he was washed and purified. There were other problems. "The bearded centre forward who first kicked the ball was forbidden to return to, and thus defile, his home. He went to live with relatives."[73]

Cricket, too, involved a leather ball and the taint of blasphemy. Since the ball had to be handled rather than kicked, the staff of the school faced a real problem. The solution was to allow the pupils to catch the ball with their hands up their sleeves. It was awkward, but it did avoid direct pollution. Tyndale-Biscoe and his colleagues throughout the length and breadth of British India persisted, and cricket became popular at missionary schools.

Military men and officers of the Indian Police Service also did their bit to introduce cricket to the adult members of the Indian elite. H. T. Wickham, stationed in Northern India from 1904 to 1922, condescendingly described some of the not entirely satisfactory results:

At three o'clock in the afternoon [the] Maharajah himself would come down to the ground, the band would play the Kashmir anthem, salaams were made and he then went off to a special tent where he sat for a time, smoking his long water pipe. At four thirty or thereabouts he decided he would bat. It didn't matter which side was batting, his own team or ours. He was padded by two attendants and gloved by two more, somebody carried his bat and he walked to the wicket looking very dignified, very small and with an enormous turban on his head.[74]

Errors committed by the Maharajah were overlooked.

For the prince who refused to make even a token effort, the British had only contempt. Charles Kincaid, an administrative officer in the tiny state of Nawanagar, dismissed the titular ruler as "an unattractive figure. He had had every advantage. . . . Yet he never learnt to play any game properly. Nor did he ever show the least interest in sport."[75]

Far more serious about cricket—and about a host of other sports as well—was Prince Rajendra Singh (1872–1900), Sikh ruler of Patiala (whose Punjabi peoples were mostly Hindu and Muslim). "The traditional princely sports were polo, pig-sticking and shikar (hunting)," but Rajendra took to cricket as well. His son Bhupendra was even more enthralled by the game. "In the grounds of his palace, which also housed three hundred wives and concubines and a scented swimming pool, there was a cricket field, the Bardari Palace Oval, in an area larger than Lord's and with facilities that rivalled the best of country-house cricket available then in England. Elephants were sometimes used to roll the wicket."[76]

Although the prince's love of cricket was never in doubt, he, like the British whom he emulated, used the game to make a political point about the need for Patiala's mutually hostile religious communities to overcome their animosities and to work together; he fielded religiously mixed elevens. Hindus, Muslims, Parsees, and Christians bowled and batted for the same team. As president of both the Board of Control of the Cricket Club of India and the Indian Olympic Association, he used his wealth and status to promote sports—especially cricket. He organized, financed, and captained a team that toured the British Isles (1911). He selected and coached the first official team sent to England (1932). He paid the bills for an Australian eleven to tour India (1935–36). His son, Yadavendra Singh

(1913–74), combined an active career as a cricket player with political work with Gandhi and Nehru for the cause of Indian independence. He captained the Indian team that visited Australia in 1935–36; he chaired the All-India Council of Sports; he founded the Asian Games Federation.[77]

The most famous of all Indian players was a man patronized by Prince Yadavendra's grandfather—K. S. Ranjitsinhji (1872–1933). Although "Ranji," as he was known to cricket fans, claimed to have been a prince, he was actually the grandson of a cousin of the ruler of Nawanagar. Thanks to a subsidy he received from his royal relative, who had once considered him as an heir, Ranji was educated at Cambridge. Leaving India in 1888 as a boy of fifteen, he lived in England until 1907. At Cambridge he won his "blue." After leaving the university, he played for Sussex and was selected many times to represent England in Tests against Australia. He must have been a marvelous player. "When he batted," wrote Neville Cardus, "a strange light was seen for the first time on English fields." It was "a lovely magic . . . not prepared for by anything that happened in cricket before Ranji came to us."[78] In 1907, after the Jam Sahib of Nawanagar died without an heir, Ranji became the prince he had always pretended to have been.

His fame as a cricketer disposed the British to choose him over rival claimants. In addition, Ranji was politically sound. His love of England inspired him to deny cultural difference: "I do not consider myself a foreigner in Cambridge."[79] His attitude toward the Empire was manifest in a comment he made in 1897: it was, he averred, "a pride to him to know that, while he was playing cricket against Australia, a relative—and a dear one, his uncle—was fighting for his Queen on the frontier in India." Cricket, he thought, was "among the most powerful of the links which keep our Empire together."[80] Significantly, it was *our* empire. After he had ascended the throne of Nawaganar, he constructed a new cricket pitch and did his best to promote the game. His nephew, Prince K. S. Duleepsinhji (1905–59), also played for England. In all, there were thirteen princes among the 143 men who participated in Test matches during the first century of Indian cricket.

Richard Cashman, upon whom I have relied for much of this account of Indian cricket, has concluded that cricket was attractive to India's princes "because it was a game which was susceptible to the distinctions of social class and which upheld traditional notions of social hierarchy."[81] I doubt that cricket was *intrinsically* more susceptible to hierarchical distinctions of social class than other games, but it *was* associated, more than any other sport, with the British ruling class. Rugby, too, was a game associated with Oxford and Cambridge and the amateur ethos of Victorian England, but cricket had intrinsic advantages in the eyes of higher-caste anglophiles; cricket required neither rough physical contact with opposing players nor an extreme of physical exhaustion incompatible with princely dignity.

After partition and independence, newspapers, banks, and other corporations replaced British officials, missionary educators, and Indian princes in the role of cricket promoters, but the game's corporate sponsors have continued the British (and Gandhian) opposition to religiously divisive communal cricket. The official emphasis has been on cricket as a symbol of national unity. Drawing attention away from the divisions of religion and caste that have plagued Indian democracy, cricket—like the English language—is one of the few things shared the length and breadth of the subcontinent.

In fact, cricket is now played on every continent and in most countries, but its popularity remains limited, for the most part, to what was once the British Empire. Why has cricket been less widely adopted than soccer? One can only speculate. It may be that cricket was disadvantaged by the greater complexity of its rules, but I incline toward an explanation that stresses extrinsic rather than intrinsic factors. I suspect that cricket's handicap was that its initial diffusion occurred at a time when it was by no means clear that Great Britain was destined to emerge victorious from the imperial wars of the eighteenth and nineteenth centuries. When the British exported cricket to their American colonies in the eighteenth century, Spain, Portugal, and France ruled most of the western hemisphere and the protectionist trade policies of mercantilism limited the activities of foreign entrepreneurs. By the time that British sailors began to kick soccer balls on foreign beaches, Britannia ruled the waves and Great Britain was—as another of those annoying slogans phrased it—the world's workshop. In other words, Victorian Britain had become a truly hegemonic power. The liberal doctrines of *laissez-faire* economics, supported by the awesome power of the British navy, had opened the world's markets, and British entrepreneurs were ubiquitous. Manchester's economic—and cultural—influence extended far beyond the limits of London's political control. And Manchester's favorite sport was soccer football.

2

SOCCER

The diffusion of soccer football is an excellent case for careful study because the game is complex enough not to have been invented independently by a number of premodern cultures and yet simple enough to have become unquestionably the world's most popular team sport. "What diffusion," asks a French geographer, "is more universal than football's, whose grounds can be seen in every latitude—in the center of huge industrial cities and in the most isolated villages of Third World countries?"[1]

While something akin to modern soccer was played in ancient China,[2] the game's direct antecedents can be traced back to medieval Europe, where folk football, a rough sport that maimed many of its participants, was played in one form or another in the peasant villages of England and France. Royal edicts banned football in 1314, 1349, 1389, 1401, and many subsequent years. The necessity for repeated prohibitions suggests that the game was too deeply rooted in the soil of customary behavior to be eradicated by royal decree. Like other traditional games, the rules for folk football, which were never codified, varied from place to place and from time to time. Common to all versions was a level of physical violence responsible for the vain efforts at prohibition.

It was by no means merely the peasantry that was addicted to football. In 1615, Sir Thomas Overbury complained of the game's unhealthy popularity at Oxford and Cambridge. According to Overbury, the typical student was contemptuous of "the meere scholar. . . . The antiquity of his University is his creed, and the excellency of his Colledge (though but for a match of foot-ball) an article of his faith."[3]

The modern form of the game is a nineteenth-century adaptation of folk football (which persisted, in some parts of England and Scotland, into the twentieth century). In 1848, fourteen collegians who had played a number of different ball games at Eton, Harrow, Rugby, Winchester, and several other schools met in Cambridge and agreed upon a common set of rules that enabled them to play together.[4] The role of the universities was crucial for the diffusion of soccer. "Without the unifying influence of the universities, which acted as a 'relay station,' organized games could not have emerged in the schools with the same speed or to the same degree that they did in the years 1830–80."[5] The name of the game—Association ("soccer") Football—derives from the fact that the sport was organized and promoted by the Football Association, founded in London on October 26, 1863, a day that scholars agree was "the most important date in the modern history of football."[6]

In its modern form, the game began as a middle-class pastime. Of the first club, founded in 1855, Eric Dunning and

Kenneth Sheard have commented, "Most members were old boys of Sheffield Collegiate School." The Old Harrovians, who established their club in 1860, were obviously another group with "public school" origins.[7]

The "old boys" wanted to keep the game for themselves, but soccer was quickly diffused downward through the social strata. Aston Villa FC and the Bolton Wanderers, both founded in 1874, were typical of the many clubs that recruited their first members from the congregations of churches and chapels. Within a few years, other clubs destined to figure grandly in the annals of English sports were organized by the employees of industrial enterprises. Manchester United began as Newton Heath FC, founded in 1880 by railroad workers, and Coventry City FC had its start as a club organized by the workers at Singer's bicycle factory. In 1895, laborers at the Thames Iron Works founded a team that became West Ham United FC. The Football Association's Cup Final, which represented the national championship, was won in 1883 by Blackburn Olympic FC, whose somewhat pretentiously named team included three weavers, a spinner, a cotton operator, an iron worker, a plumber, and a dental assistant.[8]

By 1888, the solidly middle-class directors of the Football Association's member clubs implicitly acknowledged that soccer had become "the people's game" when they reluctantly accepted the openly professional clubs of Football League. By the early twentieth century, the connection between soccer and the working class was so strong, and the feelings for the game were so intense, that "it was no exaggeration for some to describe football . . . as a 'religion.' The football grounds of England were the Labour Party at prayer."[9]

TO THE CONTINENT

"In the years after 1880," writes Ruud Stokvis, a Dutch sociologist who has closely studied ludic diffusion, "English sports were adopted on the European continent by young members of the elite and the upper middle class."[10] Others followed. Geographers describing the process refer to a well-known S-curve pattern: innovations of all kinds are initially slow to spread among a population; then there is a phase of rapid adoption followed by a long period in which the laggards are gradually won over to the new technique or mode of behavior.[11] On the continent, it was the anglophile segments of the upper class that responded initially to the new game, the middle classes that quickly spread the word, and the workers and peasants whose tardy arrival at the soccer pitch completed the process of diffusion. Once *they* began to kick the ball about, players from the upper and middle classes dropped their gear and moved on to greener and more exclusive ludic pastures. For many of them, rugby was an acceptable substitute for soccer.

There has been some confusion about exactly who introduced soccer football to the European continent. In a classic essay entitled "Gymnastics and Sports in *Fin-de-Siècle* France," Eugen Weber wrote that

> English boys attending private schools in Geneva, Lausanne, and St. Gallen, as well as Swiss graduates of Oxford and Cambridge, established [soccer] in Switzerland before it appeared elsewhere on the Continent: La Chatelaine of Geneva was founded in 1869; the St. Gallen Football Club in 1879; and the Grasshoppers of Zurich in 1886.[12]

The palm for priority seems to have been awarded wrongly. Soccer was played in Belgium as early as 1863, the year of the foundation of England's Football Association.

Although adult Englishmen resident in Belgium organized a number of sports clubs, including the Antwerp Football and Cricket Club (1880), the principal mechanism for the diffusion of soccer throughout the kingdom was the network of Roman Catholic schools established for the sons of the nation's elite. English students are sometimes said to have played Belgium's first game of soccer on the Ten Boschplein in Brussels in 1865, but they seem to have been anticipated by the boys of a Jesuit school in the town of Melle (in the vicinity of Ghent). At the *Maison de Melle,* which catered to the scions of the nobility and the upper middle class, the game was introduced in 1863 by Cyril Bernard Morrogh, an Irish pupil from Killarney. According to a memoir published by Jules Dubois in 1923 in the *Blad van de Vereniging der Oud Mellisten* (an alumni magazine), enthusiasm for the new game was so great and play was so wild that the ball soon "exhaled a resounding 'pouf,' its last sigh."[13] Thomas Savage brought a new one from London, play resumed, and Savage's Belgian classmates quickly learned a version of English "more useful than the beautiful poetry of Shakespeare that they pounded into us in the classroom."[14]

For more than a decade, the taste for soccer seems to have been limited. Then, in 1880, Pater Germain Hermans returned to Belgium after a year in Croyden, where he had played goalie on a team at St. George's College (a Jesuit school). Employed by the *Collège de Saint-Stanislaus* in Tirlemont, he explained the rules of football to his pupils and organized the first game. The police stepped in to quell what they perceived as youthful disorder, but the mayor seems to have heard enough about the ways of mad dogs and Englishmen to let the boys have their fun. In 1884, Hermans carried the game to his new post at the *Collège Saint-Matherne* at Tongres and from there he moved on, in 1886, to the *Maison de Melle.* Since the original Mellian game of 1863, developing in relative isolation, had become rather eccentric, Hermans imposed the official rules of the Football Association. Meanwhile, in 1885, students at the *Sint-Francis-Xavier Instituut*, who had begun to play soccer in 1868, joined with students from the *Koninklijk Atheneum* to form a combined team and boldly challenge the Red Caps of the English College of Brussels. Six years later, students at the *Collège Saint-Bernard*, with the help of some local Britons, founded an organization to which they gave an English name: the Brussels Football Club.

By the time the *Union Belge des Sociétés de Sports Athlétiques* was founded in 1895, the sport was popular in many if not most of the nation's elite schools.

The Dutch pattern was an interesting variant of the Belgian. "The introduction of sports such as cricket, football, and tennis and the establishment of clubs to practice them . . . was the work of Englishmen resident in the Netherlands and of the Dutch who had been to England."[15] C. H. Bingham, a cycling enthusiast who became the first director of the *Nederlandsche Vélocipédisten Bond* (1883), was British while J. R. Dickson Romijn, founder of Deventer's Utile Dulce Cricket Club (1875), was educated in England. His father, who had been a Dutch consul there, took the lead in forming the *Haagsche Cricket Club* (1878). Pim Mulier, who had studied at an English boarding school, founded the *Haarlemsche Football Club*, Holland's first, in 1879. At the time, he was only fourteen years old. By the time Mulier was twenty-two, he was a veteran leader in the *Nederlandsche Voetbalboond,* which he helped to organize.[16]

In the port city of Rotterdam, soccer was played by dock workers who had been inspired by the example of British seamen, but historians eager to learn more about their games have been frustrated by the paucity of documentary evidence. Longshoremen and other workers who took up the game "formed fluid soccer teams and played irregularly under changing names and without having club houses, standardized uniforms or fixed playing fields."[17]

Because Dutch educators at the secondary and the collegiate level were generally opposed to sports and strongly committed to noncompetitive gymnastic exercises, these mainstays of middle-class culture were far less disposed than their Belgian counterparts to encourage the mania for English sports. During the eighties and nineties, gymnastics teachers, who had formed a national organization in 1862 in order to propagandize for their version of physical education, condemned Holland's emergent sports clubs as "a cancer" afflicting the nation's youth.[18] Their antipathy was based on more than divergent ideas about the importance of competition. The physical educators came mostly from the working class while the first enthusiasts for modern sports, including soccer, came predominantly from the upper middle class or from the titled aristocracy. For models of physical activity, the educators looked to Germany, where the tradition of noncompetitive gymnastics (*Turnen*) had originated; their affluent pupils, unimpressed by regimented exercise, took their cues from England.

German physical educators were no more able than their loyal Dutch admirers to dampen the fire of the *Fussballmanie* that raged in their schools. Boys who were bored by the deadly routines of *Schulturnen* (educational calisthenics) responded eagerly to the excitement of soccer. Konrad Koch, an eighteen-year-old student at Braunschweig's *Gymnasium Martino-Katharineum,* introduced the game in 1874. Although Koch was influenced by Thomas Arnold of Rugby, whom he wrongly imagined to have been a believer in sports as an inculcator of manly self-discipline, he was realistic enough to understand that the game's English origins were a drawback in that period of intense German nationalism. Koch attempted to translate the lingo of soccer into German and to trace the game back to some acceptably Teutonic sources. His stratagem was apparently successful. The middle classes of the school formed a team in 1875. Some of the students were worried about a loss of dignity and resisted the lure of the rough-and-tumble game until 1879, when their teachers, realizing that boisterous play on the pitch was preferable to unruly outbursts in the classroom, sternly ordered the recalcitrant youths to go out and have a good time.[19]

A passion for the sport slowly began to spread from school to school. Wherever the educational authorities were hostile, boys formed teams for out-of-school play, but their "wild" clubs had a tendency to disappear after a single season. Soccer was not, at first, as popular or as firmly institutionalized as another sport derived from England. The aura of the Henley Regatta and the example of British business representatives in seaports like Bremen and Hamburg inspired thousands of middle-class and upper-class Germans to become oarsmen. When the rowers organized their *Deutscher Ruderverband* in 1883, they far outnumbered the soccer players.

By that time, however, soccer was more than a sport for schoolboys. In the commercial centers of northern Germany, Britons and Germans of the mercantile and professional classes founded the first soccer clubs for young adults. Bremen and Hamburg had theirs in 1880, Hannover followed a year later. Berlin's first club, the *Berliner Fussball-Club Frankfurt 1885*, received its unusual name because its founder, the artist Georg Leux, brought the game with him when he arrived from Frankfurt am Main. Leux was also a leader in the *Bund Deutscher Fussballspieler*, which united the city's British and German clubs in 1890. Other regional federations sprang up as if, in the German idiom, "stamped from the ground." Archibald S. White, a Scottish minister living in the elegantly international resort town of Baden-Baden, became the first president of the *Süddeutsche Fussball-Union*. In nearby Karlsruhe, Walter Bensemann founded the *Kickers* and inaugurated international play against teams from Belgium, Holland, France, Switzerland, Hungary, and—boldest move of all—England. After a number of failed attempts to found a national organization, eighty-six mostly middle-class delegates met in Leipzig on January 28, 1900, and formed the *Deutscher Fussball-Bund*.[20]

A tournament to determine the national champion took place three years later. It was marred by the first of many soccer scandals. A few days before Karlsruhe's team was to meet Prague's in Leipzig, the former received a telegram: "Game postponed. Information follows." The team from Prague waited vainly in

Leipzig; the telegram was a fake. The sponsors of the tournament allowed Prague to advance to the final because Karlsruhe had not been clever enough to see through the hoax.[21]

It was not, however, until working-class adults took to the "completely unfamiliar" sport that soccer began really to flourish.[22] This did not happen until a quarter century after Koch introduced the game at the *Gymnasium Martino-Katharineum* in Braunschweig. One reason for the relatively late acceptance of the game was initial resistance on the part of the *Arbeiter-Turn-Bewegung*, the socialist gymnastics federation organized in 1893 in opposition to the middle-class gymnasts of the *Deutsche Turnerschaft*.[23] While the high-minded leaders of the socialist federation deplored football's competitiveness, which they likened to capitalism's, rank-and-file workers had little interest in ideological consistency. The history of one of Germany's most famous professional teams, *Schalke 04*, is instructive. The club, which lies in the heart of the heavily industrialized Ruhr Valley, traces its origins back to May 4, 1904, when fifteen-year-old Heinrich Kullmann and fourteen-year-old Gerhard Kloop organized a group of their friends into a "wild" club that they named *Westfalia Schalke*. (The Ruhr Valley is part of Westphalia.) It was not long before the boys' fathers—miners and steel workers—noticed what their sons had done. One can imagine Herr Kullmann and Herr Kloop pausing on their way home from work, wondering what their sons were up to, laying down their lunch pails, and joining the game.[24]

In the first ten years of its existence, Schalke had forty-four members whose occupational status is known to us. Half of them were miners and fifteen others were factory hands or artisans.[25] In other clubs as well, the German evolution recapitulated the English, which had taken twenty-five years to shift its demographic center of gravity from the upper middle class to the working class (i.e., from the foundation of the proudly amateur Football Association in 1863 to the creation of the openly professional Football League in 1888). Soccer became, in Germany as in England, a basic constituent of working-class culture, part of what it meant to be *"ein guter Kumpel"* ("a good fellow worker").[26]

L'invention britannique arrived in France no later than 1872, when the British residents of Normandy, led by F. F. Langstaff of the South West Railway, formed the Havre Athletic Club (HAC). Since most of the members were Oxford or Cambridge men, the club's colors "combined the blues of the two universities." A rival claim to priority has been made by the Breton town of St. Servan, which began to attract English tourists after the Southampton-St. Malo steamship line was inaugurated in 1864. Joseph Gemain, who was one of the early players, testified that soccer was introduced in the sixties by members of the town's British colony. The first team was called *"les Anglais de Saint Servan."*[27]

Like many of the early enthusiasts, the members of the first clubs were often unsure about exactly which kind of football they wanted to play. On November 18, 1884, ten members of the Le Havre club voiced a preference for soccer, two were for rugby, and twelve members—resolutely undecided—voted for a combination of both games. Eventually, in 1891, the club divided into soccer and rugby sections.[28]

Britons living in Paris formed a Paris Football Club in 1879, but it collapsed five years later "for lack of rivals." The British in Paris tried again with the International Athletic Club (1887) and the Paris Football Association Club (1887). The White Rovers (1891), named after the Blackburn Rovers, winners of the Football Association's Cup Final, were followed a few months later by the Standard Athletic Club (1892), which was probably the most successful; in 1894 it won a national tournament reluctantly sponsored by the *Union des Sociétés Françaises de Sports Athlétiques* after a number of soccer clubs threatened to secede from the organization to protest the *USFSA*'s discriminatory policy. There was only one Frenchman on the Standard Athletic Club's championship team. When the *Racing-Club de Paris* defended its goal against the attacks of the Richmond Town Wanderers in 1906, the "home" team had four Frenchmen. (The defense cannot have been very impressive; *le Racing-Club* lost by a score of 15–0.)[29]

Inspired by the British clubs in Paris and by a visit to Eton by two of their number, pupils of the *École Monge* began to contemplate forming a team of their own, which they did on October 28, 1888. The first schoolboy game was played on the *Pelouse de Madrid* on December 10.[30] In 1892, Georges Duhamel, later to become an important man of letters and the author of a history of French soccer, formed a team of pupils recruited from the *Collège Chaptal* and the *Lycée Jeanson-de-Sully*. Several of the boys had had an *"éducation sportive"* in England or Scotland. Charles Bernat and Eugène Frayasse, for instance, had played for St. Joseph's College in Dumfries.[31] By the turn of the century, there were clubs in most French cities. Paris alone had twenty-five, most of them founded by teachers of English or—as was the case in southern cities like Marseille and Nîmes—by students returning from an English sojourn. During the *fin de siècle*, nearly all of the players came from the politically dominant urban bourgeoisie, which doubtless explains why the president of the republic appeared among the spectators at the first game played by the boys of the *École Monge*.[32] In these early years, the game was so closely identified with the British that casual spectators listening to the players' excited exclamations often assumed that the *écoliers* were British lads with an admirable command of colloquial French.

For the provincial bourgeoisie who had neither visited England nor come into contact with one of the British teams based in France, the press provided rudimentary instruction. On the other hand, the most powerful athletic organization of the day, the *Union des Sociétés Françaises de Sports Athlétiques*, did little to promote the game.[33] Paschel Grousset, Pierre de Coubertin's great rival for leadership in French sports, overcame his dislike for English sports and organized a national tournament for schoolboys (won by the *Lycée de Rouen*), but it went against Grousset's chauvinist grain. When forced by the sports engagement of its members to accommodate itself to imported British games, the USFSA indicated a preference for rugby, which became immensely popular in the southwest of France. In the Gironde and in Provence, peasants seem to have perceived the rough-and-tumble of rugby as a bracing contrast to the urban effeteness of soccer.[34]

The industrial workers of Lille and the dockers of Marseilles were much slower to develop a passion for soccer than their British or German counterparts. As an essentially middle-class sport, an "amusement for young men from good families," soccer was able to attract only some two thousand spectators to a 1903 match that was to decide the national championship; two years earlier, 100,000 Britons had jammed London's Crystal Palace for the Football Association's Cup Final. Although the Germans' *Fussballverband* was formed in 1900, it was not until 1919 that the *Fédération Française de Football* was constituted.[35] Until that time, soccer, lacking its own national structure, was simply one of many sports sponsored—rather reluctantly—by the *Union des Sociétés Françaises de Sports Athlétiques* or—more enthusiastically—by regional leagues.

Although soccer has never been as popular in France as in Great Britain and Germany, the game has served the French well as a vehicle of acculturation and ethnic integration. The first and second divisions of the national soccer league have always fielded a higher percentage of foreign professionals than its European counterparts have. From the thirties to the eighties, about 20 percent of the players have been foreigners, recruited mostly from Eastern Europe and from Latin America. Unfortunately for gallic pride, foreign stars are ineligible for the

national team, which has never done very well in international competition.[36]

The Italian story differs from that of the northern Europeans in that students played less of a role in the diffusion of soccer than was the case in France, Germany, and the Low Countries. British sailors had introduced the game in the eighties when they docked and went ashore in Genoa, Leghorn, Naples, and other peninsular ports, but it was Britons "in trade" in Turin and Milan, the industrial and financial centers of northern Italy, who first organized viable teams. The role of British entrepreneurs was important enough to justify Antonio Papa's neat formulation: "With remarkable precision, the map of soccer retraces the map of foreign capital in the peninsula."[37]

The industrial city of Turin was the home of the first Italian known to have been captivated by the charm of soccer. In March 1887, Edoardo Bosio returned from a business trip to England with a soccer ball and some lively memories. Recruiting the employees of his firm, he arranged for a game. In 1891, Bosio's group fused with a team of equally anglophile local patricians who had begun to play two years earlier. Since foreigners were welcomed to this as to the other teams founded by Italian enthusiasts, the result was an international club whose lengthy name was popularly shortened to *Football Club Torinese*. In Genoa, it was British businessmen and consular officials who took the initiative in the summer of 1896 and added soccer to the array of sports offered by their four-year-old Cricket and Athletic Club. Soccer quickly became so popular that the members renamed themselves the Genoa Football Club. Simultaneous with the change of name came a change in policy: upon the urging of Dr. James Spensley, the club's goalie, Italian members were admitted. A year later, British expatriates founded the famed Juventus Football Club of Turin. Englishmen and Italians joined forces in 1899 to create another club destined for prominence in the history of the game: the Milan Cricket and Football

Club. Still another collaboration occurred in 1900 when Ignazio Pagano, son of a prominent Sicilian lawyer, came home from a year of study in London. Determined to put into play the ball that he had brought with him, Pagano spurred Palermo's foreign colony into forming the Anglo-Palermitan Athletic and Football Club. Another famous team, Pro Vecilli, was organized in 1903 without the benefit of a stay in England or intercourse with the expatriate British, but Albion's influence was nonetheless easy to trace. A member of the town's fencing and gymnastics club, a student named Marcello Bertinetti, had visited nearby Turin, seen a soccer game, and returned to Vercelli with a soccer ball that he had somehow managed to buy, borrow, or steal.[38]

The names chosen for the first teams were but one indication of the game's English origins. The measurements of the field (in yards rather than meters), the temporal divisions of the match-es, and even the code for the deportment of the spectators were the results of English influence, an influence that later proved to be a source of embarrassment for Italian chauvinists. In the period of Fascist rule, efforts were made to rewrite the history of the game, but only the most gullible Italians were persuaded to deny soccer's English origins and to derive calcio from the Renaissance pastimes of the Florentine aristocracy.[39]

On April 15, 1898, clubs from Genoa and Turin, rejecting any impulse to think in small terms, created the Federazione Italiana del Football. The president was an Italian, the secretary an Englishman. Two months later, the infant seven-club asso-ciation sponsored its first "national championship." Genoa, which fielded a rugged team bolstered by five foreigners, won this and five of the next six championships. In 1908, the feder-ation decided to bar foreign players from its annual tourna-ment, but a boycott by the powerful clubs from Genoa, Milan, and Turin led to a quick reversal of the rule. Nationalism did score a point in 1909, however, when the federation changed its name to the Federazione Italiana Gioco del Calcio.[40]

Nationalism was one brake on the game's accelerated diffusion from the classes to the masses. Another was the widespread (and correct) perception that modern sports in general and soccer in particular had been imported from a predominantly *Protestant* culture. Giovanni Semeria cleared the way for hesitant Roman Catholics by obfuscating the issue. Belittling the English origins of soccer, he explained that the relationship of the captain to his obedient teammates is analogous to the position of the pope in relation to the great mass of faithful believers. Semeria's publications seem to have cleansed soccer "from the taints of both Protestantism and 'modernity.'"[41]

Whether reassured by sophistic argumentation or simply lured by the excitement of the game, industrial workers took to soccer and greatly increased the options available to the selectors of the national team. On May 15, 1910, the Italian team made its debut in Milan's *Arena Civica*. The team was strong enough to defeat the French visitors by a score of 6–2. In a second match, which took place a mere eleven days later, the team encountered stiffer opponents. Charles Löwenrosen, a schoolboy whose parents had emigrated from Hungary to England, had brought a soccer ball with him when he visited Budapest in 1896. Löwenrosen's hometown friends must have been impressed; three months later, they formed Hungary's first football team. By 1910, when the Hungarians hosted the Italians in Budapest, their game was so far advanced that they trounced the visitors by a score of 6–1. Some Italian partisans claimed that their players had been unfairly distracted by the erotic presence of women in the crowd of 15,000 Hungarian spectators.[42]

By this time, there was an international federation to supervise the diffusion of the sport. It seems rather "a paradox, when one considers the weakness of the French game," that the impetus for global organization came from France. In 1903, Robert Guérin, a leader in the *Union des Sociétés Françaises de Sports Athlétiques* suggested to Frederick Wall, secretary of England's

powerful Football Association, that an international federation be formed to propagate their beloved recreation. To his chagrin, Guérin discovered that neither Wall nor any other Englishman was interested in the idea. Wall's response was pompous and condescending: "The Council of the Football Association can- not see the advantages of such a Federation, but on all such matters upon which joint action [is] desirable they would be prepared to confer."[43] Guérin characterized his efforts to per- suade A. F. Kinnaird, the FA president, as "like beating the air."[44] Undeterred, Guérin went ahead in 1904 with the forma- tion of the *Fédération Internationale de Football Association* (FIFA), which has grown into the largest and most important of all the transnational sports federations. Charter members in addition to France were Belgium, Holland, Denmark, Spain, Sweden, and Switzerland.[45] The four British soccer federations, whose members far outnumbered those of any continental nation, refused to join the organization, a haughty attitude typ- ical of those who felt that their invention of a game gave them patent rights to it. The British federations did join FIFA in 1906, but they twice departed in fits of principle, first in 1920, when the federation declined to expel its German and Austrian members for their role in World War I, and then in 1928, when FIFA allowed "broken-time payments" to remunerate amateur players who missed work in order to compete in matches. Insu- larity did not end until 1946, when the British rejoined FIFA.[46]

LATIN AMERICA

Although we have grown accustomed to the idea of North Amer- ican penetration of Latin American markets, British entrepre- neurs dominated the economic scene for most of the nineteenth century. The pound sterling was then the world's medium of exchange. In "Argentina, Uruguay and Chile, the British pres- ence was so thick on the ground as almost to make them part of the informal empire." Needless to say, wherever they went, the

British took their games with them. By the end of the century, modern sports were an integral part of Latin American culture.[47] Argentinians, who thought of themselves as rather more cosmopolitan than other *Latinos*, were especially eager to adopt cricket, soccer, rugby, polo, and a number of other British sports.

In 1806, during a forty-five-day military occupation of Buenos Aires, British soldiers reduced the boredom of their duty with cricket matches. The troops left, the merchants arrived. The wool trade brought Thomas Hogg, owner of a Yorkshire textile factory, to the city. No wool gatherer he. The energetic merchant helped to found a British commercial center, a British library, a British college—and, in 1819—a cricket club. The initial reaction of the local public was amused dismissal; the headquarters of the club was referred to as the "insane asylum." Within a few years, ridicule changed to emulation. As early as 1832, Argentine youths returning from study abroad founded a cricket club of their own.[48]

Cricket continued to be fashionable, but the cosmopolite leisure class soon had a variety of other sports from which to choose. If Swiss marksmen failed to win adherents to *El Tiro Suizo*, if French gymnasts and fencers lured relatively few natives to the *Club de Gimnasia y Esgrima*, a great deal of the credit for the Argentine preference for modern British sports has to go to the aforementioned Thomas Hogg, who reared his sons to be as active as he was. Young Tómas Hogg was a founder of the Dreadnought Swimming Club, which had its first contests in 1863. In 1866, he took up squash. With his brother James, he organized the Buenos Aires Athletic Society, which had its first track-and-field meet on May 30, 1867. At some point in the next decade, Tómas seems to have been responsible for Latin America's first golf club. He also participated in an inaugural rugby game played at the Buenos Aires Cricket Club on May 14, 1874. Brother James was on hand in 1880 when the recently invented game of lawn tennis arrived

in Argentina. It is impossible not to imagine that Tómas, rac-
quet firmly in hand, was on the other side of the net.[49]

British sailors on shore leave had played some kind of football as early as 1840, at which time the local newspaper, *La
Razón*, informed its readers that this odd pastime "consisted of
running around after a ball."[50] The next reference to the game
seems to have come a generation later. When the Buenos Aires
Football Club first took to the field, on June 20, 1867, the ath-
letically ubiquitous Hogg brothers were the mainstay of one of
the eight-man teams while William Heald captained the other.
According to *The Standard* for June 23, the Hoggs, wearing colored caps, defeated Heald's white-capped players four goals to
none. H. J. Barge led the "white caps" in the second match, but
the change in leadership was only marginally helpful. The
Hoggs won the second match by 3–0. The sport received a set-
back in 1874 when the members of the Buenos Aires Football
Club voted, unanimously, to shift to rugby football. (One of the
two rugby teams was, inevitably, captained by "Señor Hogg.")[51]
Among the boys at British schools in Argentina soccer made
good this loss of favor, especially after 1881, when Alexander
Watson Hutton arrived from Scotland to join the faculty of St.
Andrew's College. Hutton moved on to establish the Buenos
Aires English High School, which opened its doors in 1884.
Before long, the school had a physical-education teacher, a soccer pitch for the boys, and tennis courts for the girls. When a
shipment of regulation soccer balls ordered by Hutton arrived
in Buenos Aires, puzzled customs officials did not know how to
classify them and were said to have fabricated a new customs
category: the leather objects were listed as "items for the crazy
English." It was also said that neighborhood wits thought it
appropriate that the school's sports facilities were located in the
vicinity of a madhouse. In light of the enthusiasm upper-class
Argentines had already expressed for all sorts of British recreations, one suspects that Hutton—the source of a number of

ful team, *Real Madrid*).[53]

In nearly every case, the first clubs were formed at British schools. The year that Hutton introduced soccer in the Buenos Aires English High School, his colleagues did the same in Rosario and Santiago. By 1890, "one could say that football had conquered the student population." At St. Andrew's, where the school club was founded in 1890, the Scottish headmaster, the Reverend Mr. J. William Fleming, was notoriously strict; absence from church in the morning meant exclusion from soccer in the afternoon. Strictness must have paid; a year later, St. Andrew defeated the "Old Caledonians" to win the first national championship.[54]

Employees of British-owned railroads were also active in the diffusion of soccer in Argentina (and in much of the rest of Latin America). Famous clubs like *Rosario Central* and *Excelsior* were founded by British and, eventually, Argentine workers of the *Ferrocarril Central Argentino*, the *Ferrocarril Sud*, and other railroads. Between the railroad workers and the students at schools and colleges, challenges went back and forth. In Santiago in 1890, the representatives of *Ferrocarril Nordeste Argentino* lost a famous 1-0 match against the youths of the *Colégio Nacional*. In 1891, an Argentine Association Football League, presided over by F. L. Wooley, a member of the Buenos Aires and Rosario Railway Athletic Club, came into being.[55] Long after the railroad workers followed the students to the pitch, the sport's British imprint remained legible. For decades, soccer stories remained a monopoly of the English-language press. "The first soccer notices in the national idiom appeared

anecdotes—aggrandized his own role by exaggerating the puzzlement of the locals. At any rate, whatever hostility to the game existed diminished sufficiently by 1893 for Hutton, "the faher of soccer in the Argentine," to launch the Argentine Football Association.[52] (This was, incidentally, five years before Spanish students organized what became their country's most success-

[in *El País*] in January 1901." During the first championships, organized by the Argentine Association Football League, "everyone spoke English." It was not until 1905 that the association's name was changed to Spanish. As late as 1914, British names far outnumbered Spanish ones on team rosters.[56]

Across the Río de la Plata, in Uruguay, modern sports arrived in more or less the same way. In Montevideo as in Buenos Aires, cricket preceded soccer, introduced by British soldiers during their brief occupation of the city in 1807. Subsequently, businessmen and diplomatic personnel played informal games until the foreign population was large enough to support a club. On June 4, 1842, the *Britannia and Montevideo Reporter* announced that a group of British residents had met on May 31 to establish the Victoria Cricket Club, cleverly named for both the Roman goddess and the young queen who had ascended the throne five years earlier. The VCC was "the first sports club to make a real impression on the public."[57] The Montevideo Cricket Club, composed mostly of native Uruguayans, was formed on July 18, 1861. Seven years later, the MCC began a famous series of annual matches with the Buenos Aires Cricket Club.[58]

From the very start, members of the MCC seem to have played soccer as well as cricket. Ship's crews did their bit to popularize the game in the seventies, but the real "take-off" came after the creation of the Central Uruguay Railway Cricket Club on September 28, 1891. This club, like the MCC, was devoted to cricket in the summer and soccer in the winter. The players wore black and yellow—the colors of the railroad's signal of distress—but there was little reason to fret about the future of soccer. Teams sprang up, it seemed, wherever rails were laid down. It was an annoyance, however, that so many of the railway workers were aliens. In order to "snatch sports from the hands of foreigners," patriotic Uruguayans organized the rival *Club Nacional* on May 14, 1899. Ten months later, the

Uruguay Football Association was founded. Montevideo host-ed, and won, the South American championship in 1916, but Uruguay's greatest sporting successes came in 1924, 1928, and 1930, when the national team, led by José Leandor Andrade, triumphed in the final matches of the Olympic Games (against Switzerland and then against Argentina) and in the first FIFA-organized World Cup (against Argentina).[59]

In Chile on the Pacific as in Argentina and Uruguay on the Atlantic, "English commercial houses and colleges were the great propagandists for the sport that, in time, became the pas-sion of the multitude."[60] The first club seems to have been the Valparaíso FC, created in 1889 by David N. Scott. Teams then sprang into life at English schools like Mackay and Sutherland in nearby El Cerro Alegre and in firms like *la Casa Rogers*, importers of White Rose Tea. By 1893, a few ethnic Chileans were also to be seen in the distinctive shorts and shirts worn by all self-respecting (and self-advertising) soccer players. That year also saw the first games between Valparaíso and Santiago as well as the first encounter against a team from Argentina. The 1–1 tie between Chile and Argentina was less international than it seemed because all the players involved were either British born or of British descent. Needless to say, the Football Associ-ation of Chile, chartered in 1895, was another organization dominated by *los ingleses*. Within a year, however, Santiago had its first purely Chilean clubs. Students at the *Instituto Nacional* and the *Escuela Normal de Preceptores* led the way to the "nationalization" of the game. The foundation of the *Asociación de Fútbol de Chile*, in 1912, can be taken as a sign that the Chileans were finally on their own.

Brazil's discovery of soccer was similar, but there were some unique aspects to the game's early development. Charles Miller, born in Sao Paulo of English parents, was sent to study in Eng-land in 1884. After ten years abroad, he returned to Brazil, bringing a pair of footballs with him. "Soccer then—to his sur-

prise—was virtually unknown; even the resident British firms preferred to play cricket." Miller, obviously not one to sit and brood about the lack of opportunity, promptly recruited some adventurous teammates from Sao Paulo Railways, the English Gas Company, and the London Bank. "Then he cajoled the Sao Paulo Athletic Club, a cricketing affair, to play soccer."[61] All the players of the first game, which took place on the grounds of the local cycling club, were English. By 1902, Sao Paulo had a football league whose players—mostly British—were expert enough to trounce a visiting team composed of Britons who had settled in South Africa.[62]

Meanwhile, the British in Rio de Janeiro had created *Flumi-nense*, a socially exclusive club destined to become one of the most illustrious in Brazilian history. In 1910, *Fluminense* invit-ed its British counterpart, the strictly amateur "old boy" Corin-thians, to Rio. The visitors went on to Sao Paulo, where they inspired their hosts to create another of Brazil's most famous teams: the Sao Paulo Corinthians. Although most of Brazil's early players stemmed from the middle and upper classes, the new Corinthians did not; they were recruited mainly from the employees of the Sao Paulo Railway Company. By 1914, Brazil-ian soccer had developed so rapidly among all classes in the urban centers that the national team was able to defeat Argenti-na in the first of their many bitterly fought encounters. In 1919, Brazil won the South American championship.[63]

Unlike the Argentines and the Uruguayans, most Brazilians can claim African origins. Not long after slavery was legally abolished, in 1888, black Brazilians began to appear on the ros-ters of the smaller soccer clubs. They were not always welcome. When the America Football Club of Rio accepted its first black player, "a number of players and supporters left for Flumi-nense."[64] Responding to such manifestations of elitist racism, the city's poor created their own club, *Flamengo*, whose symbol is a black vulture.[65] In time, of course, Brazilian soccer came to

be dominated by black players, of whom Edson Arantes do Nascimento—better known simply as Pelé—is unquestionably the most famous. He, the idol of the Brazilian masses, presumably spoke for them when he informed the *Jornal do Brasil* that soccer is "the greatest joy of the people."[66]

AFRICA

In the course of the nineteenth century, which can fairly be referred to as "an Age of Imperialism," Africa became the most colonized of continents. In the race to carve out colonies, protectorates, and spheres of influence, the British were more successful than the other Europeans. And their sports, especially soccer, spread more swiftly than those of other imperial powers. One reason for the more rapid ludic diffusion was "the sharp contrast between the role of sport in the ethos and make-up of the British colonial administrator on the one hand and his colonial counterparts from other European countries."[67] French officials, for instance, while emphasizing physical education to improve the health of the native population, discouraged "the creation of teams and clubs and the organization of sports competitions." When Frenchmen upset by the relatively poor performance of the national team at the 1928 Olympic Games looked to the African colonies for "a reservoir of athletes," the army, which was in charge of physical education, sabotaged their efforts to recruit native athletes.[68]

Behind the success of the British and the relative failure of the French in the diffusion of soccer and other modern sports to the African continent was—quite simply— the British mania for sports. In their passionate commitment, the British in Africa were motivated in part by the intrinsic pleasures of their pastimes and in part by the ideology of empire. When the Reverend J. E. C. Welldon announced his belief that "England has owed her sovereignty to her sports," he was by no means an unusual or eccentric spokesman.[69] It was widely assumed that sturdy

shoulders were needed to bear the "white man's burden." If Britannia were to rule the savannahs and the rain forests as well as the waves, one had to be true to the games ethic, to the belief that sports—especially team games—created the kind of character needed to meet extreme physical and psychological challenges and to impose European civilization upon what Kipling referred to as "lesser breeds without the law." If French and German colonizers were far less obsessive in their approach to sports, it was not from a lack of concern for *ordre administratif* or *Ordnung und Disziplin*; it was rather that the French and the Germans were less certain than their British rivals that modern sports created moral fiber along with muscle mass.

From 1910 to 1948, men recruited for administrative work by the Tropical African Service were selected with an eye to "character" and character was equated with athletic ability demonstrated by the candidate at a "public school." Between 1899 and 1952, Eton, Harrow, Winchester and the other elitist foundations supplied more than 90 percent of all the officers in the Sudan Political Service.[70] The administrative attention paid to sports was extreme. R. D. Furse, a sports fanatic who had studied at Balliol College, Oxford, handed out application forms with a special section for sports. Furse was by no means unusual. "In the Sudan the provincial governor of Kassala, R. E. H. Baily, who had played cricket for Harrow and Cambridge, used to circulate a leather-bound book among his staff every morning, in which they were expected to indicate against their names the particular form of exercise they would be taking that afternoon."[71] The men who had won their "colours" at Oxford and Cambridge were so prominent in the Political Service that wits referred to the Sudan as "the Land of Blacks ruled by Blues."[72] We can be quite certain about the prevalence of the "games ethic" in the British colonies. We have a reasonably clear view of the pattern of its institutionalization in these colonies. The historical details, however, are often obscure. Anthropologists

have provided us with numerous studies of traditional African sports; historians have published relatively little on the transition from traditional to modern sports. Although the introduction of soccer was "an epoch-making event in the same way as the introduction of cocoa to the Gold Coast a century and more ago," no one has been able to identify "the originator of soccer in colonial Africa."[73]

We are not wholly in the dark. We know that wherever the British went, from Capetown to Cairo, they took their games with them. Kenya seems to have been typical of the African colonies. Britons

built up a sport culture in Kenya which was a copy of the one in Britain. . . . Even the smallest European community had its own club house, golf course, swimming pool, and tennis and squash courts. Where there were sufficient numbers, team games like rugby, cricket and field hockey were also played. The only drawback to all of this was that these facilities and the sport and social intercourse which they provided were open only to Europeans.[74]

No matter what the sport, colonial officers, military as well as civilian, preferred to compete among themselves and occasionally to indulge their more athletic wives and daughters in a game of field hockey or tennis. Although most natives were excluded from these attempts to replicate British culture in the tropics, there were exceptions—African soldiers and policemen were introduced to modern sports as part of their fitness programs and children educated at missionary schools were taught to play cricket, rugby, and soccer.

The latter exception was especially important because these church-run schools trained the boys—and to a lesser extent the girls—who became the native elite. Some colonial administrators left the missionaries to their own devices. Others, like Sir Frederick Lugard, the atheist governor-general of Nigeria, went beyond a laissez-faire attitude and actively encouraged the churches to include sports in the schools they established

throughout the colony. In these clerical schools for native chil-dren, Lugard hoped that sports might serve as a means to pro-duce what Mangan refers to as "atheistic athleticism."[75]

The athleticism cannot be doubted. The masters of institu-tions like the Alliance School in Nairobi, Kenya, and the Church Missionary Society Grammar School of Freetown, Sier-ra Leone, were physically active men who took their sports seri-ously. Headmaster Francis Carey of Alliance School recalled that "Christianity and games were only a part of the life of the school but were indeed its most important elements."[76] A for-mer student of the Freetown School in Sierra Leone remem-bered, "Games were compulsory. . . . We played cricket in the dry season, and football in the rainy season, under the supervi-sion of the appropriate master."[77] According to the General Sec-retary of the Uganda Olympic Committee, soccer was brought to the natives of Kampala in 1910 "by missionaries from the United Kingdom, our former colonial masters."[78] These mis-sionaries seem to have been anticipated by A. G. Fraser, who carried a soccer ball to Uganda in 1900 and laid out a soccer field, four years later, at King's School in Budo, a school estab-lished for the sons of Ugandan chiefs. When Fraser moved on to Achimota College in the Gold Coast, he arranged for the stu-dents to have the civilizing benefits of two cricket ovals and four football fields.[79] In Nigeria, too, British clerics and lay teachers emphasized soccer and other modern sports as an instrument of acculturation.[80] It was not just schoolmasters who spread the gospel of modern sports. Marion Stevenson, a Scottish missionary at Tumutumu in Kenya, "played her small part in the diffusion of British games—in the interests of disci-pline and more importantly of purity." Soccer, she alleged, dis-tracted the boys from dances and fistfights.[81]

It should, however, be emphasized that the main target for the games-mad British missionary was the son of the native chief. Throughout British-ruled Africa, ordinary people were

(unless they seemed too intimately a part of pagan ritual). Modern sports festivals, like Empire Day, first celebrated in Nigeria in 1893, did gradually supplant traditional games, but the organization of regular year-round play came slowly. For the white settlers of South Africa, a Football Association was established in 1892; it was not until 1922 that the Football Association of Kenya, which may have been the first African sports federation for black players, was founded. The Nigeria Football Association did not come into existence until 1945.[82]

The British were, of course, not the only actors in the drama of sports diffusion throughout Africa. In the years just before World War 1, missionaries introduced soccer into what was then the Belgian Congo and is now Zaïre.[83] In 1919, French colonists organized a team, for Europeans, in Brazzaville, the capital of the French Congo. In the twenties, the Belgians and the French played one another, and the natives were quick to form their own teams. On Bastille Day, 1930, the players of Kinshasha's *Mutuelle* crossed the Congo River to challenge Brazzaville's *L'Etoile,* thereby inaugurating the area's first African-built soccer field. A year later, a sports federation was founded in the French colony to encourage native participation in modern sports. Since the authorities were leery about the formation of native teams and generally opposed to interracial contests, European volunteers acted as coaches, trainers, and officials. The organization foundered when the colonial administration allocated most of the available funds to the European members of the *Club Athlétique Brazzavillois.* An additional brake on the diffusion of soccer was the colonizers' demand that the Africans play without shoes, allegedly to prevent savage injury to civilized shins. In response to this indignity, some disaffected natives left to join the *Fédération Athlétique Congolais,* which the Church established in 1933. The clergy, it seems, had no objection to all God's children wearing shoes.[84]

The Congo was not the only French colony with a contingent of European and native *soccer players*. In the twenties, a handful of Senegalese seem to have been accepted as members of *le Racing-Club Dakarois*, which included soccer among its sports. In the thirties, at a time when the colonial authorities were scouting unsuccessfully for African track-and-field talent, a number of Senegalese were forming soccer clubs in the cities of Dakar, Saint-Louis, and Bamako.[85] There were also native teams in Cameroon as early as 1927.[86] On the whole, however, the diffusion of modern sports through the French, Belgian, and Portuguese colonies of sub-Saharan Africa was far slower than in the contiguous British-ruled territories.[87] In German-ruled Africa, which was a large part of the continent before 1914, gymnastics was the preferred form of physical recreation and modern sports were more likely to be discouraged than promoted by the white minority.[88]

Everywhere in sub-Saharan Africa, Europeans who promoted modern sports among the indigenous peoples had to reconcile themselves to the persistence of what seemed to them incongruous beliefs and behaviors. Decades after the introduction of soccer, magic continued to play a role.

It is a fact accepted by one group living on the Zaire River upstream from Kinshasha that each team in a soccer match starts out with a preordained number of goals. In the days preceding the match, team magicians do battle with medicine and supernatural force to steal the opponent's points and to defend their own. Actual play is the public enactment of what the magician's combat has already determined. Cameroonian soccer players kick up the ground around their opponent's goal in an effort to uncover the magic that keeps the ball from going in.[89]

Modern sports radiated somewhat more quickly, and with less of a magical penumbra, throughout French-ruled North Africa, where the army's role was less prominent than in the sub-Saharan colonies. Morocco, Algeria, and Tunisia had rel-

atively large European populations and Islamic culture seems to have been somewhat more receptive to modern sports (for men) than were the indigenous cultures south of the Sahara. An additional reason for the comparatively rapid diffusion of soccer in North Africa was the early realization on the part of Arab nationalists that sports clubs were an excellent nucleus for political organization. In Algeria, which had been seized by the French in 1830, the colonists formed clubs for marksmen, for gymnasts, and—eventually—for rugby and soccer players, but "the practice of sports and related physical activities was strictly reserved for Europeans." With the rise of anticolonialist nationalism, sports became, in the words of an Arab scholar, "a phenomenon of appropriation." That which was not freely offered by the colonizer was seized from him." In 1926, Arab nationalists in Algiers organized the *Étoile Nord-Africaine* as a center for sports and politics. By 1928, Algerian soccer had become a predominantly Arab sport with unmistakable anticolonial overtones. In the FLN's struggle for Algerian independence, soccer became "an instrument of sedition."[90]

In Tunisia, which became a French protectorate in 1881, soldiers rather than settlers were initially responsible for "the eruption . . . of western sports," but the colonists who crossed the Mediterranean from France and Italy soon established a civilian network of sports clubs. In 1921, the *Ligue Tunisien de Football* brought together a medley of sports organizations whose names indicated their ethnic identity: *Jeune France, Stella d'Italia, le Foot-ball Club Sionniste, La Musulmane.* Beneath the cooperative multicultural surface lay the political differences destined to end European rule. They were differences of which everyone was keenly aware. "Every Tunisian sports victory against the European sports organizations," wrote Ben Larbi Mohamed and Borhane Errais, "contributed to the destruction of the myth of colonial power."[91]

Soccer is such an important example of global diffusion that a brief summary is in order. Although Europeans of many nationalities participated in the process, the initial diffusion of soccer football was accomplished principally by British military men, diplomatic personnel, businessmen, missionaries, and secular educators. They packed the game with the rest of their cultural baggage and took it with them to the farthest posts of empire and to countless other "places never under the Union Jack."[92]

The pattern of ludic diffusion confirms the generalizations of Everett M. Rogers, the leading sociological authority on "the diffusion of innovations."[93] The sequence of events he posits is clearly observable in the process of ludic diffusion. In almost every instance, the first to adopt soccer and other modern sports were the cosmopolitan sons of the local elites, many of whom had been educated at English schools in their own country or abroad. Seeking status as well as diversion, the bourgeoisie, many of whom were employed by British-owned firms, followed. From the panoply of different games imported by the upper and middle classes, the industrial workers of Europe and Latin America, like the indigenous population of Africa, appropriated soccer football as their own. That soccer, like other modern sports, was "first the province of the elite and then taken over by other sectors of society only underscores the fact that culture is competed for."[94] Did soccer appeal to the working class because of the game's aura of rough masculinity or did soccer acquire connotations of rugged virility because it was played, roughly, by sturdy villagers and a tough urban proletariat? The latter explanation seems more plausible. In any event, the scholastic amusement that began on the greens of nineteenth-century Oxford and Cambridge is now the passion of the stadia—and the back streets—of Genoa, Sao Paulo, Nairobi, and a thousand other cities.

§

ORIGINS

If Abner Doubleday is still remembered as the mythic progenitor of a game that he may never have played, the misinformation can be credited to one of baseball's greatest entrepreneurs—Albert Goodwill Spalding. As a former player, coach, manager, and owner, as a manufacturer of equipment and publisher of guidebooks, Spalding had a financial and emotional stake in baseball. In order to scotch rumors that America's "national game," derived from traditional British children's games (which, in fact, it did), Spalding, in 1905, named a six-man investigatory commission headed by his friend Abraham G. Mills. Their task was to determine who invented baseball.

The commission, relying on the memory of an octagenarian named Abner Graves, reported in 1907 that Doubleday was the man and Cooperstown the place. The legendary event occurred, according to the commission, in 1839. The good news of a purely American genesis was announced in Spalding's *Official Baseball Guide* for 1908 and was repeated in his book, *America's National Game*, published three years later (and still in print). Baseball, proclaimed Spalding with satisfaction, was "a game too lively for any but Americans to play." How absurd to imagine that stolid John Bull was capable of inventing Uncle Sam's lively pastime![1]

Careful readers of *America's National Game* will, however, come upon the name of Alexander Joy Cartwright, to whom Spalding attributed the organization of the first baseball club on September 23, 1845. Most historians now agree with Harold Peterson's contention that Cartwright, a twenty-five-year-old New York bank teller, did more than merely organize the Knickerbocker Base Ball Club; he drew up a set of rules distinctive enough from those of earlier games for us to say that the activity that occurred on Hoboken's "Elysian Fields" on October 6, 1845, was *baseball* and not rounders or town ball or "cat" or any one of a number of other traditional bat-and-ball games whose origins can be traced back to medieval times.[2] The Knickerbockers, unlike the Cooperstown urchins of cherished myth, were ordinary middle-class gentlemen; about one third of them were merchants. "They were more expert with the knife and fork at post-game banquets than with bat and ball on the diamond."[3]

No matter that our founding athletes turn out to have been gourmets. Alexander Cartwright still deserves the laurels posthumously awarded to Abner Doubleday. The "New York game" spread quickly and the Knickerbocker Club was soon overshadowed. The Gothams (1850), originally dubbed the Washington Club, were followed by the Excelsiors (1854) and a

number of other middle-class teams. The first viable plebeian clubs seem to have been the Eckfords of Greenpoint and the Atlantics of Jamaica, both founded in 1856. It was they—the dockworkers, teamsters, bricklayers, and carpenters, not the bank clerks and young professionals—who became the new sport's typical players. The game's pre-Civil War popularity among the working class can be conjectured from an 1857 song, "The Baseball Fever":

Our merchants have to close their stores
Their clerks away are staying,
Contractors too, can do no work,
Their hands are all out playing.[4]

The urban worker at play was an annoyance to his employers and fair game for perennially vote-hungry politicians. The New York Mutuals, organized in 1857 by the volunteer firemen of the Mutual Hook and Ladder Company, were directed by William Marcy Tweed, who subsequently used the team as a cog in his Tammany Hall machine.[5] Office-seekers began to scramble aboard the ludic bandwagon. The least an alderman could do for his working-class constituents was to cheer from the bleachers and toast the team's unparalleled accomplishments at the postgame festivities.

By the end of the decade, partisans of the "New York game" had won over the adherents of the "Massachusetts game" (which had slightly different rules). Twenty-two clubs formed the National Association of Base Ball Players in 1857. Contrary to what one might have expected, the Civil War, rather than hindering the diffusion of the game, actually accelerated it. Baseball alleviated the boredom of life in a military camp. Thanks to the enforced geographical mobility of the war, soldiers and sailors from the Northeast were able to spread the good news far and wide. They taught the game not only to the men of Midwestern regiments but also to Confederate troopers with whom they fraternized in prisoner-of-war camps. Ironi-

cally, it was often immigrants born in County Kerry or in Bran-
denburg who explained the rules of the new "national game," to
fellow citizens whose ancestors had arrived on the *Mayflower*.
Although the postwar years were the heyday of the "cult of
domesticity," a surprisingly large number of young women
acquired the ability not only to bake and sew but also to wield
a bat and field a line drive. At Vassar College in the spring of
1866, twenty-three students formed a pair of teams—the Lau-
rel Base Ball Club and the Abenakis Base Ball Club. A decade
later, in 1875, there were at least three clubs: the Sure-Pops, the
Daisy-Clippers, and the Royals. That same year, at Smith College, Minnie Stephens and her friends organized a team. When
they failed in an attempt to steal a bat from a group of Northampton boys, they did the proper thing and bought one. "The
athletic, robust, healthy, competitive woman," writes Gai I.
Berlage, "was the antithesis of the [era's] ideal and yet, by the
1890s, sports for women—and especially baseball—were part
of college life."[6] The privileged students at Vassar, Smith, Bryn
Mawr, Radcliffe, Wellesley, and other women's schools were
obviously not typical of their sex, but there were scattered indications that other women were hardy enough to play the
national game. In the eighties, an entrepreneur named Harry H.
Freeman sponsored a short-lived team of female professional
baseball players and a number of women had brief careers as
semiprofessionals. The invention of softball more or less halted
the growth of women's baseball, but a time of glory began in
1943 when Philip Wrigley, owner of the Chicago Cubs, en-
livened the wartime doldrums of major-league baseball with an
All-American Girls' Baseball League. The league, which inspired the film *A League of Their Own* (1992), lasted for nearly a
dozen years.[7]

It is a commonplace among historians that the tempo of industrialization was quicker in the United States than it had been in
England. We can see a similar acceleration in the evolution of

American sports. If one dates the "invention" of soccer football from 1848, when the Cambridge Rules were drafted, then base-ball was born three years before "the people's game." Baseball's national association of amateur players preceded soccer's by six years. When overtly professional soccer began in England with the creation of Football League in 1888, baseball's developmen-tal lead had increased to twelve years. In 1876, William A. Hul-bert had brought the owners together in the National League of Professional Base Ball Clubs. Baseball's more rapid march toward modernity might have been interpreted by the prescient, even then, as an omen of Great Britain's eventual displacement by the United States as the premier exporter of modern sports.

JAPAN

When one considers how culturally different nineteenth-centu-ry Japan was from the United States, one has to be astonished that baseball was introduced in the Meiji era and not—as many Americans assume—as a result of the postwar occupation of the islands by forces under Douglas MacArthur. The military pres-ence that loomed behind the diffusion of baseball was Com-modore Matthew Perry, whose "black ships" arrived in Japan in 1853 and confronted the shogunate with the brute fact of Amer-ican naval might. As part of the "Meiji Restoration" that returned political power from the shogun to the emperor, Japan's leaders embarked upon a campaign of modernization that included the complete reorganization of the educational system.

The high-minded preamble to the Educational Code promul-gated in 1872 made no mention whatsoever of *physical* educa-tion, which the imperial authorities considered an unnecessary frill. Japanese students shared their elders' attitudes: "They are contemptuous of their bodies," commented Nobuo Hiraiwa, "as if strength of physique were tantamount to savagery or animal-istic power."[8] The foreign teachers engaged by the Japanese, however, had their own ideas about the place of sports in the

educational system. In 1873, Horace Wilson introduced the game of baseball at Kaisei Gakkō (now Tokyo University). Transportation was another sector undergoing rapid modernization. It must, therefore, have seemed almost inevitable that Hiroshi Hiraoka, an engineer who had studied in Boston and become a Red Sox fan, would assemble the first regular baseball team, in 1878, from members of the Shimbashi Athletic Club (an organization formed for the benefit of supervisory personnel of the Shimbashi Railroad).[9]

Initially, baseball had some competition from cricket, introduced to Japan on October 16, 1869, when eleven British residents of the bustling port city of Kobe met a team from H.M.S. Ocean. A cricket club was organized three days later, thanks largely to the initiative of Arthur Hesketh Groom, but the British, who set the tone in Kobe, lost out, in sports as in the economic sphere, to the Americans whose most active colony was located in Yokohama.[10] Before the end of the century, baseball had won the allegiance of most of the members of the Yokohama Cricket and Athletic Club.[11]

Baseball, for which "the initial campus response was less than overwhelming,"[12] received an enormous boost in 1896 when some Tokyo schoolboys arranged for a "kokusai shiai" ("international contest"). Five years earlier, Ichikō ("First Higher School") had issued a formal challenge to the Yokohama Athletic Club, but the challenge was haughtily rejected. One of the students described his injured feelings:

The foreigners in Yokohama have established an athletic field in their central park into which no Japanese may enter. There, playing by themselves, they boast of their skill in baseball. When we attempt to challenge them, they refuse, saying, "Baseball is our national game" or "Our bodies are twice the size of yours."[13]

After five years of frustrating negotiations, William B. Mason, an English teacher at Ichikō, overcame the condescension of the other Americans at the Yokohama Athletic Club. A match was

arranged. By the time the game was played, on May 23, 1896, the air crackled with emotional tension. Lingering illusions about good sportsmanship vanished when the spectators at the Yokohama Athletic Club jeered the arrival of the nearly uni- formed Ichikō students and taunted them as they warmed up for the game. The haughty Americans, anticipating an easy rout of the impudent challengers, experienced a humiliating upset. Wielding their bats with skill and determination, the boys smashed stereotypes and won by a lopsided score of 29–4. "While gloom pervaded Yokohama, Ichikō athletes returned home to a rousing welcome marked by banzai chants, choruses from the national anthem, and overflowing cups of sake."[14] The Japan Weekly Mail found an excuse for the boastful Americans' poor performance: "School-boys with their daily opportunities for practice, their constant matches, and sparer figures have always the advantage over a team of grown men . . . who have not played together."[15]

The students won a June 5 rematch with a score of 32–9. A third encounter was scheduled. The emotional stakes rose. A team of sailors from the cruiser Detroit was dispatched to Tokyo for this third game, played on June 27 before nearly ten thou- sand Japanese spectators. Ichikō triumphed again, this time by a score of 22–6. American honor was finally redeemed, partial- ly, when the battleship Olympia steamed into port with a crew noted for athletic prowess. On the Fourth of July, the reinforced American squad managed a narrow 14–12 victory over their adolescent opponents.[16]

Students like those of the First Higher School were the most eager of the early players. Japanese baseball did not become an intercollegiate sport until the end of the century. Keio Universi- ty, one of Japan's premier institutions of private higher educa- tion, had a team in 1885, but Waseda University, Keio's great rival, had none until 1901. Keio and Waseda began to play one another in 1903 in a series that even today excites emotions

comparable to those aroused in this country by the annual Harvard-Yale football game. Together with Meiji University, Keio and Waseda formed an intercollegiate league in 1914. This organization, later expanded to include six of Tokyo's most prestigious universities, became the athletic equivalent of the Ivy League (upon which it was modeled). When Nels Norgren of the University of Chicago led a collegiate team to Japan in 1922, he reported in amazement that baseball "is more the national sport of Japan than it is of America."[17] Norgren, who spent more time with Japan's educated elite than with the nation's rice farmers and factory hands, overstated the popular appeal of the game, but *bēsubōru* had certainly become a part of campus life.

Inevitably, the collegians wanted to do what the boys of *Ichikō* had done: "to beat them at their own game." After Waseda lost a match to the University of Chicago in 1910, Suishu Tobita, a student who eventually became known as "the god of Japanese baseball," vowed revenge. Years after his graduation, he left his job as a journalist in order to coach Waseda's team. He was a harsh taskmaster. "If the players do not try so hard as to vomit blood in practice," he claimed, "then they can not hope to win games. One must suffer to be good." They did suffer, they were good, and they did win. In 1925 they defeated the University of Chicago three times in a four-game series (the fourth game was a tie). Tobita's conclusion, reminiscent of some recent opinions voiced in Japan, was that the Americans lacked spirit.[18]

By 1915, *bēsubōru* had become widespread enough for an Osaka newspaper, *Asahi Shimbun*, to sponsor a national tournament for high-school teams.[19] The annual competition became the schools' most fanatically pursued extracurricular activity. Two years after a memorable 1934 tour by an American team that included Babe Ruth, a professional league was launched. In the summer of 1941, a few months before the attack on Pearl Harbor, the militarists who controlled the Japanese government

disbanded the league. Baseball fell out of favor. Shortly after the devastating Japanese attack, an angry editorial in *The Sporting News* concluded that we Americans had generously given the gift of our national game to a pack of ingrates. The ethos of the sport had never "penetrated their yellow hides."[20] Had J. G. T. Spink, owner and publisher of *The Sporting News*, lived long enough to observe the revival of baseball during the postwar occupation, he might have been more sanguine about the game's long-term influence on Japanese culture. In 1950, the Japanese established a two-league system akin to ours. Every fall the champions of the Central League and the Pacific League compete in the "Japan Series."

Now that baseball is unquestionably Japan's most popular sport, drawing more participants and spectators than any of its rivals, scholars have attempted to explain this surprising popularity. Donald Roden believes that the game "caught on" because it "seemed to emphasize precisely those values that were celebrated in the civic rituals of state: order, harmony, perseverance, and self-restraint."[21] The Japanese adopted the game because these perceived values were familiar ones. While Roden's analysis is certainly possible, I incline to the contrary opinion that baseball was seized upon by the Japanese because it seemed to embody values that were *not* traditionally Japanese. Had they wanted to reaffirm their indigenous culture, they should have seized *kendō* swords and *kyūdō* bows rather than baseball bats. The American game, which Roden sees almost as a stately ceremony, Mark Twain characterized as "the outward and visible expression of the drive and push and rush and struggle of the raging, tearing, booming nineteenth century!"[22] Twain was surely right; baseball symbolized—for both the Japanese and their American contemporaries—not tradition but modernity. Like the telegraph, the telephone, and many other technological marvels of that era, the ludic import bore the magical stamp: Made in America. Whether or not the

Japanese enthusiasm for baseball will ebb away now that they perceive the United States as a nation in rapid decline is anybody's guess.

THE CARIBBEAN

Rafael Leónidas Trujillo Molina, the right-wing dictator of the Dominican Republic from 1930 to 1961, shared a passion for baseball with Fidel Castro, the left-wing dictator of Cuba from 1960 to who knows when. Similarly, Carlos Cuadra Clachar, the *Sandinista* who served as Nicaragua's commissioner of baseball, admitted that brutal Anastasio Somoza García deserved credit for at least one contribution to the nation he tyrannized and looted: as a fan, a player, an umpire, and—eventually—as owner of the *Cinco Estrellas*, he promoted "nuestro béisbol."23 One indicator of the more or less nonpartisan popularity of Caribbean baseball is the number of Hispanic players who have had major-league careers in the United States. Cuba's Orestes "Minnie" Minoso, Puerto Rico's Roberto Clemente, Venezuela's Chico Carrasquel and Luis Aparicio, the Dominican Republic's Juan Marichal, and Mexico's Fernando Valenzuela are only six names selected at random from the long list of Hispanic players who achieved stateside stardom in the major leagues.

Cubans were apparently the first Caribbeans to catch the baseball virus from the *Norteamericanos* and they were certainly active in spreading the fever. *When* the game crossed from the United States to Cuba is a matter of some dispute. The claim that American merchant sailors introduced baseball at Matanzas in 1840 is hard to credit because Alexander Cartwright's rules had not yet been formulated. Rounders or some other bat-and-ball game may have been played in 1840, but it would be another twenty or so years before Cuban students, not American seamen, planted the sport on the island and saw that it was firmly rooted. Among the upper-class Cuban youths sent to study in the United States was Nemesio Guilló; he is said to have intro-

duced baseball to Havana when he returned home in 1864. The first historically attested game took place between the Habana Base Ball Club and a team from Matanzas. The report published in *El Artista* for December 31, 1874, appeared over the name of "Henry." Whoever he or she was, "Henry" sprinkled English terms throughout the account of Havana's 51–9 victory.[24] Cuban teams were numerous enough by 1878 for Havana's Emilio Sabourín to organize the *Liga de Béisbol Profesional Cubana*, whose first and second annual tournaments were won by *El Club de Habana*.[25] An 1887 tour by the Philadelphia Athletics also helped to popularize the game.[26]

The first *aficionados*, who were members of the creole upper class, had to deal with the disapproval of the Spanish authorities who preferred that they devote themselves to the gymnastic exercises brought home from France in 1842 by José Rafael de Castro.[27] Drill seemed more compatible with good discipline than the exuberant disorder of a ballgame. The colonial administration also suspected, quite correctly, that sports had political implications. Opposition to Spanish rule came largely from upper-class nationalists who looked to the United States for their sports as well as for political ideals and funds. When armed resistance to Spanish rule brought an array of repressive countermeasures, baseball was banned (in 1895). Cuban patriots did not lose heart. Wenceslas Gálvez y Delmonte, "a ballplay-er turned writer," predicted in 1897 that baseball would surpass bullfighting and cockfighting, "centuries-old pastimes imported from Spain." His prophecy about ludic futures had unmistakable political overtones.[28]

Emilio Sabourín, the organizer of the *Liga de Béisbol*, personified the intimate connection between sports and politics. He was part of an underground organization that gathered and repaired weapons discarded by the Spanish troops. The weapons were then smuggled from Havana to the insurgent forces in the countryside. Sabourín and his friends also raised money for the rev-

olutionary party José Martí founded in 1892. Saburín was arrested in 1895, convicted of subversive activities, and exiled to a prison in Ceuta (in Spanish Morocco). There he died of pneumonia on July 5, 1897. A fellow prisoner, Juan Gualberto Gómez, praised him as "an enthusiastic partisan of this 'sport' that regenerates the human organism" and as "a passionate lover of his country's liberty." In almost equal degrees, Saburín was devoted to "el Base-Ball, su Familia y su Patria."[29]

When the island passed from Madrid's rather ineffectual rule to Washington's pervasive "protection," Cuban baseball (like North American economic investment) "took off." A viable amateur league was formed in 1914 and a professional one in 1917. There was soon a two-way traffic in ballplayers. Two light-skinned Cubans, Rafael Almeida and Armando Marsans, were signed by the Cincinnati Reds in 1911. In 1922, an entire team, the Cuban Stars, became a part of our eight-team Negro National League. In the fifties, Cuban and American *béisboleros* made the Havana Sugar Kings a contender in the International League. A number of *yanquis* who failed to make major-league rosters in the United States tried their luck on the island.[30]

Since Cuban baseball had a winter rather than a summer season, many major-leaguers welcomed the chance to play for Cuban teams. The infamous "reserve clause," which denied major-league players the right to bargain with any club other than the one that owned them, kept salaries so low that Americans were eager to earn extra dollars in "winter ball." Cuban players like Luis Tiant, Sr. had a chance to compete against major-league stars like Tris Speaker and Rogers Hornsby. The money and the climate were not the only attractions. Havana, in the days of dictator Fulgencio Batista, was renowned for its nightclubs, casinos, racetracks, and brothels. And the Cubans' more relaxed attitudes about racial differences made it possible for major-leaguers, all of whom were white, to compete against Josh Gibson and other stars of the Negro National

League: "For the Negro leaguers, Cuba served as an escape valve from repressive racism. In Cuba the players led more 'normal' lives: they played a single game each day and their travel was negligible. Then too, they were experiencing de facto integration."[31]

(The milder air did not, however, soften everyone. When Johnny Dunlap of the Boston Braves invited Early Wynn to have a drink with him and Willie Wells, a black player, Wynn responded, "I don't drink with niggers," whereupon Dunlap broke Wynn's jaw.[32])

Although Mexicans, too, became as enamored of baseball, there was a time when cricket seemed a more likely candidate for the title of national game. British mine owners and other businessmen set up the Mexico Cricket Club in 1827. A number of well-to-do Mexicans tried their hand at the game after French troops installed an Austrian Archduke as emperor of Mexico in 1864. An old photograph shows Ferdinand Maximilian and his court, accompanied by the British ambassador, Sir Charles Wyke, behind the stumps. The pitch, comments Julian Barnes, "seems to need not so much a roller as a gang of stone breakers."[33] Conditions were doubtless primitive in the early years of play, but amenities did come. A few years after the unfortunate Maximilian had been dispatched by a firing squad, the Mexican Cricket Club "arranged special trolley service [from the capital] to its pitch at Napolés, and it held a formal breakfast at 1 P.M. between innings."[34] The amenities may have been excessive; in 1868 the club did poorly in a match against players from various British-owned companies. The star of that game, M. J. Trigueros, was the only Mexican player. He was also the prime mover of the Victoria Cricket Club, which he formed from the ranks of his fellow students at the Escuela de Artes y Oficios. A number of other clubs sprang into life, but, later in the century, cricket went into decline, irrevocably replaced in upper-class Mexican affections by baseball.

By the time that American investors in the Mexican economy surpassed British entrepreneurs in the value of their holdings, which occurred in 1890, baseball had already made an appearance. "Doubleday's heirs and the carriers of his legend were the Yankee employees of the Mexican National and the Mexican Central railroads, who organized company teams in the summer of 1882 to play scrimmage games. A challenge match pitted the National Baseball Club against the Telephone Company, Sunday morning, July 28."[35] The railroad men prevailed by a score of 31–11.

On that Sunday morning, Mexicans were limited to the role of spectators, but they were not content to remain on the sidelines. A passion for American sports became a hallmark of what historians refer to as the "Porfirian persuasion" (a reference to Porfirio Díaz, the dictator who ruled from 1876 to 1911). "This temper showed a rush to accept European, and especially American, activities. . . . Baseball particularly reflected the growing influence of the United States."[36] The first Mexican teams were formed no later than 1886, when a game was played at Corazón de Jesus to collect funds for the city's poorhouse. By 1895, Mexican players in the capital were skillful enough to win the city's championship against the American Base-Ball Club and the Cricket Club (whose English players "adjusted more or less successfully to American rules").[37] The winners were by no means the city's only native team. Others who took to the game were the Victoria Club, the Cyclist Union Club, and teams representing the Colégio Militar and the Escuela Preparatoria.

Five years before the championship series played in Mexico City, three Cuban teenagers introduced the game to Yucatán. In 1892, two years after this first match, the upper class of Mérida formed El Sporting Club. A regional league appeared in 1905, but it soon disintegrated—not because of lack of interest but rather because of the intense rivalry between the Escalante family, which stocked its club with Yanqui players, and the Molina

family, which stocked *its* club with Cubans. In fact, the flow of Cubans to Yucatán was so strong that the Cuban championship was left high and dry. The island's tournament was canceled.[38]

In 1904, Mexican teams established two leagues. The first, for amateurs, played during the summer months; the second, for the semiprofessionals, was for winter ball. *El Record*, the winners of the 1906–7 season, had their moment of glory when they competed against the Chicago White Sox, the first major-league team to conduct spring training outside the United States. Although the Mexicans, whose team included two Americans, lost by a score of twelve to two, local fans were nonetheless proud of them. After all, the White Sox had won the 1906 World Series against the favored Chicago Cubs.[39]

The demographic base for turn-of-the-century Mexican baseball was narrow. Neither the peasants nor the urban poor were of the "Porfirian persuasion" and neither paid much attention to the game (or to any other modern sport). The outbreak of revolution in 1910 diverted the attention of the middle and upper classes to graver matters than a three-two count with bases loaded. When the spasms of political unrest became less severe, in 1920, baseball revived. By 1924, the capital had at least fifty-six teams, some of which now attracted working-class players and fans. A visit to Mexico City by Byron Bancroft Johnson, the founder of the American League, left him "so enthusiastic that he decided to donate a trophy to encourage the sport."[40]

While Johnson encouraged the amateur game with this and other benefactions, Mexican entrepreneurs established a new professional league, which began operations in 1925. Officialdom encouraged such enterprises. The *Partido Nacional Revolucionario* announced in 1932 that it had a "sacred obligation" to seek physical as well as economic and social progress.[41]

By the forties, the level of play and of salaries in the *Liga Mexicana* were both high enough to cause a crisis in major-league baseball in the United States. A Vera Cruz millionaire, Jorge

Pasquel, became president of the *Liga* and determined to mount a real challenge to the *gringos*. Since a number of Mexican players had had successful careers in the United States, Pasquel concluded that turnabout was fair play. Aided by his four brothers and a willingness to pay players two or three times what they earned north of the Río Grande, Pasquel began to raid not only the Negro National League, which had always been easy prey for Hispanics eager to stockpile talent, but also the major leagues. Players like New York Giant pitcher Tom Gorman were impressed when tens of thousands of dollars were placed on the table—literally. The *Liga Mexicana*, which the Pasquel brothers expanded from six teams to eight, flourished. Major-league baseball's Commissioner Albert "Happy" Chandler blacklisted the "jumpers" but was unable to dam the southward flow of players or entice the defectors to return.

> A measure of Pasquel's power was displayed after Ray Dandridge left for the States after a salary squabble with him. Dandridge soon received a shock. While he was in a train compartment near Monterrey, the Mexican army stopped the train and came looking for him! The explanation was simple enough: Pasquel had changed his mind and was prepared to raise Dandridge's salary.[42]

Unfortunately for the ambitious Pasquel brothers, the largest Mexican stadium, the capital's, held only 22,000 fans. Too few tickets were sold to pay the recklessly inflated salaries. There were no television networks to offer multimillion-dollar contracts. The Pasquels began to cut costs in 1947 and the "jumpers" begged Chandler to take them back, which he did when a successful legal challenge to the blacklist threatened baseball's antitrust exemption.[43]

Despite the continued successes of the game in Cuba and in Mexico, the Dominican Republic has become the center of gravity for Caribbean *béisbol*. The game came early to the island. Cuban patriots who had fled their homes after the failure of their first war for independence (1868–78) sought solace in baseball during their exile in Santo Domingo. The first Dominican clubs to enjoy more than an ephemeral existence were formed in 1891 by Ignacio and Ubaldo Alomá, iron workers from Cuba. The clubs were officially entitled *El Cauto* (from a Cuban river) and *Cervecería* (from the local beer). When Dr. Samuel Mendoza y Ponce de León took the game to the interior of the island in 1893, he adopted the nicknames that the fans had given to the two Cuban teams because of their blue and red uniforms—the *Azules* and the *Rojos*.[44]

A group of boys, mostly from the upper class, organized what became one of the island's most successful teams—*El Club Licey*—in 1907. The city of Santo Domingo held its first championship in 1912, a year after *Licey* defeated a team from San Pedro de Macorís in one of the first interurban encounters. Santo Domingo also produced the first team to vanquish a visiting American nine. In 1914, Dominicans rejoiced as Enrique Hernández of *El Club Nuevo* pitched a no-hit, no-run game against a team of Americans from the U.S. Navy cruiser *Washington*.[45]

From 1916 to 1924, the United States carried out one of its periodic military occupations of the Dominican Republic. Even before the Marines landed, James Sullivan, the American ambassador, saw that baseball might pacify the natives. "The importance of this new interest to the young men in a little country like the Dominican Republic should not be minimized. It satisfies a craving in the nature of the people for exciting conflict, and [it] is a real substitute for the contest in the hill-sides with rifles."[46] Ignoring the ambassador's sage counsel, the State Department refused to make the diffusion of baseball a matter of public policy, but the game flourished nonetheless.

During the twenties, American baseball waxed and cricket, which the British had introduced in the nineteenth century, waned. American popular culture became so pervasive that two cricket teams in the town of Consuelo were dubbed the

Twentieth Century Foxes and the Metro Goldwyn Mayers.[47] Against the baseball tide, soccer made no more headway than cricket did. While still a child, Juan Estaban Vargas—a gifted athlete whose subsequent career took him to Cuba, Panama, Columbia, Venezuela, Canada, and the United States—abandoned *fútbol*, because—as his cousin later explained—baseball had more *acción*.[48]

From 1922 to 1936, *Licey* employed an American black, Charles Dore, as its field manager, but Cuban influence continued to be remarkably strong throughout the island. When *Licey* imported several Cuban players, *Escogido* responded by bringing in a real star, Martin Dihigo, who may be the only player enshrined in the Halls of Fame of Cuba, Mexico, and the United States. The rush to recruit Cuban stars became so frantic that the *Estrellas Orientales* of San Pedro de Macorís were transformed into a completely Cuban team except for three Dominican players. Thanks to its imported talent, San Pedro's *Estrellas* won the championship. This was too severe a blow to the dictator's prestige. Trujillo merged the two leading teams of the capital, *Licey* and *Escogido*, into a new club privileged to bear the dictator's name. *Ciudad Trujillo* included eight African Americans from the United States, six Cubans, a Puerto Rican, and a lone Dominican.

Trujillo's raids on the Pittsburgh Crawfords and the Homestead Grays brought him the players he needed and disrupted the season of the Negro National League. Trujillo paid Josh Gibson, James "Cool Papa" Bell, and the other black stars far more than they were able to earn in the United States, and he expected great things from them. Legend has it that the dictator told Satchel Paige "to pitch a shutout or face a firing squad."[49] According to another anecdote, "when Trujillo's team lost a series to Santiago, his players returned to their hotel to discover a squad of angry militiamen, firing their rifles in the air. 'You know you are playing for El Presidente,' they shouted, and more shots rang out."[50] The stories may be apocryphal. And maybe they are not. The highly motivated *Ciudad Trujillo* players won the island's championship in 1937. The dictator seems, however, to have decided that such glory was overpriced. Having made his point, he put an end to professional baseball until after World War II.[51]

With the revival of the professional league in 1951, the flow of baseball players reversed direction. American players continued to be actively recruited for the island's teams, but they were soon outnumbered by the Dominicans who sought fame and fortune on the mainland. The first of many hundreds was Ozzie Virgil, hired by the San Francisco Giants in 1956.[52] A number of factors combined to tighten the bonds between the island and major-league baseball. The racial integration of American baseball, which had begun in 1947, opened doors for Dominicans of African ancestry. For Cuban players, white and black, the doors to major-league baseball slammed shut in 1960 when contacts between the United States and Castro's Cuba were broken. After 1960, the Dominican Republic became North American baseball's chief source of Caribbean talent.

Relations between the islanders and the mainlanders moved into a new phase when free agency came to major-league baseball in 1976. A year after the restrictions of the "reserve clause" were finally loosened by a combination of legal action and labor-management negotiations, the Toronto Blue Jays opened a Dominican baseball camp run by Epifanio ("Epy") Guerrero, a former major-leaguer. By 1991, one third of all the Blue Jays had flown north from the Caribbean.[53] By 1989, fifteen other major-league franchises had followed Toronto's lead and established "academies" on the island. (The maelstrom of cultural interactions must not have been turbulent enough with sixteen American teams roiling the Dominican waters; a Japanese team, the Hiroshima Carp, has taken a leaf from the American notebook and opened a Dominican baseball camp.)

The most elaborate "academy"—*Campo Las Palmas*—is owned by the Los Angeles Dodgers. Dreams of glory pull and desperate poverty pushes young Dominicans to the gates of the camp. From the hundreds of youths who aspire to play in the United States, Cuban-born Ralph Avila selects a few to spend thirty days at *Las Palmas,* after which the best of them are signed for a bonus of $4,000 to play for six months in the island's minor leagues (for $700 a month). The best of *these* players advance to the *Estrelles Orientales* or another of the island's six major-league teams. Since each of the American major-league franchises has a limited allotment of only twenty-four visas with which to bring foreign players into the United States, only a few hundred of the thousands of young aspirants can realize their dream of "a ticket off the island." Most of those who arrive in the United States spend their careers in the minor leagues, but islanders who have made it to the National and American Leagues are numerous enough for Santo Domingo and San Pedro de Macorís to claim proudly that they are, on a per-capita basis, the world's leading source of baseball talent. Dominicans now playing for the Dodgers and other major-league teams, sixty-five of them in 1990, are the magnet that draws thousands more to the gates of the training camps.[54]

Although the young men continue to arrive, not everyone is happy with these establishments. The camps have been characterized (by a North American critic) as "the baseball counterpart of the colonial outpost, the physical embodiment overseas of the parent franchise."[55] They are "as recognizable a mark of foreign domination as the sugar mill."[56]

In 1990, American economic influence on Dominican baseball was manifested in another form. The "Caribbean World Series" was deflected from its traditional orbit. The championship, which had been regularly contested in Mexico, the Dominican Republic, Puerto Rico, and Venezuela, was transferred to Miami's Orange Bowl (designed for football, the stadium is a poor place to play baseball). The main argument for the move seems to have been the number of television sets in South Florida. This particular instance of Yankee domination was bitterly resented throughout the Caribbean. On the other hand, ire at Yankee arrogance and greed have not diminished the Hispanic love of *béisbol*. The attitude of many of the Caribbean's *fanaticos* is well represented by the Dominican journalist Pedro Julio Santana in an interview with Rob Ruck: "You must understand that baseball is not thought of as the sport of the Yankee imperialists. That is a stupid way of thinking. Baseball is the national sport of the United States, and it is the greatest thing that the United States has given us and the other countries of the Caribbean. [The Americans] have not given us anything else that, in my opinion, is of any value."[57]

AUSTRALIAN BASEBALL

Basketball is the most Americanized of Australian professional sports ventures from the perspective of the players' nationality and golf is probably the Australian sport most completely dominated by foreign (in this case Japanese) ownership of the facilities. Regular-season National Football League games can be seen on Australian television and the amateur version of the American game is now played in Victoria, New South Wales, and South Australia. Baseball is, however, the best sport for a case study of outside penetration into what was once an almost exclusively British sphere of cultural influence because baseball is perceived as a distinctly American sport in direct competition with its near relative cricket, the archetypically English game.[58]

Australian baseball, popularly believed to have been inspired by the presence of American servicemen stationed in Queensland during World War II, actually dates from the mid-nineteenth century. A decade after the discovery of gold at Sutter's Mill in California, a number of "Forty-Niners" hurried on to Australia to try their luck in another gold rush. Some of them were foresighted enough to pack a few balls and bats along with their picks and shovels. Of their first games we know very little, but two teams of Americans, who may or may not have been miners, laid out a baseball diamond in Sydney's Moore Park in 1882. They played the first historically attested game of Australian baseball.[59]

Australians were exposed to a more professional version of America's "national game" in 1888 when Albert G. Spalding took the Chicago White Sox and the "All-Americans" on a round-the-world tour. There had been an earlier expedition to England in a vain attempt to convert the English, in 1874, but this venture was far more ambitious. Spalding's team was the first literally to circumnavigate the globe. Embarking in San Francisco, they stopped for exhibition games in Hawaii and then sailed to New Zealand, where they entertained the Aucklanders on December 10th. From there they proceeded across the Tasman Strait to Australia. Led by Chicago's redoubtable Adrian "Cap" Anson, they performed in Sydney, Melbourne, Adelaide, and Ballarat.[60]

"Performed" is the correct word. The visitors entertained their hosts not only with expertly executed home runs and double plays but also with parachute jumps from a balloon and the antics of Clarence Duval, an African-American boy who confirmed the audiences' cultural stereotypes by singing, dancing, and twirling a baton. Whether attracted by song and dance or by athletic prowess, crowds were large and seemed to be enthusiastic. At the Melbourne Cricket Grounds, reported Harry Palmer, "we played to pretty nearly twelve thousand people, and the degree of interest they manifested in the game was a gratifying surprise to each and every member of our party."[61]

Some Australian journalists expressed an interest in the game, others sneered that it was merely a debased version of rounders. American assumptions of superiority were galling. The editors of the *Sydney Referee* were unable to contain their irritation at

American airs. On January 27, 1889, the *Referee* complained "that Americans think baseball the only game worth playing. [They] abuse and revile [Australian rules] football, and ridicule cricket. They think the players the only people on earth, and that all the world should bow down and worship them."[62] Spalding, whose promotional flair rivaled Phineas T. Barnum's, was probably guilty as charged. Once back in the United States, he opined in his familiar self-assured way that cricket was a game for the elite and baseball one for the masses.

One member of Spalding's entourage, Harry H. Simpson, stayed behind to test this belief in baseball's potential for mass appeal. He began to organize Australian baseball games. Teams from Victoria and South Australia met twice in April of 1889. In the nineties there may have been as many as fifteen teams active in Adelaide, Melbourne, and Victoria. By 1897, the game was popular enough for an Australian team led by Harry Musgrove to set off for an ambitious twenty-six-game tour of the United States. The "Kangaroos" were disappointed to discover that they were no match for their American opponents. They were also miffed that their hosts did not provide banquets and receptions comparable to those enjoyed by Spalding's group a decade earlier. On the way home, the star-crossed Australian team stopped in London, where the manager absconded with their funds. "The tour was judged to be a disaster from all points of view."[63]

Australian baseball did better at home than abroad. A Metropolitan Baseball Association was formed in Sydney in 1898. At Melbourne Girls' Grammar School, Gwynneth Morris added baseball to the array of sports in her physical-education classes.[64] Interest in the game rose to the point where South Australia, New South Wales, and Victoria were able to launch an Australian Baseball Council in 1912. At first, the promoters of the game wisely avoided direct conflict with cricket; baseball was played during the continent's relatively mild winters while the summer months were left to the cricketers (some of whom doubled as baseball players when their season ended). Although Australia in the twenties seemed to many "a backwater awash"[65] with films and radio programing from the United States, the domain of sports continued to be steadfastly British. Baseball remained a marginal activity through the thirties and forties. The advent of television in 1956 advanced the process of "Americanization," but it was not until 1973 that the Australian Baseball Council was confident enough of the sport's appeals to switch to summer play—a direct challenge to cricket.[66]

The next phase began in 1989, exactly a century after Spalding's tour, when the eight-team professional Australian Baseball League was formed. American involvement was direct and indispensable. In addition to an infusion of American players (four to a team), each of the eight original franchises was able to rely upon financial and administrative support from an American major-league club (see Table 3.1).

After the first season, during which the league drew 376,650 spectators, the Sydney Metros were sold and renamed the Sydney Wave. In a move to Australianize the team, the Melbourne Monarchs were dubbed the Melbourne Bushrangers. The Gold Coast Clippers were acquired by a Japanese firm and renamed the Daikyo Dolphins. It was obvious almost from the start that tick-

Table 3.1
AMERICAN SPONSORSHIP OF AUSTRALIAN
BASEBALL TEAMS, 1990–1991

Australian Team	American Sponsor
Waverley Red	Cincinnati Reds
Melbourne Monarchs	California Angels
Parramatta Patriots	Pittsburgh Pirates
Sydney Metros	Chicago Cubs
Brisbane Bandits	San Diego Padres
Gold Coast Clippers	Milwaukee Brewers
Adelaide Giants	Los Angeles Dodgers
Perth Heat	Baltimore Orioles

et sales (at five Australian dollars each) were inadequate to keep the league afloat, but the Pepsi-Cola Company signed a sponsoring deal worth $500,000 and Channel Nine TV purchased the rights to the 1990–91 final series.[67] In 1992, Channel Nine also began telecasting major-league games from North America.[68]

In response to the American invasion, defenders of Australian cricket mounted a counterattack. They began a media campaign to promote their game and win back its departed fans, but there are few signs of success. In fact, the aggressive adoption of Madison Avenue techniques and the rapid commercialization of Australian cricket have been cited by some analysts as a *cause* of the game's loss of ground to American baseball: "The once hegemonic amateur ideology has become increasingly marginal and residual, as all professional (men's) sports have been reorganized on the basis of management science with executive directors and specialists in advertising, marketing, and public relations."[69] According to this theory, the Australian media entrepreneur Kerry Packer undermined cricket's defense against baseball's incursions when he began to telecast one-day professional World Series Cricket matches on Channel Nine, matches packaged and publicized on the American model. Packer's innovations allegedly cost cricket a good deal of its pristine amateur allure.[70] When cricket "was dragged into the commercial world of international sport, the last handicap to American-style baseball in Australia was removed."[71]

This novel theory about the unexpected negative consequences of modern marketing is not persuasive. Baseball's successful penetration of a cultural domain long thought to be solidly British can be explained, in part, by a postwar influx of European immigrants who are not particularly interested in an Australian replication of British life. These new immigrants seem especially susceptible to the lure of baseball, whose third-strike-dropped-ball rule is no more arcane than cricket's leg-before-wicket regulation, but the immigrants are by no means the only ones to experience the permeation of Australian life by American popular culture. "In the twentieth century, the United States has sold its culture—its films, music, language, cars and many other products—effectively and often aggressively to Australians."[72] In short, baseball's most important advantage, one that cricket can never hope to overcome, is quite simply that baseball is an American game.

4

BASKETBALL

ORIGIN

Cricket, soccer football, and baseball are all sports that evolved from traditional games. They were "invented" only in the weak sense that someone sat down, pen in hand, and codified a set of rules from which the modern version of the sport has more or less continuously evolved. Basketball was invented in a much stronger sense. It had no recognizable antecedents. It was made to order, cut from whole cloth in response to a specific request.

It happened in 1891 in Springfield, Massachusetts, at the School for Christian Workers (later renamed the International Young Men's Christian Association Training School and still later renamed once again as Springfield College). Basketball's inventor was a thirty-year-old Canadian immigrant named James Naismith. The game was, in Naismith's words, "a synthetic product of the office. The conditions were met, and the rules formulated…before any attempt was made to test its value."[1] Naismith had been given the task of inventing the game by the twenty-five-year-old superintendent of the school, Luther Halsey Gulick, who encouraged Naismith's ingenuity by arguing, with illustrations drawn from the chemistry of synthetic drugs and dyes, that novelty is merely the result of new combinations of known elements. Specifically, Gulick challenged the young instructor to devise a game complicated enough to maintain the interest of adults and spatially confined enough to be played indoors when New England winters daunted faint-hearted Christians. Naismith tried prisoner's base, sailors' tag, rounders, town ball, battle ball, and leapfrog, but all failed the first criterion; adults lost interest. He tried indoor baseball, football, soccer, and lacrosse, but all failed the second criterion; they caused too many injuries when played in the confined space of a gymnasium. Whereupon the resourceful Canadian invented basketball. It was, in his own words, "a deliberate attempt to supply for the winter season a game that would have the same interest for the young man that football has in the fall and baseball in the spring."[2]

In a 1914 article published in the *American Physical Education Review* and in a short book entitled *Basketball*, which appeared in 1941 to celebrate the fiftieth anniversary of the game's invention, Naismith reconstructed the sequence of logical steps he took as he reasoned his way to the solution of the problem presented to him by Gulick. Perhaps the best indicator of his instrumental approach was the placement of the basket (which was, in 1891, quite literally a peach basket). Fearful of potential injury from balls hurled forcefully at a ground-level vertical goal (like soccer's), Naismith elevated the goal above the players' heads and designed it so that its aperture was horizontal and narrow. The ball *had* to be propelled softly—in those pre-dunk-shot days—if its arc was to pass through the center of the basket. Constructed rule by rule, basketball represented a rational design.

The invention succeeded beyond Naismith's expectations. The first game was played in the school's gymnasium on December 21, 1891, a date that anthropologists a millennium hence will undoubtedly recognize as the ritually significant winter solstice. The YMCA's *Triangle* published Naismith's original rules on January 15, 1892, the *New York Times* decided on April 26 that a description of the game was fit to print, and Amos Alonzo Stagg, better known today for his long career in football, introduced the game at the University of Chicago in 1893. Intercollegiate basketball began on February 9, 1895, when Hamline lost to the Minnesota State School of Agriculture. By the end of basketball's first decade, Columbia, Cornell, Harvard, Princeton, and Yale had organized the Intercollegiate League. Amherst, Dartmouth, Holy Cross, Trinity, and Williams had joined together in the New England League.

Women's basketball began at Smith College in Northampton, only fifteen miles from Naismith's Springfield gymnasium. Senda Berenson, a graduate of the Boston Normal School of Gymnastics, altered the rules to make the game acceptable for young ladies.[3] At first, the game was played as an intramural sport in which the seniors coached the sophomores for their big game against the junior-coached freshmen.

> In order to protect the players from the embarrassment that might be caused either by the bloomers and black stockings that they wore...or by the nature of the exertion demanded in the game of basket ball, all men aside from President [L.C.] Seelye, who was expected to give the game an air of dignity, were barred from the gymnasium on the day of the game. Lines formed outside of the gymnasium as early as an hour before the game was to start. The audience filed in in an orderly fashion. Every inch of the gym was occupied.

The supporters of each class sat on opposite sides and wore their team's chosen colors. Because cheering was "not included in the present scheme of womanliness," the audience took to enthusiastically singing songs.[4]

Women's basketball spread almost as rapidly as the men's game. Within four years of the formulation of women's rules, the first intercollegiate game was played, on April 4, 1896, between Stanford and the University of California. A month later, the *New York Journal* for May 17 ran a headline: BASKET BALL—THE NEW CRAZE FOR ATHLETIC YOUNG WOMEN. The illustration showed Vassar girls "in their Field Day game of basket ball."[5]

Berenson's adaptation of the rules was certainly not unique. Once it had sprung full-blown from the high-minded Mr. Naismith's brow, basketball was continuously reshaped by the YMCA, the Amateur Athletic Union, the National Collegiate Athletic Association, the National Basketball Association, and various other national and international bureaucratic organizations anxious to perfect the game and to enhance its attractiveness and profitability. One result of this instrumental approach to play is that the historian can chronicle the development of the rules in the minutest detail. The pivot was allowed in 1893, the dribble in 1896. At first, fouls were penalized by points, but the free throw was introduced in 1894 as an added element of suspense. Naismith began with nine players to a side (because his YMCA class consisted of eighteen), but the AAU reduced teams to five in 1897. The peach-basket goals of the first game made retrieval of the ball something of an inconvenience; the problem-solvers knocked out the basket's bottom. The modern net, "basket" in name only, was introduced in 1906. The out-of-bounds rule was imposed in 1913 to end mad scrambles for the loose ball. There is no need to trace the steps from Naismith's clever placement of the basket to the twenty-four second rule and the three-point shot. My primary concern is the game's trajectory once it departed for foreign shores.

Basketball reached Asia before it established a firm beachhead in Europe because Naismith's first teams included future missionaries to China, India, and Japan. In its early years, Chinese basketball was nurtured almost exclusively by the YMCA. Dr. Willard Lyon, who established the first Chinese YMCA at Tientsin in 1895, was also the organization's athletic director. A few months after his arrival, he introduced the Chinese to Naismith's newly invented game. "As early as 1896, the Tientsin YMCA embarked on a program of promoting athletic competition in [Chinese] schools."[6] When C. H. Robertson arrived to assume responsibilities in Tientsin, in 1902, he spent part of his time in the local Chinese schools and saw to it that "an American teacher of physical education was placed by the Association on a full-time basis in the Tientsin school system."[7] To stimulate interest on the part of the Chinese, the Americans in Tientsin organized an Annual Athletic Meet for YMCA members and students at the local schools.

When the YMCA organized China's first national athletic meet, in which 140 teams would compete, at Nanking in October of 1910, basketball was part of the program (along with track and field, tennis, and soccer). Although the officials were Americans, the athletes were Chinese, a pattern quite different from that of Latin America, where the first championships in soccer and many other modern sports were contested mostly by foreigners. By the time the Chinese were deemed ready for their first national championships, the most energetic promoters of basketball were located in Shanghai, where Dr. Max J. Exner had arrived in 1908 as the Chinese YMCA's first National Physical Director. Although the YMCA never had more than fifteen or twenty "physical secretaries" for all of China, they were amazingly influential "as coordinators of programs in Chinese and mission schools, as promoters of athletic meets, as trainers of native leadership personnel, and as propagandists for increased support for physical education programs among government officials and private citizens."[8] Exner, who returned to the United States in 1911, seems to have been especially effective. The YMCA was also responsible for the inauguration of the Far Eastern Championship Games, the first of which were held in Manila in February of 1913. The principal organizer was Elwood S. Brown. "Probably no other [YMCA] physical director . . . had greater impact on a foreign country than Elwood S. Brown had on the Philippines, where he was privileged to serve for almost a decade (1910–1918)."[9]

Brown had arrived in the Philippines in 1910 "with a volleyball and an indoor baseball."[10] Within a year he had organized the Philippine Amateur Athletic Association. When Filipino government clerks complained about the heat, even at the summer capital in the mountains, Brown concluded that these pampered white-collar workers had lived under the indolent Spaniards and "knew nothing of occupying their idle time in vigorous physical exercises."[11] He took action against idleness and the natives began to play ball (in how many senses?) with the Americans. Brown, a boundlessly energetic exemplar of "muscular Christianity," decided that the next step was to stage the Far Eastern Games and thereby to bring together three traditionally hostile peoples in a spirit of unaccustomed mutual respect. Invitations went out to the Chinese and to the Japanese, whose interest in basketball was fostered by the YMCA's Franklin Brown.[12]

International athletic meets were not a high priority of the Republic of China, which was then a mere two years old, but J. H. Crocker and other American YMCA workers in China arranged for a team to be present at this and subsequent Far Eastern Games. Since the Philippines were then under American rule and far more influenced by American sports than the Chinese or the Japanese, it was hardly a surprise that the home team, which greatly outnumbered the visitors, won most of the events, including the basketball championship. Despite the drubbing, the Chinese—or their American mentors—volunteered to host the Second Far Eastern Games, which were held in Shanghai in 1915. Once again, the Filipinos were victorious in the basketball competition. The president of the republic was struck less by the maiden appearance of female athletes (as baseball players) than by the apparent disappearance of political strife. He expressed his astonishment that "the medium of athletics had induced Chinese from such politically hostile districts as Canton, Shanghai, and Peking to stand shoulder to shoulder as the champions of a common China."[13]

In 1918, the YMCA opened a short-lived college in Shanghai to train Chinese physical educators. The ambitious project failed; the school closed its doors a year later because of financial problems, the unfortunately timed furloughs of key American personnel, and a rising tide of anti-American sentiment that drastically reduced the scope and effectiveness of all the YMCA's programs. When J. H. Gray returned to the United States in 1927, "the YMCA ceased its active role in Chinese physical education, and an era was brought to an end." By this time, the Roman Catholic schools were ready to take up the slack. At Shanghai's St. John's University, Philip B. Sullivan coached the national championship team that went on to represent China at the 1923 Far Eastern Games in Osaka, Japan. Until 1927, when China's civil war disrupted Shanghai's sports program, Sullivan's charges defeated most of their Chinese and Japanese rivals. In that civil war, both sides trumpeted their determination that the Chinese forge their own national destiny, but neither side meant by this an exclusive commitment to traditional sports like archery. Basketball remained among the sports actively promoted by both the Nationalists and the Communists throughout the decades of their struggle for power and by the Communists since their victory in 1949.[14]

In the summer of 1896, Ernst Herrmann, director of physical therapy at the Massachusetts Hospital for Dipsomaniacs, paid a visit to his father, who was a physical-education teacher at the *Martino-Katharineum-Gymnasium* in Braunschweig and an active member of a national committee to propagate sports. Among the American novelties in his baggage was a basketball. August Herrmann and his colleague Konrad Koch, the man who had introduced soccer football to Germany more than twenty years earlier, were enchanted by the younger Herrmann's demonstration of the game and they introduced it, in 1897, to their physical-education classes. F. W. Fricke, who taught at nearby Hannover, did the same. Unlike the YMCA workers who had invented the sport a mere five years earlier, the Germans saw basketball as a game more suitable for girls than for boys. The rules they published in 1901 were apparently based on those Berenson had devised at Smith College. Players were limited to three dribbles; the court was divided into three zones, each of which had three players who were not allowed to move from one zone to another. *Korbball* did not prosper. By the twenties, the game was more or less forgotten.[15]

Basketball did not fare much better in England. In 1895, Swedish-born Martina Bergman-Osterberg experimented with the girls' version of the game at the Hampstead Physical Training College, which she had founded a decade earlier. The game was modified, called netball, and promoted by a national organization created in 1902. At the first major international athletic meet for women, the *Olympiades Féminines* held at the Sporting Club of Monaco in the spring of 1921, a team of English women defeated the French by a score of 8–7, thereby winning the basketball tournament.[16] Despite this success, despite a tournament sponsored by the Central London YMCA, interest in both the men's and the women's game remained limited. In

1936, an Amateur Basketball Association was formed, but there were still, forty years after the arrival of the game, only thirty-four basketball clubs in all of England and Wales.[17]

Since basketball was invented under the auspices of the Young Men's Christian Association, it was appropriate that a major propagating impulse came from "YMCA officials who accompanied the American Army in the First World War."[18] Elwood S. Brown, the YMCA activist who had organized the 1913 Far Eastern Games, was named as director of athletics for the American Expeditionary Force that President Wilson dispatched to France. Barely a month after the Armistice that ended the bloodshed, Brown wrote to Colonel Bruce Palmer, a member of General John Pershing's staff, and suggested that an athletic festival might do wonders to bring "divers peoples together" and cement the wartime alliance. Brown's suggestion met with approval, the *Stade Pershing* was constructed in the *Bois de Vincennes*, and the soldiers of eighteen different nations gathered on June 22 for the Inter-Allied Games.[19] Basketball was included in the program.

Opposing the American team, whose victory was all but certain, were some novice Italian and French basketball players. Italian officers had asked the YMCA to teach the game to the troops and the YMCA had gladly complied with the request. *Pallacanestro* seems to have been an instant hit with the men from Milano, Roma, and Napoli. The French were less eager than the Italians to learn *le basket*, but at least they were more receptive than they had been in 1895 when Emil Thiess, a YMCA worker, vainly attempted to introduce the game to some apathetic Parisians. James Naismith, who served in France as a YMCA adviser to the American Expeditionary Force, was sure that the ice of French indifference was about to thaw.

> Once he observed a crowd of Frenchmen watching American servicemen play. When the game ended, several spectators tried their hand at shooting baskets. "They were at first quite awkward in their

attempts," Naismith commented, "but the rapidity with which they learned to pass and shoot was astonishing."

Neither the French nor the Italians learned rapidly enough. The outcome of the 1919 tournament was a foregone conclusion. In the third and last of the three games played, the Americans vanquished the hapless French by a score of 93–8.[20]

It may have been prophetic that the Italians also defeated the French (by the somewhat less alarming score of 15–11). Within two years of the Inter-Allied Games, Italian players joined the Swiss as the principal sponsors of the *Fédération Internationale de Basketball Amateur*.[21] Switzerland's Léon Buffard was the first president and Giorgio Asinari di San Marzano served as vice-president. Asinari di San Marzano acted as one of basketball's most ardent advocates in the long campaign for recognition by the International Olympic Committee. (The appeals bore fruit in 1936 when the Olympics included their first official basketball tournament.) Another sign of Italian interest was their victory in an international tournament for students (held in Turin in September of 1933). The Italians defeated the French, 52–32.[22]

Thanks in part to Italian influence, basketball was able to put down deeper roots in Germany than had been the case when Ernst Herrmann tossed out the first ball at the turn of the century. Hugo Murero, a German army officer, learned about the game while he was on detached duty in Italy. Returning to the army's school at Wünsdorf, near Berlin, he became the *Referent für Basketball*. In 1935, his men took on a team from the University of Berlin, where Chinese and Japanese students had introduced the new game in 1927. (By such indirect routes do sports spread after the initial years of their diffusion.)[23]

Noncommissioned officers at the air force's school in Spandau joined in the fun and the three-way competition in Berlin led to a "national" tournament at Bad Kreuznach in 1935, won by the noncoms from Spandau. Bad Kreuzbach was chosen as the site for the tournament because Hermann Niebuhr, a member of the *Turnverein 1848 Bad Kreuzbach*, had encountered the game while teaching at a German school in Turkey. Missionary friends at Istanbul's Robert College had converted him to the exciting new sport. Together with Hugo Murero and Dr. Siegfried Reiner from the University of Breslau, Niebuhr trained the German team that competed in the 1936 Olympic Games. (James Naismith awarded the medals, which went to the United States, Canada, and Mexico. Germany finished a disappointing seventeenth.) By this time, Nazi propagandists were ready to overlook the game's YMCA origins and to give it their stamp of approval on the grounds that it required not only speed and stamina but also the spirit of aggressive *Kampf* that allegedly characterizes the true German. Section Four of the Ministry of Sport took administrative responsibility for basketball. Section Four was headed by Richard Herrmann, who may have been related to the Ernst Herrmann who had brought basketball to Germany a generation earlier.[24]

By 1936, basketball was played throughout Europe, but a markedly more rapid growth in participation came after 1945, when American popular culture began to wash over the continent in successive waves. The British, who had been largely immune to the basketball virus, began to weaken, but amateur teams proliferated slowly until the creation in 1972 of the National Basketball League. Beginning with six amateur teams, England's NBL grew, in its first sixteen years, to fifty-two teams, some of them professional. Paid attendance climbed from a mere 7,500 in 1972–73 (for the entire NBL) to a respectable 330,000 in 1984–85. By the nineties, teams that had struggled along with subsidies from local businessmen were signing sponsorship contracts with Fiat, Sharp, and other multinational corporations. American influence was obvious in the campaign to publicize the game in the print media and to package it for television audiences. Peter Sprogis, an NBL official, boasted to a *Daily Mail* reporter that the league was run "the way pro-basketball football and soccer are run in the United States." American influence also accounted for the cheerleaders and the Disney-inspired courtside mascots. If the players dribbled, passed, and shot like Americans, the reason was that 30 percent of them, including all ten of the top scorers, were born in the United States.[25] Like thousands of their countrymen, these expatriates are part of an explosively expanding international labor market for athletic talent.[26]

The modest success of British professional basketball had an effect on the amateur game. The number of players in schools and clubs, which was 240,000 when the NBL was launched, increased nearly five-fold in the course of the decade. Although no one can claim that basketball has become one of the kingdom's major sports, its proponents have at least established a British beachhead.[27]

Basketball has been more of a success on the continent. National Basketball Association stars are "lionized in Italy, Spain and France, where glossy magazines with names like *Maxi-Basket* (published in LeMans), *Nuevo Basket* (Barcelona) and *Super Basket* (Milan) keep almost breathless tabs on every aspect of the NBA." In Italy, the professional game has attracted millions of *tifosi* ("fans"; literally, "those infected with typhus"). Since 1987, basketball has been the nation's second most popular spectator sport. Italy's thirty-two-game professional league draws two million fans to its games; twenty-five percent of the television audience follows the championship games. The Italian league is backed financially by some of the country's wealthiest men. Rome's *Il Messaggero*, named for the city's leading newspaper, is owned, together with the newspaper, by Raul Gardini, a financier who controls "a $22 billion conglomerate that does business on six continents." Gardini demonstrated the status of Italian basketball in 1989 when he

TABLE 4.1.

THE POPULARITY OF BASKETBALL IN EUROPE

Spain	(1990)	2
Italy	(1983)	3
Turkey	(1983)	3
Belgium	(1987)	3
Bulgaria	(1980)	4
Yugoslavia	(1990)	4
Ireland	(1983)	6
Iceland	(1983)	6
Luxembourg	(1986)	6
Poland	(1972)	6
France	(1985)	7
Czechoslovakia	(1985)	8
Sweden	(1969)	9
Finland	(1985)	11
The Netherlands	(1987)	15

acquired Danny Ferry, an All-American from Duke University who had been drafted by the Los Angeles Clippers. Ferry joined Brian Shaw, whom Gardini had just lured away from the Boston Celtics.[28]

Large numbers of Italians and other continental Europeans are now playing as well as watching basketball. Maarten van Bottenburg, a Dutch authority on the "differential popularization of sports," has recently published some intriguing statistics on the number of sports participants in twenty-two European countries. In fifteen of these countries, basketball was among the top fifteen sports. On the basis of Bottenburg's data, basketball's rank can be seen at a glance in table 4.1.

In fourteen of these fifteen countries, soccer was the most popular sport and soccer is likely to remain in first place for the foreseeable future. The Italian case is typical. The number of Italian basketball players increased by approximately 350 percent between 1974 and 1983, but the number of soccer players increased almost as rapidly. Since there are still approximately five times as many Italians kicking soccer balls as dribbling basketballs, the gap between the sports is not likely to close soon—unless there is another quantum leap of American influence like the one that occurred in the era of the Cold War. Nonetheless, basketball has probably become Europe's most popular indoor sport.[29]

5

A M E R I C A N   F O O T B A L L

If we were concerned simply with the quantitative expansion of American sports in Europe, we might focus on volleyball, which has grown phenomenally in the postwar period. In the Netherlands, for instance, membership in the volleyball federation has increased at a rate more than twice that of rival organizations. In Italy, soccer is the only participant sport more popular than volleyball, which is played by both men and women. If we wished to emphasize the diffusion of "postmodern" sports, we might concentrate on the almost instantaneous adoption by young Europeans of what French sociologists refer to as *sports de glisse* or *sports californiens* (surfing, wind-surfing, "hot-dog" skiing, skate-boarding, hang-gliding). These and similar activities offer "acrobatic mobility and the vertiginous pleasures of speed and risk."[1] For two reasons, however, gridiron football seems especially appropriate as an example of ludic diffusion impelled by American power. First, the game has been promoted in Great Britain and on the continent by means of a well-organized mass-media campaign. Electronic and print journalism have been carefully coordinated to win almost immediate popularity. Second, its promoters have not been satisfied to place their product in the interstices of European sports (which is where *les sports de glisse* tend to be located). They have sought to displace firmly rooted British sports not only on the European continent but in the British Isles as well. Just as Australian baseball has gained ground at the expense of cricket, European football—American-style—has seduced participants and spectators long enamoured with soccer or rugby. The irony, of course, is that American football itself is an adaptation of the very ballgames it now seeks to drive from the field.

A brief retrospect may be helpful. In 1657, Boston's magistrates imposed a twenty-shilling fine for "playing at foot-ball in the streets."[2] In all probability, students at Harvard College engaged in some sort of kicking and running game in the seventeeth and eighteenth centuries. New Haven was also a venue for football. "An engraving of Yale College in 1807 showed students in beaver hats and swallow-tailed coats playing football on New Haven Common, while an elder who closely resembled college president Timothy Dwight looked on with an air of disapproval."[3] At Harvard and Yale as at other antebellum colleges, the president and the faculty did their best to encourage studious piety and to discourage boisterous play. The forces of propriety won many battles. On July 2, 1860, students at Harvard College, with mock solemnity, buried "Football Fightum," a casualty of professorial disapproval.[4] "Football Fightum's" age at the time of decease was given as "LX Years." But, in the long run, the students were victorious. Compulsory chapel has vanished from most American campuses, and the "football weekend" has assumed the status of a secular ritual.[5]

Celebrators of American football sometimes cite the Princeton-Rutgers contest of November 6, 1869, as the first intercollegiate game, won by the latter with a score of 6–4, but that historic game was an approximation of what we now call soccer. Something akin to modern rugby was brought to the United States five years later when students from McGill University, in Montreal, met a team from Harvard. On May 15, the schools struggled to a scoreless tie. This contest occurred only two years after Oxford and Cambridge inaugurated their rugby rivalry.[6]

The new game was immensely attractive to boisterous young men in need of some way to demonstrate the masculinity that their fathers and older brothers had recently proved on the bloody battlefields of the Civil War. On November 26, 1876, representatives from Harvard, Columbia, Princeton, and Yale met at Springfield, Massachusetts, and formally adopted the rules of rugby football as they had been formulated by their English counterparts (whose Rugby Football Union dates from 1871).[7]

Rugby evolved very quickly into what was for a time referred to as "gridiron football." That term derived from the accelerated modernization of the transplanted game. Americans divided the relatively continuous play of the English game into a series of "downs" and continued possession of the ball was made contingent upon the team's ability to move it forward a specified number of yards. Chalked lines enabled the players to calculate whether or not the ball had indeed been carried far enough, and the lines gave the game its distinctive name—until the American version was so dominant in the United States that it became simply "football." In time, of course, the ball was carried and thrown much more often than it was propelled by the foot, but avid partisans of the sport worried as little about misnomers as basketball fans did after the replacement of the primordial baskets with bottomless nets.

In a famous essay, "Football in America: A Study in Culture Diffusion," sociologists David Riesman and Reuel Denney explained the transformation of British rugby into American football as the result of a lack of tradition. Since there were no experienced older players who knew how to deal with such ambiguities as the unintentional "heel-out" (which allowed a player to scoop up the ball and run with it), it was necessary for the ball to be "hiked" into play from a stationary line of scrimmage. It may be that the lack of tradition accounted for the more extreme rationalization of the American game, but we should recall that the first American game of rugby was contested a mere three years after English players banded together to create Rugby Football Union—hardly time for hoary tradition to have done its work. More persuasive is another conjecture offered by Riesman and Denney: The "procedural rationalization" of the American players "fitted in with other aspects of their industrial folkways."[8] Since those "industrial folkways" were themselves part of a comprehensive rationalizing process that encompassed much more than the economic sphere, I prefer the term modernization, but the important point is that rugby eventually returned to England transformed into the unmistakably American game of gridiron football.

On his famous around-the-world tour of 1888–89, Albert Spalding had tried vainly to convert John Bull from cricket to baseball.[9] On *his* 1924 baseball tour to the British Isles, New York Giant's manager John J. McGraw cajoled a favorable prediction about the game's future from Arthur Conan Doyle (who proved himself better at detective fiction than at sports prognostication).[10] The British, in short, had been given (and had scorned) opportunities to convert to baseball.

In contrast, American football was hardly known in Great Britain before 1982, the year in which Channel 4 television introduced seventy-five minutes a week of NFL football. American network videofilms were edited by Cheerleader Productions. The firm's marketing director, Andrew Croker, was enthusiastic about the project because he felt football to be, technologically, "the best-covered sport in the world." Coverage of British sports seemed stodgy in comparison to American television's fast-paced presentations of football action. With American models in mind, Cheerleader Productions provided colorful graphics and a lively rock 'n' roll soundtrack for the edited videotapes of regular-season play. The NFL-inspired innovations introduced by Croker and his colleagues at Channel 4 eventually impressed the producers at the BBC and Independent Television. "Sport coverage," comments Garry Whannel, "appeared to take on some of the characteristics of what some call postmodern culture—disjointed juxtapositions, a focus on surface appearances, and a tendency for form to subsume content." And, of course, a tendency for faces in the crowd to draw attention away from inaction on the field.[11]

Attracted by the form or the content or by both, Britons took note of the novelty. The average weekly audience for the first season's telecasts was slightly more than one million; by 1987–88, the number had risen to 3,700,000 and Super Bowl XXII, carried live, drew more than six million British viewers. This may not seem like very many compared to the audience of twelve million soccer fans who followed the telecast of the Football Association's annual Cup Final, but gridiron football was more popular with British viewers than such archetypically British sports as cricket and rugby. This was especially true for younger Britons, 26 percent of whom told surveyors that they enjoyed watching the American sport. Demographically, the fans of gridiron football—compared to those for other sports—are also disproportionately male and affluent. Since wealthy young men like these are also likely to be avid readers of sports journalism, the promoters of the American game offered them *Touch-*

down and a number of other magazines, one of which, *The Daily Telegraph American Football Magazine*, soon had a weekly circulation of 100,000. The *Daily Telegraph,* which underwrote the costs of editing the American videotapes, also distributed free guidebooks to the game. Yearbooks, the first of which appeared in 1983, rounded out the print campaign.[12]

Almost simultaneous with the appearance of the Dallas Cowboys and other NFL teams on "the telly" was the birth of the first English team: the London Ravens (in 1983). A year later, two leagues were formed: the British American Football Federation and the American Football League U.K. They merged in 1985 to become the thirty-eight team British American Football League. (I assume that the abbreviation—BAFL—is not meant as a cockney comment on the game's mysteries.) At this point, Anheuser-Busch, which had underwritten Channel 4's production costs for telecasts of NFL games, entered the fray and organized the semiprofessional Budweiser League. Originally, the brewing company owned 51 percent of the shares in the league and in the individual clubs, which numbered seventy-two in 1986 and nearly two hundred in 1988. Many of the teams—like the Dunstable Cowboys—sported American names. For sponsors, clubs in the Budweiser League tend to enlist multinational corporations like Johnson & Johnson, American Express, Toshiba, Minolta, and Hitachi.[13]

Beginning in 1986, the National Football League (of the United States) took a further step toward ludic conquest of the British Isles. At hallowed Wembley Stadium, historic scene of soccer's Cup Final, the Dallas Cowboys and Chicago Bears clashed in a preseason exhibition game entitled, appropriately enough, the American Bowl. For this encounter, which American Express, Budweiser, and TWA sponsored, 80,000 tickets were sold in a single week.[14]

NFL Productions, a subsidiary which licenses the use of the organization's name and logo, also elbowed its way into the

TABLE 5.1.

AMERICAN FOOTBALL TEAMS IN WESTERN EUROPE, 1990

Country	Number	Year League Was Formed
Italy	114	1978
Germany	170	1978
Finland	31	1980
France	60	1981
Switzerland	13	1982
Britain	152	1983
Ireland	12	1984
Netherlands	30	1985
Spain	12	1988

British market. Among the products touted are clothing for adults and children, watches and clocks, coffee mugs, books, magazines, calendars, posters, stickers, jigsaw puzzles, painting-by-numbers games, playing cards, skateboards, roller-skates, bean bags, cookies, chocolate bars, and bubble gum. Skeptics might question the value of the NFL's endorsement of bean bags and bubble gum, but a 1988 Gallup Poll found that 91 percent of Britain's sixteen-to-twenty-five-year-olds considered NFL-licensed products to be as good as or better than the competition's brands.[15]

As can be seen from Table 5.1, the NFL's efforts to bring gridiron football to Britain are part of a grand strategy to diffuse the game throughout the European continent.[16]

Television is an essential aspect of what Joseph Maguire calls the "media-sport production complex." To publicize its product, the NFL has arranged for continental European television coverage of these nascent leagues and of a number of regular-season NFL games. The arrangements are complicated. "TWI [Trans World Sport], the company involved in selling the NFL highlights package to European broadcasters, is, in fact, a sister company of the IMG [International Marketing Group], the

NFL's marketing agent for Europe."[17] TWI does not have a monopoly. NFL games can also be seen on Scanset in Scandinavia, on Tele 5 in Germany and Austria, on Canal Plus in France and Belgium, and on other stations the length and breadth of the continent. Dubliners and Muscovites, should they find themselves in the same airport lounge, may soon discover a common passion for the Dallas Cowboys.

Or the Barcelona Dragons. The World League of American Football, which played in the spring and summer months, came into existence in 1991 with NFL-sponsored franchises in Barcelona, Frankfurt, London, Montreal, and six American cities. In their first season, the London Monarchs had an average home-game crowd of more than 40,000. Their victory over the Barcelona Dragons, by a score of 21–0, was dubbed "a jolly good show." Roger Goodell, a spokesman for the NFL, denied that the league had economic motives: "We do not see the World League as an instrument for profit. . . . We see it as a tool to make American football more popular."[18]

Skepticism about the NFL as a nonprofit organization is in order. The brief history of the World League of American Football indicates an interest in bottom lines as well as goal lines. Midway in the second season, the Frankfurt Galaxy was drawing an average of 34,495 fans—more than those who attended the home games of Frankfurt *Eintracht*, the city's entry in Germany's *Bundesliga*. The London Monarchs, playing in Wembley Stadium, drew large crowds. Other teams, however, did less well. Despite an initial NFL investment of $28,000,000 and a TV contract for $14,500,000, the World League of American Football suffered a cash-flow crisis and had to be bailed out by the parent organization. Each NFL franchise contributed another $500,000. Even after this financial infusion, the WLAF was in serious economic trouble.[19] Play was suspended at the end of the 1992 season and the European future of American football thus remains in doubt. Rugby has lost ground to its American cousin, but there is "no evidence," even in Great Britain, where the promoters of the American game have made the most strenuous efforts, "that the emergence of American football has led to the cultural marginalization of soccer."[20]

The National Football League, undaunted by the British loyalty to "the people's game," has plans to revive the World League as a purely European operation. Paris, which already has a Disneyland, is a likely home for a new team. And then? "Ultimately," explained Roger Goodell to *Sports Illustrated*, "we'd like to expand to the Far East and Latin America."[21] It may be that the intrinsic characteristics of the game—its complexity, for instance, or its extraordinary physicality—will limit the proposed expansion, but the globalization game is not one that the NFL intends to lose by default.

6

THE OLYMPIC GAMES

BEGINNINGS

The modern Olympic Games began as a European phenomenon and it has always been necessary for non-Western peoples to participate in the games on Western terms. In the terminology of Talcott Parsons, there was from the very start a contradiction between the universalistic ideals, which called for participation by "the youth of the world," and the particularistic forms, which are unquestionably those characteristic of modern sports.[1]

Although a number of nineteenth-century Europeans had endeavored to revive the ancient games, none of their efforts bore much fruit. An Englishman, Dr. W. P. Brookes, inaugurated a series of annual "Olympian Games" in Shropshire in 1849, but they were purely local affairs.[2] In 1859, the Greeks made the first of several attempts to resuscitate the athletic contests that had expired some fifteen hundred years earlier; their games, local and limited to ethnic Greeks, went unnoticed by the rest of the world.[3] In 1891, John Astley Cooper proposed a Pan-Britannic and Anglo-Saxon Festival, to which athletes from the British Empire and the United States were to be invited. His intention was to celebrate Anglo-Saxon superiority and to strengthen the bonds of Anglo-Saxon solidarity. It was not until 1930 that his dream was partially realized in the form of the first quadrennial British Empire Games (subsequently rebaptized as the Commonwealth Games).[4]

Baron Pierre de Coubertin, who possessed a more inclusively cosmopolitan vision and greater organizational skills than any of his predecessors, succeeded where they had failed. One reason was his willingness to use hallowed memories of the ancient games for some distinctly modern ulterior political ends. Schooled like every educated European in the lore of classical civilization, he exploited the aura of antiquity in order to further his goal—international peace and reconciliation.[5]

Considering the lengths to which he went in order to dazzle the participants of the congress he convened at the Sorbonne in 1894, one wonders that the delegates did not complain of ideological manipulation. On the eve of the congress, Coubertin published an essay in the *Revue de Paris* in which he eloquently advocated the revival of the Olympic Games. When the seventy-eight delegates from nine nations gathered together on June 16, they were seated in a grand auditorium whose walls had recently been decorated with classical murals by Pierre Puvis de Chavannes. The delegates were aurally seduced by the ancient "Hymn to Apollo," discovered the previous year at Delphi, translated into French by Théodore Reinach, set to music by Gabriel Fauré, and sung by Jeanne Remacle and the chorus of the *Opéra français*. In this heady atmosphere of high culture, there seems to have been unanimous approval for Coubertin's suggestion that an International Olympic Committee (IOC) be organized to bring to life a new version of the old games.[6]

Coubertin chose a Greek scholar then resident in Paris, Demetrios Bikelas, to be the first president of the IOC. (He served until 1896, after which Coubertin took the office and served for nearly thirty years.) The first Olympic Games of the modern era were scheduled for Athens, where, thanks to the generosity of wealthy George Averoff, the ancient stadium of Herodes Atticus was rebuilt in pentelic marble. Consciously Hellenizing, Coubertin arranged for the Olympic program to include contests in hurling the javelin and the discus—two events that had not been a part of modern track-and-field matches. Accounts by Herodotus and Plutarch of the Greek victory over the Persian invaders in 490 B.C. inspired one of Coubertin's friends, Michel Bréal, to donate a trophy to be given to the winner of a twenty-two-mile race beginning at the site of the battle and ending in the Olympic stadium.

Coubertin, however, was no antiquarian pedant. To the first modern games he invited not only track-and-field athletes and wrestlers but also swimmers and weightlifters, fencers and gymnasts, none of whose events had been a part of the ancient games. In other contests, oarsmen, cyclists, sharpshooters, and tennis players used equipment unknown before the nineteenth century. There were other indications that Coubertin's Hellenism had its limits. When the Greeks themselves, initially somewhat reluctant to sponsor the modern games, became enthusiastically proprietary and announced their intention to keep the quadrennial celebrations in Greece, Coubertin and his colleagues on the IOC were adamant about Olympic internationalism. If the games were truly to summon "the youth of the world," the invitation had to come not from a single permanent site but rather from all points of the cultural compass. The games had to be celebrated in various places in order to propagate the Olympic ideal, to spread the light.

Coubertin was by no means the only one to emphasize cultural continuity in order to make a political point. For the 1936 games, celebrated in Berlin, the German sports administrator and scholar Carl Diem introduced the torch relay. The message was plain: from the pure Hellenic source at Olympia, the sacred flame, symbolizing life itself, was carried to the site of the games, where architecture and statuary made an overbearingly emphatic statement about the classical genealogy of the modern games.[7]

A good deal of what happened in 1936 was staged for the benefit of Leni Riefenstahl's monumental documentary film, *Olympia*, made to commemorate the Berlin games. In the film's prologue, naked maidens dance and a loin-clothed youth ignites the symbolic torch at the Olympic altar. Across hills, along the seashore, through tiny Greek villages and the great urban centers of Bulgaria, Hungary, Austria, and Czechoslovakia, Riefenstahl's camera follows the flame from Olympia to Berlin while Herbert Windt's Wagnerian music swells and thunders to underscore the alleged kinship between the ancient Greeks and the modern athlete. The torch relay is only one element of a romantic Hellenism so intense that it teeters on the edge of the absurd. After showing film credits that appear to be carved in stone, *Olympia* shifts from a classical landscape to the Parthenon and other ancient ruins and then to Greek statuary. The marble of Myron's famed discus-thrower metamorphizes into a living German athlete who twists, turns, and hurls the disk skywards. Symbolically, the whirling bronze discus carries the Olympic spirit from its birthplace in the Peloponnesus to the site of the games in Berlin, where fifty thousand spectators wait in the grandiose neoclassical stadium for the arrival of the flame.[8]

Coubertin insisted that the quadrennial games be peripatetic in order to demonstrate the universality of his ideal. At each successive site, the spirit of Olympism was to be rekindled. Following the initial success in Athens, the world's athletes were called to Paris, to St. Louis, to London, and to Stockholm (after which the games were interrupted by World War I). It was not until 1956, however, that the summer or the winter games were celebrated any place other than Europe or the United States, and Melbourne was hardly a hotbed of non-Western culture. Tokyo and Mexico City, which hosted the Olympics in 1964 and 1968, were chosen in part belatedly to realize Coubertin's aspirations to universality. Similarly, one reason for the choice of Moscow for the 1980 games was that the IOC wished to prove its ideological neutrality. Had the IOC not been attracted by Sydney's presentation and repelled by China's violations of human rights, the games of the year 2000 would have been celebrated in Beijing.

What of Africa? Although he was far more cosmopolitan than most of his countrymen, Coubertin, like most Frenchman, believed that France had a "civilizing mission" in Africa. Sports were one instrument to accomplish this "sacred" mission. Coubertin was especially anxious to involve the African continent in the Olympic movement. In fact, the effort was, in his words, "the final battle . . . in sport's conquest of the world."[9] Early in 1923 he appointed a committee to investigate ways to bring modern sports to Africa. At the IOC's 21st Session (Rome, April 1923), this *Commission d'Afrique* recommended two concurrent series of biennial games—one set for indigenes and the other for European residents. The first regional games were planned for Algiers in 1925, but they were shifted to Alexandria, postponed until 1929, and then canceled. The Egyptians asserted that the IOC had been uncooperative, which it may have been under Coubertin's successor, Belgium's Comte Henri Baillet-Latour. A more important reason for the cancellation seems to have been the "reticence of the colonizers to promote sports in their colonies."[10] Regional games took place only after decolonization.

Although modern sports came to British-ruled Africa before the French propagated them in their colonies, France took the lead in the sixties in encouraging sports competitions among the newly independent states. The continent's first important international athletic meet, the *Jeux de la Communauté*, was held at Tananarive, Madagascar, in April of 1960. The success of these games encouraged African sports administrators to organize the *Jeux de l'Amitié* at Dakar in 1963 and then the *Jeux Africains* at Brazzaville in July of 1965. These last games, which Jean-Claude Ganga described as the "decisive departure" of African sports, had the strong support of IOC President Avery Brundage. Although Brundage has often been vilified as an out-and-out racist, Ganga, who led the Supreme Council for Sport in Africa, praised him as a "true patriarch worthy of respect"; Ganga credited Brundage with persuading the International Amateur Athletic Federation, then headed by the Marquess of Exeter, to lend its essential support to the venture.[11]

Africa's anglophone elites organized the African Games in 1973, held successfully at Lagos in the former British colony of Nigeria. That year, the IOC established "Olympic Solidarity," an organization to distribute economic and technical aid to the National Olympic Committees of Third World nations. This aid has accelerated the diffusion of modern sports throughout the continent, but no African city has ever been entrusted with the Olympics and it is extremely unlikely that any will be in the foreseeable future.

As the games moved from Athens to other European and North American cities, their symbolism evolved and became somewhat less eurocentric. Christian worship, which was introduced in 1908 and conducted in the stadium as a part of the opening ceremony in 1912, became peripheral in 1928 when the Dutch concluded that Protestant services were inappropriate at a festival to which athletes of every religion were invited. The interlaced rings of the Olympic flag, flown in Antwerp in 1920, were designed by Coubertin to symbolize the unity of the globe's five continents. The baron noted proudly that the colors of the rings represented those of the world's national flags. The ceremonial lighting of the Olympic flame, first ignited at Amsterdam in 1928, drew upon the universal symbolism of fire.

In 1964, at the first Olympics to be celebrated in a non-Western nation, the Japanese introduced their own identifying logo, and every subsequent host has done the same. In general, the culturally specific elements of the opening ceremony—Gershwin's music in Los Angeles in 1984, a taekwando display in Seoul in 1988, flamenco in Barcelona in 1992—have become increasingly prominent. As John J. MacAloon remarked, with the 1988 games in mind, "the processes of global interconnection and cultural differentiation occur everywhere simultaneously."[12]

And what of the athletes whose physical presence is the *sine qua non* of the games? In theory, the IOC's call has always gone out to "youth of the world," but, in practice, only those athletes already involved in the system of modern sports were in a position to hear and to respond to the idealistic summons. At the first games, a Chilean and an Australian may have been alone among the more than three hundred original contestants in that they were born neither in Europe nor in the United States.[13] In fact, references to "Europe" are imprecise; athletes from Eastern Europe played a negligible role in the early decades of the Olympic movement. Although General A. D. Butowsky was a member of the original IOC, Czarist Russia did not send a team until 1908. The five Russians who competed at these games were scarcely noticed; the British hosts fielded a team of 710 athletes.[14]

Data on the exact number and nationality of the early Olympians are unreliable, but it seems that the first African athletes to compete in the Olympic Games were a pair of Zulu marathoners, Lentauw and Yamasani, who finished ninth and twelfth in the 1904 games (celebrated in St. Louis). Because South Africa was then under British rule, the Zulus wore the uniform of the British team. All three of the Africans who sailed to London for the 1908 games and nineteen of the twenty-one present in Stockholm in 1912 were white South Africans. The other Africans who participated in 1912 were an Egyptian fencer and an Algerian marathoner. They competed under the flags of the colonial powers—as did another Algerian, Mohammed El Quafi, who won the marathon in Amsterdam in 1928.[15] That year two Egyptians also won gold medals: Ibrahim Mustafa in Greco-Roman wrestling and Said Nasser in weightlifting.

The French, whose athletes did not fare well at the 1928 games, began to wonder about their African colonies as a "reservoir" of athletic talent. When the French team was badly outclassed at the 1936 games in Berlin, the journal *L'Auto*—the equivalent of *Sports Illustrated*—urged that the colonies be scouted for black track-and-field talent of the caliber of Jesse Owens. The army, which was in charge of colonial physical education, was more cooperative than it had been when similar suggestions were made a few years earlier. Marcel de Coppet, governor-general of *Afrique Occidentale Française*, did all he could to promote sports and locate athletic talent in Senegal and other colonies in his jurisdiction, but the project foundered. The main reason was the generally wretched health of the undernourished natives.[16]

It was not until after World War II that African athletes were more than a token presence at the Olympic Games. It was 1960 before the first black African was awarded a gold medal; Abebe Bikila of Ethiopia achieved this honor when he won the marathon. He repeated his triumph in 1964.[17] Kenya burst upon the scene as a track-and-field power as dramatically as the Japanese had, in 1932, as swimmers. At the 1968 games in

Mexico City, Kenya's Kipchoge Keino defeated world-record holder Jim Ryun in the 1500-meter race and came in second over 5,000 meters. Amos Biwott and Naftali Temu won gold medals in the 3,000-meter steeplechase and the 10,000-meter run. Wilson Kiprugut and Benjamin Kogo took silver medals in the 800-meter race and in the steeplechase, and the 4-by-400-meter relay runners triumphed in their event. Bronze medals in the 5,000-meter race (Naftali Temu) and in featherweight boxing (Philip Waruinge) brought the total number to nine. As late as 1988, however, African athletes received only about one percent of the medals awarded at the Olympics.[18]

At the first Olympic Games in 1896, Chile's Luis Subercaseaux was the only Latin American athlete among the three hundred contestants. Subsequently, Chileans managed to win silver medals at the games of 1928, 1952, and 1956, but only two Latin American nations can boast of a significant number of Olympic victories. Between 1908 and 1976, Argentina's flag was raised for thirteen gold, eighteen silver, and thirteen bronze medals. (The first golds came in 1924 with a victory by the polo team and in 1932 when Juan Zabala finished first in the marathon.) In 1976, Argentine athletes were surpassed by the Cubans, who returned from Montreal with six gold, four silver, and three bronze medals. The Cubans had starred as fencers in 1904, when they won five of six possible medals, but it was Fidel Castro's Communist regime that made Olympic victory a real priority.[19]

It will surprise no one to read that Japan, the first Asian nation to undergo the process of modernization, was also the first to send athletes to the Olympic Games. A four-man team participated in 1912. Although the Japanese were expected to perform better than "less advanced" Asians, their astonishing achievements at the 1932 games in Los Angeles took their European and American opponents by surprise. In every one of the men's swimming races, three Japanese reached the finals; they won eleven of the sixteen medals. In 1936, Kitei Son, a

Korean forced to bear a Japanese name and to compete as a member of the Japanese team, won the marathon. The athletes of no other Asian nation figured prominently in the first half-century of modern Olympic history.[20]

Female athletes, whom Coubertin wished completely to exclude from the games, made their appearance in 1900 as golfers and tennis players, in 1912 as swimmers and divers, and in 1928 as gymnasts and track-and-field athletes. Nearly all of these women were from Europe, North America, or Australia, but one Asian woman made her mark early. Japan's Hitomi Kenue was the star of the 1926 *Jeux Féminins* held in Göteberg, Sweden, where she won gold medals in the long jump and the standing long jump and silver ones in the discus and 100-meter dash. In the first Olympic 800-meter race, in Amsterdam in 1928, Kenue placed second behind Germany's Lina Radke. It was another twenty years before Latin American women began to appear among the winners. In 1948, Argentina's Noemi Simonetti won a silver medal in the long jump; eight years later, Chile's Marlene Ahrens was second in the javelin. The first Hispanic woman to earn a gold medal was Cuba's María Caridad Colón; at the 1980 games in Moscow she cast her javelin the Olympic-record distance of 68.4 meters. Women from sub-Saharan Africa began to mount the victory platform in the eighties. Zimbabwe's field-hockey team, for instance, was memorable 1980 both for the women's victory at the games and for their reward; to each of them, upon their return, an ox was given. Islamic women have been the last to ascend Olympic heights. They can hardly be faulted for their tardy appearance. As late as 1992, Algeria's Hassida Boulmerka had not only to outrun her rivals but also to surmount the psychological barrier of fundamentalist death threats in order to win the 1500-meter race in Barcelona.[21]

One reason for the paucity of Africans, Asians, and Latin Americans in the early annals of Olympic history was the requirement that athletes be selected and sent to the games by National Olympic Committees officially recognized by the IOC. There were long delays before these committees, which had formed quickly in Europe, North America, Australia, New Zealand, and South Africa, appeared elsewhere. Egypt's NOC won recognition in 1910, Japan's in 1912, Argentina's in 1923. Until the global decolonization that occurred after 1945, most African and many Asian athletes competed under the aegis of European NOC's.

If we examine the dates when each of the NOC's was granted official recognition by the IOC, the pattern of diffusion observed *vis-à-vis* the athletes emerges once again. Almost all of Europe and the larger states of Latin America were a part of the Olympic movement by 1920. The smaller Latin American republics were brought into the fold between 1945 and 1960. Most of Asia and Africa followed during the period of postwar decolonization, i.e., between 1960 and 1980. In the eighties and early nineties, the number of NOC's soared as the IOC granted quick recognition to committees from a number of dependent ministates (like American Samoa and the British Virgin Islands) and to the successor states that were created as a result of the political disintegration of the Soviet Union, Yugoslavia, and Czechoslovakia.

Like the constituent parts of other organizationally complex transnational entities, the IOC and the NOC's are often at loggerheads. Two of the most serious clashes have been over the IOC's universalistic attempts to *include* athletes whom the NOC's wished to *exclude*. These two conflicts were tests of strength that pitted Third World NOC's against an IOC dominated by a coalition of Western Europeans, North Americans, and members from Australia and New Zealand. The first of these two clashes occurred when the government of Indonesia, then ruled by Sukarno, refused to allow the Israeli and the Nationalist Chinese teams to participate in the Asian Games which took place in Jakarta in 1963. The Indonesian NOC failed to oppose its government's discriminatory policy and was unable to protect India's IOC member, G. D. Sondhi, from the Jakarta mob that formed to protest the IOC's interference in what the mob considered to be Indonesian domestic affairs. An outraged IOC suspended the Indonesian NOC, a punitive action to which the IOC had *not* resorted when Israel was denied participation in successive postwar celebrations of the *Jeux Méditerranés*. After a period of defiance during which Sukarno, with the support of the People's Republic of China, staged "Games of the New Emerging Forces" (GANEFO), the Indonesian NOC offered its apologies and the suspension was lifted. Eventually, however, as Asian and African participation in the Olympic movement became increasingly important, the IOC submitted to pressure and acquiesced in the Asian Games Federation's continued exclusion of Israel and the Republic of China.[22]

The growing influence of the African and Asian NOC's was also felt in the long apartheid crisis that threatened and then fractured the Olympic movement. The suspension and subsequent expulsion of the South African National Olympic Committee (SANOC) was the IOC's reluctant response to the Afrikaaner-dominated South African committee's refusal to take a stand against its government's policy of racial segregation in sports. In 1970, after years of procrastination and maddeningly inconclusive negotiations, the IOC finally responded to the demands of Jean-Claude Ganga and other leaders of African sports. SANOC was expelled.[23] South Africa's Springboks did not return to Olympic competition until 1992—after the South African government officially repudiated its racist policies and guaranteed the participation of a multiracial team.

In 1972, threats of an African boycott were sufficient to force the IOC to alter its policy and bar a Rhodesian team—already present in Munich—from the Olympic Games, but the limits of African influence were demonstrated four years later when the

Organization for African Unity demanded that New Zealand's Olympians be excluded from the Montreal games because a team from New Zealand had played rugby against a team from South Africa. Rejecting the IOC's argument that rugby was not an Olympic sport and was not, therefore, controlled by New Zealand's NOC, twenty-eight African NOC's announced a boycott and removed their athletes from Montreal. The New Zealanders competed (and John Walker won the 1500-meter race against a field diminished by the absence of Filbert Bayi and other African middle-distance runners).

The IOC itself remains a restricted club (to which women were first admitted in 1981). Its composition is an even better indicator of Western hegemony than the percentage of European and American athletes or the dates of recognition of the National Olympic Committees. The original IOC was as demographically narrow as the contingent of athletes at the first games. Twelve of the original fifteen IOC members were Europeans. The others were Professor William Milligan Sloane of Princeton University, Argentina's José Zubiaur (who never attended a single meeting), and Leonard A. Cuff of New Zealand.[24] Having chosen a coterie of men most of whom were titled or wealthy or both, Coubertin sought to enlarge the committee and to extend its geographical and cultural influence by having it elect members to serve as delegates to nations that had not sent athletes to the 1896 games. (The fiction that the members are delegates *to* rather than representatives *of* their nations was maintained until after World War II.)

Latin America was an obviously fallow field upon which to sow the seeds of Olympism. Miguel de Beistegui, a Mexican, was tapped for the IOC in 1901. The IOC extended its influence into the non-Western world when Turkey's Selim Sirry Bey joined the ranks in 1908. A year later, Jigoro Kano was added to the rolls. (The Japanese scholar, who had studied English language and literature at Kaiseijo University, created the sport

TABLE 6.1.

IOC MEMBERS BY REGION

Area	1894	1954	1993
Africa	0	2	16
America	2	16	18
Asia	0	10	15
Europe	12	39	38
Oceania	1	3	4

of judo as a synthesis of traditional martial arts and modern techniques.[25]) The first men to represent Africa were Angelo Bolanaki, an ethnic Greek resident in Egypt, and Sydney Farrar, a South African of British descent. They joined the IOC in 1910 and 1913. India and China came into the Olympic fold in 1920 and 1922 in the persons of Sir Dorabji J. Tata and C. T. Wang. Despite these gestures toward universalism, the IOC remained an overwhelmingly European organization for another generation—as can be seen by Table 6.1.[26]

That the IOC became a truly transnational organization in the postwar years is due largely to the efforts of Avery Brundage, the crusty Chicago businessman who was elected to the committee in 1936 and served as its president from 1952 to 1972. Although he has been accused, with some justice, of anti-Semitism, racism, and an insensitivity to the rights of women, Brundage was actually much more ecumenically disposed than Coubertin's first two successors (Henri Baillet-Latour, a Belgian count, and Sigfrid Edstrøm, a Swedish industrial entrepreneur). Brundage was especially eager to discover Latin American sportsmen who might proselytize an area not yet embued with Olympism. He toured South America in search of administrative talent. Writing to R. C. Aldao of Argentina in 1945, Brundage, who was then IOC vice-president, noted that the committee had no members from Bolivia, Chile, Columbia, Ecuador, Paraguay, Venezuela, or any of the Central American states. Could Aldao suggest qualified people?[27] Names were supplied, and a Chilean and a Guatamalan joined the "Olympic family" (in 1948).

Brundage's ecumenicism was strong enough to overcome his lifelong personal hostility to Communism. He made it part of his mission to convert the followers of Marx, Lenin, and Mao to the tenets of Coubertin. To accomplish this purpose, he found it necessary to close his eyes to the Soviet Union's egregious violations of the amateur rule and the rule against governmental control of National Olympic Committees. Ingenuously explaining to his anti-Communist critics that the Russians had assured him of their faithful adherence to the Olympic Charter, Brundage— joined by all but three of the IOC's members—voted in May of 1951 to recognize the National Olympic Committee of the USSR. Brundage was given a harder pill to swallow when the Kremlin demanded the right to name its own representatives to the IOC. President Edström and Vice-President Brundage complained bitterly about this violation of the rules, but they eventually acquiesced in the infraction and Konstantin Andrianov took his seat among the princes, the generals, and the millionaires of the IOC.

After his election to the presidency of the committee, Brundage—aided by such influential members as the Marquess of Exeter, Comte Jean de Beaumont, and Italy's Giulio Onesti— did his best to bring representatives of sub-Saharan Africa into the IOC. Sir Adetokunbo Ademola, a British-educated Nigerian jurist, became the first black member (in 1963). Nine years later, when Brundage passed the Olympic scepter to Lord Killanin of Ireland, there were four black Africans on the IOC (and four new members from North Africa). Killanin and his successor, Juan Antonio Samaranch, continued the search for non-Western IOC members. By 1993, 16.5% of the committee members came from Asia and 17.6% from Africa. (See Table 6.1, above.) Europeans and Americans, however, continue to control the IOC. With the exception of Brundage, every IOC president has been a European.

The enlargement of the committee had some unanticipated consequences. Many European and North American nations have two (and once had three) representatives on the International Olympic Committee; many Third World states have none at all. Andrianov and his colleague Aleksei Romanov, the second Russian to be elected to the IOC, were determined to transform the committee and make the Olympic movement more globally representative. They argued forcefully in 1959 for a complete restructuring of the sixty-four-member committee. In order for the Olympic movement to become truly global, they argued, each of the National Olympic Committees and each of the twenty-five international sports federations had to have representation on the IOC. The effect of this scheme, had it been acted upon, would have been to triple the size of the IOC and to increase enormously the influence of the Communist bloc and the Third World. The plan was clearly analogous to Nikita Khrushchev's nearly simultaneous proposal that the United Nations adopt a "troika" arrangement to allow executive power to be shared among that body's Communist, non-Communist, and nonaligned factions. The IOC members from Western Europe and North America were adamantly opposed to the Soviets' initiative. When the question came to a vote at the IOC's 58th Session (1961), the reformers were defeated 35–7. At the 59th Session, a less radical request that the NOC's be allowed to send observers to the IOC's sessions was also rejected.[28]

After this rebuff, Italy's resourceful Onesti tried a flanking maneuver. He invited representatives of all the National Olympic Committees to meet among themselves just before the IOC's 60th Session in order to consider whether or not the NOC's should form a permanent organization. This meeting had to be postponed, but representatives of sixty-eight NOC's caucused in 1965 and established a Study and Coordinating Committee of the National Olympic Committees.

Brundage fought this initiative tooth and nail because he was vehemently opposed to any reform that institutionalized one-country-one-vote rule. To him it seemed absurd that Dahomey, Mongolia, and Panama should have the same weight in Olympic affairs as the United States, Great Britain, and the Soviet Union. Brundage's opposition failed to thwart Onesti, whose proposals had widespread support among Europeans as well as Asians, Africans, and Latin Americans. A Permanent General Assembly of National Olympic Committees was created at Mexico City in 1968—at a time when "Black Power" protests at the games signaled deep dissatisfaction with the IOC's traditional leadership. Brundage remained adamant, insisting to the IOC's three vice-presidents that the upstart organization "must be buried NOW" and that they should "have the courage to report that any IOC member who [wishes] to participate in the PGA activities must first resign from the IOC."[29] Others were more conciliatory. When Lord Killanin succeeded Brundage in 1972, he set up a "Tripartite Committee" to regulate relationships among the IOC, the National Olympic Committees, and the international sports federations. Today, the PGA, renamed as the Association of National Olympic Committees (ANOC), is recognized as an integral part of the Olympic movement, but it is not yet the case that every NOC is entitled to *de jure* representation on the IOC.[30]

In 1967, at the time when the NOC's were pressing hard for more control over the Olympic movement, a General Assembly of the International Federations was founded. Unlike the Permanent General Assembly of the National Olympic Committees, this organization was not formed to give greater voice to sports administrators from the Communist bloc and the Third World. The GAIF was led by Australia's Berge Phillips (representing the swimmers and divers of the *Fédération Internationale de Natation Amateur*) and France's Roger Coulon (representing the wrestlers of the *Fédération Internationale de Lutte Amateur*).[31]

The majority of the international sports federations were then controlled by Europeans and they still are. In 1993, of the thirty-one international sports federations that set the rules and regulations for Olympic sports, twenty-nine have their headquarters in Europe. One, the International Baseball Association, operates from Indianapolis; one, the *Fédération International de Natation Amateur*, from Algiers.[32]

The most important consequence of European and American control of the Olympic movement has been that all the sports included in the Olympic program have their origins in the West or are represented in the distinctly modern forms developed as a part of Western culture. Archery, for instance, has prehistoric origins on every continent, but the bows and arrows used in Olympic contests are those developed by modern technology and the targets, unlike the mimetic ones of early Islamic or premodern European archery, consist of regularly spaced concentric circles whose geometric configuration determines the points awarded for each shot.

With its power to determine the athletic program of the games, the IOC can withhold or confer a kind of ludic legitimacy. Accordingly, its sessions are frequently prolonged wrangles over the inclusion or exclusion of particular sports. As early as 1930, the prestige of the Olympic Games was so great that representatives of the international federations for baseball, billiards, canoeing, lacrosse, pelota, and roller-skating vainly petitioned for IOC recognition of their sports.[33] During the fifties, Armand Massard and Vladimir Stoytchev, influential IOC members from France and Bulgaria, campaigned for volleyball in letters to Brundage and in repeated appeals to their assembled colleagues.[34] After a heated debate in Melbourne in 1956, the volleyballers lost once again by a vote of 19–13, but the campaign finally achieved its goal with the inclusion of men's and women's volleyball in Tokyo in 1964. It was a moment of great satisfaction for the Japanese, who had campaigned for volleyball's acceptance as an Olympic discipline, when their women's team won the first-ever gold medal in that event.[35]

Although volleyball is widely played in the Third World, especially in Asia, it too was invented in the West (by William Morgan, at the Holyoke, Massachusetts, YMCA, in 1895). Judo, one of the few non-Western sports on the Olympic program, was devised by Jigoro Kano in 1882 as a compromise between traditional *jujitsu* and the modern sports that Europeans and Americans were then introducing into Meiji Japan.[36] Judo's inclusion in the official Olympic program was clearly a favor done to the Japanese hosts of the 1964 games.[37] Although the vote at the 57th IOC Session in Rome in 1960 had been an overwhelming 39–2 in favor of judo, the sport was removed from the program of the 1968 games in Mexico City. Brundage's friend, Japanese IOC member Ayotoro Azuma, had to use his considerable influence to bring the sport back into the program in 1972. Olympic judo, however, is shorn of almost all traces of its Japanese origins. Like the kayakers, whose sport derives from the pre-Columbian cultures of North America, *judokas* have increasingly adapted their martial art to the dictates of modern sports. As Michel Brousse has noted, "Modern judo has little resemblance to the judo of the Jigoro Kano, the sport's founder." The distinctive system of colored belts that seems to be a hallmark characteristic of judo and other Asian martial arts was, in fact, devised in London—in 1927. In judo as in other Olympic sports, "traditions have retreated in the face of modernity."[38] In short, the Olympic program remains essentially Western. While it is undeniably true that African and Asian athletes participate, they compete on Western terms in sports which either originated in or have taken their modern forms from the West. The catalogue of Olympic sports continues, inexorably it seems, to lengthen, but traditional games and dances survive—at the Olympics—as a marginal folkloric phenomenon.

II

RESISTANCE

7

TURNEN

ORIGINS

Modern sports are, quite obviously, only one of the countless forms of what European scholars refer to as "physical culture," "*Körperkultur,*" or "*les pratiques du corps.*" Historically, the most stubborn opposition to the diffusion of modern sports came from the proponents of German gymnastics, an activity its adherents refer to as *Turnen.* By insisting upon an ostentatiously Germanic neologism rather than simply adopting a name of Greek or Latin origin (like "calisthenics"), the *Turner* meant to emphasize the cultural uniqueness of their nationalistic physical activities.[1]

Friedrich Ludwig Jahn, who coined the term *Turnen* and many of its myriad derivatives, was an ardent nationalist whose passion for gymnastic exercises was inextricably entwined with his fanatical hatred of the French who had, under Napoleon, subjugated the various states of politically divided Germany. Although a humanistic and scientific approach to physical education was a hallmark of Jahn's immediate predecessors, the eighteenth-century *Philanthropen* who educated the children of the German elite,[2] Jahn was a fiery romantic teacher who led the pupils in his charge out of the classroom and into the woods. Setting up his *Turnplatz* in the fields near Berlin, in 1811, Jahn had no qualms about artificial apparatus provided that the towers, platforms, ropes, and rings that were constructed offered the same kinds of daring movements that have always tempted adventurous boys and girls.[3]

Although Jahn idealized the Middle Ages and despised the liberal principles of the French Revolution, he was nonetheless too much of an egalitarian for the reactionary regimes that returned to power after the Congress of Vienna in 1815. (The *Turner*, for instance, wore simple gray uniforms and addressed one another with the familiar *Du* rather than the formal *Sie*.) Jahn's defiant opinions and obstreperous behavior aroused such animosity and fear in Prussia's autocratic rulers that they imprisoned him, in 1819, and outlawed *Turnen*.

When the Prussian ban was lifted, in 1842, the *Turner* entered their most liberal phase. In the eyes of the young revolutionaries who dreamed of bringing liberal constitutionalism to a land still ruled by hereditary monarchs, Jahn, who made no secret of his hatred of *"Junker, Juden, und Pfaffen"* ("gentry, Jews, and priests"[4]), was at best an uneasy ally and at worst an embarrassment. When a number of *Turner* fought in the abortive Revolution of 1848, Jahn condemned them and was finally dismissed by them as a traitor. After the liberals' failure to bring constitutional government to Germany, the most radical *Turner* fled to America. Those who remained became increasingly conservative. While the emigrants set up their *Turnvereine* (gymnastic clubs) in the United States and volunteered almost *en masse* to fight for the Union in the Civil War, those who stayed behind founded the *Deutsche Turnerschaft* (in 1860) and became ardently nationalistic supporters of the German empire that emerged after the humiliation of Napoleon III in the Franco-Prussian War of 1870–71.[5]

The *Deutsche Turnerschaft* was so much a part of the new *Kaiserreich* that it attracted large numbers of assimilated German Jews who strove by their eager participation in gymnastic exercises and the attendant nationalistic folderol to emphasize their unambivalent patriotism. For a much smaller number of Jews, *Turnen* became the means to do exactly the opposite, that is, to affirm a distinctively *Jewish* identity. In 1898, only two years after Theodor Herzl issued the call for the establishment of a Jewish homeland, a Zionist gymnastics club, *Bar Kochba*, was founded in Berlin. On the whole, however, the Zionist clubs were never a match for their nondenominational rivals. Despite the endemic anti-Semitism of many clubs affiliated with the *Deutsche Turnerschaft*, the Zionist gymnasts had—on the eve of the Nazi seizure of power—enlisted only 8,000 of Germany's half million Jews.[6]

Simultaneous with the institutionalization of *Turnen* in thousands of clubs from Aachen to Königsberg came the *Verschulung* ("scholastification") of German gymnastics. Led principally but certainly not exclusively by Adolf Spiess, German educators transformed Jahn's boisterous open-air activity into an indoor routine closely akin to military drill. Spiess published a widely used instructional text in which he described and categorized all the imaginable ways to march, hang from a bar, move one's arms, bend from the waist, and otherwise exercise the body. Three pages of this two-volume tome were devoted to games children might play if they were not paralyzed by boredom.[7] The schools, where rows and columns of children moved in synchronized response to barked commands, became a means for the authorities to inculcate the political virtues of discipline and unquestioning obedience to authority.[8]

Conservatism dominated the clubs as well as the classrooms. It was an article of faith for the *Deutsche Turnerschaft* that modern sports were an alien import from Germany's most dangerous rival in the struggle for political and economic hegemony. "It is no accident," wrote Edmund Neuendorff, national leader of the *Deutsche Turnerschaft*, "that German *Turnen* was born in the land of Goethe and Schiller, Kant and Fichte, Beethoven and Wagner, nor is it an accident that sports originated in England, a land without music or metaphysics." What else could one expect from "the classical land of materialism"?[9] Small wonder then that the *Zeitschrift für Turnen und Jugendspiele* cautioned its readers against modern sports and the "rabid anglomania that is now horribly infecting a part of our people."[10]

The *Turner* drew up a root-and-branch indictment of modern sports, which they characterized as "a passionately pursued form of physical exercises as alien to German behavior as their name, for which there is no German word."[11] Sports were thought to encourage "pride" and "egoism" and to destroy "what the *Turner* have dedicated themselves to creating: a national community" (*Volksgemeinschaft*).[12] Sports were, in Wilhelm Angerstein's fevered eyes, "the ruin" of the gymnasts' noble efforts to promote the moral development of the German people.[13] The instrumental rationality characteristic of sports was judged to be no better than "Taylorism" (a reference to efficiency expert Frederick W. Taylor's famous time-and-motion studies).[14] Accordingly, gymnasts urged the renunciation of "concrete stadium, cinder track, tape-measure, stop-watch, manicured lawn, and track shoes. . . . In their place comes the simple meadow, free nature."[15]

The quantification characteristic of modern sports enticed the athlete to quest for records and was thus another occasion for ire. In an 1897 article published in the *Deutsche Turnzeitung*,

Ferdinand Schmidt thundered that it "cannot be our wish to post notices on our grounds of . . . records made possible by one-sided . . . preparation aimed exclusively at lowering times by fractions of a second or lengthening distances by a centimeter."[16] There were aesthetic and hygienic complaints as well. The limited movements required by sports were alleged to develop an asymmetrical and unhealthy physique. This was said to be the case with soccer football, castigated by the *Turner* as a barbaric pastime whose most characteristic physical motion resembled "*der Hundstritt*" ("kicking the dog").[17]

With the passage of time, the gymnasts experienced an erosion of support, especially among the young. Compromises were made and some contests were deemed acceptable, if the competition was not excessive, but the *Deutsche Turnerschaft* continued to prefer systematic noncompetitive collective exercise. The happy results of a strenuous gymnastic regime were demonstrated in the mass displays of cadenced movement that were the centerpiece of every gymnastics festival.

FROM GERMANY TO WESTERN AND SOUTHERN EUROPE

At the end of the nineteenth century, when Britannia ruled the waves and Queen Victoria reigned over a quarter of the earth's land surface, imperial Germany was unquestionably Great Britain's most threatening rival. To the armies that had already defeated the Danes, the Austrians, and the French, Kaiser Wilhelm sought to add a navy strong enough to challenge his grandmother's fleet. German military, naval, and industrial might enhanced the status of German culture. In the realm of physical culture, the gymnasts of the *Deutsche Turnerschaft* were taken as a model by those who feared as well as by those who admired German achievements.

Except for the French, Germany's neighbors to the west and south were strongly influenced by *Schulturnen* (educational gymnastics). In Belgium, for instance, the German system was modified by J. J. Happel and propagated by Jahn's disciple and editor, Carl Euler, who settled in Brussels in 1860.[18] A Belgian, Nicolaas Jan Cupérus, led the way in the formation of a national gymnastics federation in 1865 and a European one in 1881. His antipathy to modern sports was vehemently expressed in an 1894 letter to Pierre de Coubertin: "My federation has always believed and still believes today that gymnastics and sports are contrary things, and we have always combatted the latter as incompatible with our principles."[19]

Before his move to Belgium, Euler had been active in Holland, where he was the first teacher of gymnastics at the Royal Normal School in Haarlem. Inspired by Euler and other Germans, Dutch teachers of physical education formed a national association in 1862.[20] Looking as they then did to Germany for their model, they founded gymnastics clubs with names like *De Germaan*, *Keizer Otto*, and *Adolf Spiess*.[21] Dutch educators committed to Germanic physical training labored for decades in a vain attempt to construct an ideological dike against the successive waves of modern sports that came first from England and then from the United States.

In northern Switzerland, an area of almost unadulterated Germanic culture, gymnastics clubs appeared as early as 1820 and a gymnastic federation was formed in 1869. The dominant personality there was Adolf Spiess. He had studied in Halle and Giessen before he settled, in 1833, in the small Swiss town of Burgdorf. Eleven years later he moved to Basel, where he taught physical education. There he developed the techniques of *Schulturnen* that were eventually to sweep through the entire German educational system.[22] Gymnastics became such an important element in Swiss culture that the development of soccer football was long delayed. The *Turner* of the German-speaking cantons "despised [soccer] and at the same time felt threatened by it."[23] As late as 1978, Swiss gymnastics clubs still counted more members than the national soccer federation.[24]

Turnen reached Italy in the person of a Swiss expatriate, Rodolfo Obermann, who instituted a course in military gymnastics in Turin in 1833.[25] Italy's first gymnastics society appeared in 1844. Obermann exerted a powerful influence on Italian physical education. Encouraged by the progressive Minister of Education, Francesco de Sanctis, Obermann began to train physical educators in 1861. His normal school and that of Emilio Baumann, begun in 1877, were supposed to provide the teachers who were to implement the 1878 law mandating physical education at all levels for all of Italy's schools.[26] The law was more or less a dead letter. Some teachers were trained and they managed to introduce an occasional hour of physical education into the curriculum, but funds were scarce and reasons to divert them were plentiful. Besides, young Italians were no more enamoured of gymnastic drill than their coevals in northern Europe.

Except in Alsace, where a gymnastics club was founded at Guebwiller in 1860, French pedagogues tended to shun *Turnen* in order to follow the variant of gymnastic drill devised early in the century by Francisco Amoros. The *Société gymnastique de Lyon*, formed by Germans in 1844, inspired few Frenchman until after the nation's humiliating defeat in the Franco-Prussian War. Only then did patriotic gymnastics clubs proliferate throughout France.[27] "Feelings of revenge and the fear of renewed German aggression were reflected in the names of many of the gymnastics clubs: *La Revanche, La Patriote, La Régénératice, France!*"[28] The motto of the **Union des Sociétés de Gymnastique de France**, founded in 1873, was *Patrie-Courage-Moralité*.[29] Traditions inherited from Amoros were modified and the parades, pageantry, speeches, and gymnastic exercises of these chauvinistic clubs increasingly mirrored the practices of the hated enemy across the Rhine. "From 1879 to 1914, French gymnastics practice develops in the shadow of political power. . . . Gymnastics are politics continued by other means."[30]

Scandinavian physical educators, who were very well aware of German developments, also created an alternative to *Schulturnen*. Per Henrik Ling, the revered founder of Swedish gymnastics, was a romantic poet more influenced by one of Jahn's predecessors—Johann Christian Friedrich GutsMuths—than by Jahn. Scornful of the rings, ropes, bars, and vaulting equipment that were a prominent part of *Turnen*, Ling elaborated his own system, which his followers fiercely defended as the only "scientific" one. To propagate his version of gymnastic exercises, Ling, in 1814, established Stockholm's Central Institute of Physical Education.[31]

The French showed some interest in Ling's ideas (because almost any form of physical education was better than the German brand), but the Swedish system was never as popular in France as in England.[32] From Stockholm's Central Institute, young Martina Bergman-Osterberg journeyed to London, where she became Superintendant of Physical Education for London's schools (in 1881) and founder of the Hampstead Physical Training College (in 1885). Her influence on the physical eduation of British girls was immense.[33] Although disputes among the followers of Jahn, Amoros, Ling, and other theorists of physical education were impassioned and—to an outsider— arcane, the French and the Scandinavian variants of *Schulturnen* seem only marginally different from the German version when one compares all of them with the modern sports that all of them vociferously repudiated.

FROM GERMANY TO EASTERN EUROPE

From the thirteenth century, when Russia's Alexander Nevsky repelled the invasion of the Teutonic Knights, to the twentieth, when the Soviet Union managed to survive the onslaught of Hitler's *Wehrmacht*, Germans and Slavs contended for political,

The "Young America" Cricket Team of 1864. With the exception of Rotch Wister, whose family was of German origins, the young men have names indicating that they, like most cricketers of the period, had English origins. The C. C. Morris Cricket Library Association.

An Australian
Men's Cricket
Team (1878).
National Library
of Australia.

An Australian Women's Cricket Team (1895).
The National Library of Australia.

The Mayo College Cricket Team (1885). From V. A. S. Stowe, A Short History of Mayo College.

Schoolboy soccer players of the École alsacienne, Paris (ca. 1900). Fédération française de Football.

Young men playing soccer in the Parc de Rambouillet (ca. 1900). This picture is taken from a postcard. Collection Serget Laget.

The winners of Berlin's 1898 soccer championship: the Berliner Football Club Frankfurt 1885. The odd name is explained by the fact that Georg Leux, the captain, arrived in Berlin from Frankfurt am Main. Forum für Sportgeschichte.

The Cologne Football Club of 1899 before a home match against Newcastle United Football Club (1911). Deutsches Sportmuseum Köln.

Football Club Hertha on its Berlin Field (1909). Collection Serge Laget.

Alexander Watson Hutton, "Father of Argentine
Soccer Football." From Héctor Alberto
Chaponick, Historia del Fútbol Argentino.

Nottingham Forest Football Club versus an Argentine Team, June 1905. The signatures are those of the players. The penalty zone is hemispheric rather than rectangular. From Chaponick, Historia del Fútbol Argentino.

Club Nacional de Montevideo. Although someone has written "1908" on this postcard, the championship soccer team is from 1905. Tapabor/Kharbine.

A soccer team
from Cameroun
(1927). Centre
d'Archives
d'Outre-mer.

A baseball game at Cobden, Ontario (July 27, 1909). Arthur L. Handford/National
Archives of Canada P17 55947.

The baseball team of the First Higher School (*Ichiko*) of Tokyo
(1893). Kodansha International.

Dominican dicatator Rafael Trujillo's championship team of 1937.
The majority of the team came from Trujillo's raids on the Negro
National League. Front (left to right): Enrique Lantigua, Leroy
Matlock, Julio Vasquez, James "Cool Papa" Bell, Sam Bankhead,
Silvio Correa.Middle: Lazaro Salazar, José Enrique Ayubar (National
Congress Deputy and manager of the team), Leory "Satchel"
Paige. Rear: Josh Gibson, Harry William, Antonio Caselnos,
Rodolfo Fernandez,Bob Griffith, Perucho Cepeda, Bill Perkins.
National Baseball Library and Archive, Cooperstown, New York

St. John's University, Shanghai, China 1924-25 basketball team, the East
China Inter-collegiate Athletic Association Champions. Front: Li B. J.
second left; Zhang F. Q. center; Eu P. K. second right.rear: Zhu, L. Y. left;
P. B. Sullivan, coach, center McDonald W. Sullivan Collection.

Senda Berenson coaching women's basketball at Smith College in Northampton,
Massachusetts (1904). Smith College Archives.

The Philippine Islands versus Mexico in the basketball competitions at the 1936 Olympic Games, Berlin. Mexico won and eventually won the bronze medal. Author's collection.

Pierre de Coubertin, founder of the modern Olympic Games. Avery Brundage Collection, University of Illinois Archives.

Coubertin's three successors as President of the International Olympic Committe (ca. 1936): Henri Baillet-Latour (Belgium), Avery Brundage (United States), Sigfrid Edstrøm (Sweden). Appropriately, they stand before the globe, around which they hoped to disseminate the gospel of "Olympism."Avery Brundage Collection, University of Illinois Archives.

Kenya's Wilson Kiprugat winning the 800-meter final at 1968 Olympic Games, Mexico City. The "tape," actually a string, is held by a woman in the middle of the track because the string's reel was stuck. Bettmann Archive.

Algeria's Hassida Boulmerka winning the 1500-meter final at the World Track and Field Championships of 1991 (Tokyo). Boulmerka, one of the first Islamic women to become a world-class athlete, repeated her victory at the 1992 Olympic Games in Barcelona. Bettmann Archive.

Lithograph by Gottfried Kühn (ca. 1858). Ludwing Friedrich Jahn, the founder of *Turnen* (German gymnastics), as the patron of the gymnasts gathered to dedicate the *Trunplatz* on Berlin's Hasenheide (1811). Heimatmuseum Neu-Kölln.

Sumo wrestlers engaged in their ritual dance.
Überhorst, ed., Geschichte der Leibesübungen.

Wattussi Tribesman leaping over the head of Herzong Adolf Friedrich von Mecklenburg (right), leader of an ethnographic expedition to German East Africa (1907). G. A. C. Bogeng, ed., Geschichte des Sports aller Völker und Zeiten/Deutsches Sportmuseum, Köln.

A traditional game of
Flemish bowls. Vlaamse
Folkssport Centrale.

An urban Nuba wrestling match.
Rolf Husmann.

American football in England: the London Monarchs playing in soccer's hallowed Wembley Stadium. Sean Ryan/National Football League.

economic, and cultural domination of Eastern Europe. In the last decades of the nineteenth century, *Turnen* figured prominently in the cultural struggle because Czechs, Slovaks, Poles, and Hungarians appropriated German gymnastics and used it, as Jahn had, in their struggle for national liberation. The irony, of course, was that the Slavs resorted to a product of German culture in their efforts to liberate themselves from the political shackles of German and Austrian rule.

The two men who first realized *Turnen's* revolutionary potential for Slavic Europe, Jindrich Fügner and Miroslav Tyrs, were middle-class Czechs with complicated relationships to the hegemonic culture. Fügner's response to dual identity was to repudiate his German ancestry. His daughter Renata, who married Tyrs, quoted her father: "I was never a German. I am a citizen of Prague, a German-speaking citizen of Prague."[34] His friend and son-in-law, Miroslav Tyrs, born of parents who had forgotten their Czech antecedents, reversed the process of assimilation and changed his baptismal name—"Friedrich Tirsch"—to its original Slavic form.

Young Tyrs, a student of philosophy, took the lead in founding the first *Sokol* ("Falcon") in February of 1862, a year after his graduation from Prague's Charles University. Fügner, who sold insurance, was the club's first president. Originally, the rank-and-file members were middle-class white-collar workers while the officials were property-owners or educators, but the percentage of members who were manual workers rose above 50% by the end of the century.[35] Whatever the members' social status, the political direction of the Sokol movement was never in doubt. Both of the founders were members of the executive council of the "Young Czechs," a wing of the Czech National Party. The members of the Sokol wore red shirts as a reminder of Garabaldi's successful campaign to free northern Italy from Austrian rule. The rest of their uniform was based on traditional Slavic dress. In accord with their name, Sokol members wore jaunty hats with falcon feathers. From the beginning, Tyrs gave the movement a paramilitary emphasis. "Only a healthy nation," he wrote, "is an armed nation. A weapon in every fist!"[36]

Despite harassment from the authorities, the Sokol movement spread rapidly. In 1871, Tyrs began to edit a journal, also called *Sokol*, to publicize the movement. A decade later, thousands of Czechs and Slovaks assembled in Prague to celebrate a grand Turner-style gymnastics festival. The Bohemian Sokol Union was formed in 1889, the Czech Sokol Union in 1896. They merged in 1908, six years after the clerical elements of the movement left to create their own equally nationalistic but politically less radical organization. Shortly before the outbreak of World War I, the Prague "nest," which had begun with seventy-three members, had 128,000 "falcons." When independence was achieved in the aftermath of the war, the Sokol movement gave the new republic its first president: Thomas Masaryk. He had joined the Prague Sokol in 1890.[37]

Czechs and Slovaks were by no means the only ones to transform German gymnastics into an instrument of Slavic nationalism. A year after the birth of Prague's first club, the Slovenes of Liubliana founded the *Juzni Sokol* ("Southern Falcon"). The Austrian police closed the club in 1867 but allowed it to reopen a year later.[38] The Poles of Lemberg, also inspired by Prague's example, followed in 1866. In the western half of Poland, then a part of Germany, the Slavic clubs were tolerated, but Poles who lived under Russian rule had a more difficult time. They were not allowed to parade in their Sokol uniforms or to display their organization's symbols. When the Czarist police discovered that a number of Poles living in Odessa had dared to form a Sokol, the offenders were hustled off to Siberia.[39] In the Balkans, as in Czechoslovakia and Poland, there were numerous *Turnvereine* dedicated to the preservation of German culture, but, in the last quarter of the century, Slavic clubs sprang up all around them. The Croats of Zagreb, influenced by the Slovenes to the north, founded their club in 1874, the Serbs of Belgrade in 1882, and the Bosnians of Sarajevo in 1903.[40]

In 1879, only one year after Bulgaria broke away from the Ottoman Empire, a pair of Czech brothers, Irgi and Georg Proschek, organized a Sokol in Sofia. It seems symbolically appropriate in light of the city's history of successive conquests that the club members performed their gyrations in an abandoned mosque that had been erected on the site of a Byzantine church. The club was short-lived, but the brothers tried again in 1893, only to have their pioneering efforts overshadowed in 1895 when the Minister of Education invited twelve Swiss Turner to Sofia.[41]

While the Slavic gymnasts were unified in their opposition to Germanic culture, each ethnic group emphasized its own language and literature, its own music, its own costume, and—unfortunately— its own grievances. A Slavic Sokol Association was founded in 1912, but the polyglot organization was never as united in politics and purpose as the *Deutsche Turnerschaft*.[42]

The Slavic clubs also differed from the Turner in that their antipathy to modern sports was considerably less extreme. There *were* divisions between the proponents of gymnastics and the enthusiasts for sports. Budapest's premier athletic club, founded by Count Miksa Esterházy in 1875, split apart in a bitter quarrel over the two modes of physical culture, but Slavic gymnasts were less likely than the Turner to fight tooth and nail against the introduction of soccer and other British imports.[43]

FROM GERMANY TO THE AMERICAS

That millions of Germans migrated to the United States in the course of the nineteenth and early twentieth centuries is common knowledge. That hundreds of thousands of Germans also migrated to Latin America is less widely known—and the *Turnvereine* they founded, from Mexico to Argentina, have been less intensely studied than the clubs of the North American *Turnerbund*.

The gymnastics movement was especially strong in the "ABC" countries. Leopold Böhm seems to have taken the lead in Buenos Aires, where a *Turnverein* was organized in 1855. According to the *Deutsche Turnzeitung* for November 1, 1862, a gymnastics club had been founded in Rio de Janeiro in 1859. This club quickly expired, but another was formed in 1869 by J. A. Friedrich in Porto Alegro, the capital of the province of Rio Grando do Sul. In 1895, the nine clubs of that city formed the *Deutsche Turnerschaft von Rio Grande do Sul*. One purpose of the organization was to carry on the gymnastics tradition of *Turnvater* Jahn, "but the clubs also saw the diffusion of German culture as part of their duty." The *Deutscher Verein* in Santiago de Chile, founded in 1853, ran a school and a *Turnhalle* where members were able to perform their gymnastic exercises. The first Chilean *Turnvereine* seem to date from 1864 (Santiago) and 1871 (Valparaiso). A national gymnastics festival was held in Concepción in 1897. By the early twentieth century, there were also clubs in Mexico City, Caracas, and Montevideo, but Argentina, Brazil, and Chile were the only Latin American nations with really vigorous gymnastic movements.[44]

Numerically, the *Turner* were always outnumbered by the Latin Americans who preferred the excitement of sports contests to the noncompetitive virtues of calisthenics. Nonetheless, the disciples of Jahn, working with (and sometimes against) the proponents of the French and Scandinavian gymnastics systems, shaped the contours of Latin American physical education. The mandated number of hours for *educación física y deporte* have always been an ideal rather than a taken-for-granted reality, but the ideal has clearly been one derived, ultimately, from Jahn, Amoros, and Ling.[45]

The influence of the *Turner* on *North* American physical education was so strong that I experienced it as a schoolboy in Depression-era Chicago. Baseball, basketball, and football were unknown at James Madison Elementary School, but we marched grimly from one end of the gymnasium to the other, we did our calisthenics, we tumbled, climbed ropes, and did our best to satisfy the rather stern physical-education teacher and to pacify the spirit of Jahn (of whose existence I would remain ignorant for another thirty years).

The American roots of the activities I endured in 1938 can be traced back to 1825 when Karl Beck, a twenty-seven-year-old German schooled and skilled in *Turnen*, became a teacher at the Round Hill School that George Bancroft and Joseph Cogswell had founded two years earlier in Northampton, Massachusetts. Bancroft and Cogswell were both familiar with the German *Philanthropen* and their enlightened ideas about the importance of physical education. Cogswell had visited Christian Gotthilf Salzmann's school at Schnepfenthal. He and Bancroft, having instituted a program of physical education at Round Hill School, asked Harvard's George Ticknor, a widely traveled authority on European literature, to help them find someone to direct the new program. Ticknor recommended Beck, who constructed a *Turnplatz* for the school and led the boys in a daily hour of exercise. At night, he translated Jahn's *Deutsche Turnkunst* into English. Bancroft and Cogswell were delighted. In their *Account of the School for the Liberal Education of Boys* (1826), they boasted, "We are deeply impressed with the necessity of uniting physical with moral education; and are particularly favored in executing our plans of connecting them by the assistance of a pupil and friend of Jahn, the greatest modern advocate of gymnastics."[46]

After Harvard tried and failed to entice Jahn himself to become a member of its faculty, the college hired another of Jahn's disciples, Karl Follen, to set up a program of physical education. Follen wrote Beck on April 5, 1826, "I have commenced gymnastic exercises with the students. . . . At present

I use one of the dining halls. All show much zeal."[47] Follen soon had a regular *Turnplatz*, but the students' zeal quickly waned. Once the aura of novelty wore away, gymnastic drill seemed unutterably dreary. It was not until the massive German immigration of the fifties, after the failure of the Revolution of 1848, that *Turnen* was able firmly to secure its American beachhead.

Between 1840 and 1849, 385,434 Germans entered the United States. In the next five years, another 654,291 came. Of course, only a minority of these immigrants had been *Turner*, but many of the others became involved in gymnastics once they were in the New World. It was one way to remain German. Friedrich Hecker founded Cincinnati's *Turngemeinde* (gymnastics association) on November 21, 1848; the New York *Turngemeinde* followed one week later. Within three years, the clubs had their own newspaper, *Die Turnzeitung*. Since many of the new German-Americans had been members of the radical *Demokratischer Turner-Bund* that had been formed in Hanau in 1848, it was hardly a surprise when the New Yorkers joined nine clubs from Boston, Brooklyn, Philadelphia, and Baltimore to create the *Sozialistischer Turnerbund*, a radical organization that allied itself with the Free Soil Party in the election of 1852. At their Buffalo convention in September of 1855, the *Turner* created a political platform for the national elections of 1856. Although a delegate from Virginia cried out that "Germans in the South will be ruined if they take a stand against slavery," the majority voted their condemnation of the South's "peculiar institution." Clubs from Mobile, Savannah, Augusta, and Charleston were among the twenty-three that withdrew from the organization. The majority's radicalism did have limits. Since the *Biergarten* was as sacred to German culture as the *Turnverein*, the gymnasts broke ranks with British-American reform groups and condemned the temperance movement. If slavery was to go, one wanted to toast its demise with a hearty "*Prost!*"[48]

In the election of 1856, the majority of the *Turner* cast their ballots for Republican candidates, but not everyone was content with the new party's willingness to settle for the containment of slavery. In the eyes of some radicals, like Karl Follen and Karl Heinzen, the Republicans seemed to temporize on the question. Still, despite their doubts, most of the *Turner* supported Lincoln in his bid for the presidency. Upon Lincoln's election, the *Turner* formed part of the president's bodyguard.

In what historian Henry Adams referred to as "the great secession crisis," the *Turner* were divided. Some of those who lived in the South cheered for Jefferson Davis and readied themselves to fight for the Confederacy, but the great majority of the Germans remained loyal to the Union. When Lincoln called for troops to suppress the rebellion, they enlisted in such numbers that they were mustered into sixteen regiments. In relation to their share of the nation's population, Germans provided more men for the Union's armies than any other ethnic group, and there is little doubt that the *Turner*, many of whom had fought in the Revolution of 1848, were even more likely to volunteer than less ideologically committed German-Americans. One of the *Turner*, Carl Schurz, rose to the rank of general during the war and served in the cabinet afterwards.[49]

The politics of the postwar *Turner* were liberal rather than radical, but their national organization, the *Nordamerikanischer Turnerbund*, continued to support such reforms as a shorter workday and the end of child labor. The *Turner* also argued forcefully for compulsory physical education in the schools. Since they had a coherent argument based on decades of discussion and experience, their influence in this matter was disproportionate to their very modest numbers.[50]

The membership of the *NAT* peaked in 1893, when the organization was able to count more than 40,000 *Turner*. Their decline can be attributed, in part, to their ambivalent Americanization and, in part, to their stubborn refusal to come to terms with modern sports. As late as 1896, the organization's leaders continued to prize their German above their American identity. "The pole around which the future of German *Turnen* turns," they proclaimed, "is to be German and to act like Germans."[51] As long as the maintenance of their ethnic culture was of paramount importance to German-Americans, the *Turnverein* functioned well. Uniforms, a parade (accompanied by a stirring drum-and-fife unit), a mass demonstration of disciplined physical strength and agility, a banquet, speeches *auf Deutsch*, the singing of German *Lieder*—these elements sufficed to produce a powerful sense of communal solidarity. But, once the children and grandchildren of the Forty-Eighters commenced to think of themselves as Americans, they deserted the cause of German culture, allowed their membership in the local *Turnverein* to lapse, and seized the opportunity to play baseball. In the United States as in Latin America, *Turnen*, stripped of the emotional prop of nationalistic fervor, was never a match for modern sports.

8

TRADITIONAL SPORTS

Anthropologists are certainly well aware that there is no such thing as a "traditional society," perfectly static and exempt from the processes of historical change. All cultures evolve as a result of internal interactions, and the most isolated peoples—the Inuit of the Arctic, the Chambri of Papua New Guinea—have slowly but surely been drawn into what many social scientists refer to as the "world system." The paradigmatic dichotomy between traditional and modern sports must be understood as a contrast between two Weberian "ideal types," neither of which is perfectly instantiated in the "real world." By the time the sharp-eyed anthropologist has published her ethnographic account of the wrestling matches of the Diola of Gambia and the Njabi of the Congo, the ritualized contests have become something other than what she witnessed.[1]

Although there are exceptions to the rule, cultural change in the realm of sports is usually in one direction—from traditional to modern forms. Wherever traditional sports survive, they tend either to take on some of the characteristics of modernity or to persist in the form of what Raymond Williams referred to as "residual" (as contrasted to "emergent") culture. The religious significance of the contest wanes away to a token acknowledgement of the gods in whose honor and for whose favor the wrestlers or archers or stickball players once competed. The equipment and the facilities are rationalized to maximize performance. Players are ranked and winners are determined by objective measurements or on the basis of a point system. A bureaucratic organization emerges to administer regularly occurring tournaments and continually to adjust the rules and regulations. The modernized sport is marketed via television to spectators who have never witnessed the contest in any other form.

Articulate resistance to this process is nothing new. In 1884, Thomas Croke, one of the founders of the Gaelic Athletic Association and a vehement advocate of home rule for Ireland, wrote a stirring defense of "hurling, football kicking according to the Irish rules, 'casting,' leaping various ways, wrestling, handy-grips," and other Hibernian "exercises and amusements." He warned his patriotic countrymen against "such foreign and fantastic field sports as lawn-tennis, polo, cricket and the like."[2]

Every step on the road to modernity is contested by the traditionalists who see, rightly, that a succession of minor adjustments culminates eventually in a major transformation. Should the bat used to play *tsan*, a ballgame unique to the tiny Alpine valley of Aosta, be fabricated by a machine, which is easier and cheaper, or carved by hand, which is the way it has always been done?[3] How indispensable are the traditional (and no longer intelligible) verses chanted as Turkish wrestlers prepare to grapple?[4] How necessary are the songs that accompany the Brazilian combat sport *capoeira*, songs now deemed "useless" and "effeminate" by younger *capoeiristas* who are "focused on the agonistic interchange and how they might defeat some opponent"[5]? Those who cherish traditional sports are constantly bedeviled by such questions. Like environmentalists who fear that a single adverse decision can irrevocably extinguish an endangered species or irreparably damage a delicately balanced ecosystem, the advocates of traditionalist physical culture are haunted by the sense that all innovations are irreversible.

The process of modernization *can* be halted and even reversed, as Islamic fundamentalists have demonstrated in the political realm, but sports history does seem—for the most part—to demonstrate the opposite. One specific example of the apparently irresistible modernization of traditional sports is the evolution of the pre-Columbian stickball games once played throughout most of North America. These games were once religious rituals performed to guarantee the fertility of the earth and its inhabitants or to insure that the spring rains arrived at the most propitious time. Among the Cherokees, Choctaws, and Creeks of the Southeast, stickball players submitted to fasts, scarification, and other stringent rites of purification. They sang and danced in elaborate communal ceremonies before they were allowed to begin their contests. The game itself was a wild affair decided by priestly incantation as well as physical prowess.[6]

The game survives—in a sense. The Choctaws still play stickball, but the pre-Columbian

> rituals have vanished, along with the Great Spirit who called them forth. The teams now have uniforms, and there are officials to enforce the rules. There are boundaries, a clock, and a scoreboard. Medicine men linger on with little to do. Sitting on the sidelines, chanting their

magic incantations, they dispiritedly seek to influence the outcome of games in which hardly anyone takes much interest.[7]

One may well ask if it is the same game.

The same process of modernization was observable in Afghanistan before the ravages of civil war. The traditional sport of buzkashi, which consisted of as many as a thousand mounted tribesmen struggling to reach down and make off with the carcass of a decapitated calf or goat, has become "modern" buzkashi, a game played by two evenly matched teams of five to fifteen riders before spectators comfortably seated in an eighteen-thousand-person stadium in Kabul. In the traditional version of buzkashi, the victor was the first horseman to "break free," an act difficult to define except by the players of the game and even they were liable to quarrel about whether or not one of their number had, in fact, successfully separated himself from the mêlée. In the modernized form of buzkashi, there is a field upon which two circles are inscribed equidistant from a flagpole. One point is earned when a team lifts the "carcass" (now made of cloth or leather) from the team's own circle and carries it around the flagpole; two points are awarded if the "carcass" can be deposited once again in the team's circle. The National Olympic Committee of Afghanistan administered the yearly tournament.[8]

The most ubiquitous and hardy of traditional sports are not the equestrian games, of which buzkashi is but one example,[9] but the man-to-man (or, occasionally, woman-to-woman) combat sports, of which wrestling is probably the oldest, the most widespread, and the most varied. Wrestling seems also to be among the traditional sports most resistant to the incessant pressures of modernization. Icelandic, Cornish, Breton, Turkish, Indian, and hundreds of other kinds of wrestling have survived into the late twentieth century.[10] It is customary for their proponents to maintain—as Hans-Peter Laqueur has for the traditional Turkish variant—that their beloved sport has "successfully adapted to the requirements of modern society without losing its essence."[11] One can be skeptical about Laqueur's claim. Judgments about essences and the success or failure of ludic adaptations are often the result of wishful thinking. On the other hand, who are we to quarrel with a contented Turkish wrestler?

For a closer look at traditional sports that still retain their premodern characteristics *and* their hold on the popular imagination, nationally and internationally, one cannot do better than to look at Japanese sumo, a sport that historians have traced back to prehistorical times. On the basis of primitive terra cotta figures known as *haniwa*, P. L. Cuyler asserts that "sumo was performed as part of Shinto ritual at least from the Tumulus period (250–552)."[12] Written records of sumo begin in the eighth century, when the courtly aristocrats of Nara (near modern Kyoto) sponsored more or less secularized tournaments on the seventh day of the seventh month. The wrestlers were peasants recruited by scouts sent to scour the provinces for the best specimens of native talent.

The ninth-century version of sumo took place in a garden strewn with white sand. Tents for the combattants, who were members of the corps of imperial bodyguards, were erected on the east and west sides of the garden. Thirty-four wrestlers marched into the enclosure, followed first by twelve musicians and then by the emperor and his court. The wrestlers of the "left" wore paper hollyhocks in their hair, those of the "right" were adorned with calabash blossoms. The referees and the scorekeeper carried bows in their hands and quivers of arrows on their backs. "Following each match, the musicians of the winning team beat the drums, struck the gongs, and presented a ritual dance."[13]

By the late sixteenth century, although *shinji-zumo* ("sumo in service of the gods") was still performed at many shrines and temples, there was also a secularized version of the sport which featured professional wrestlers. An elaborate system developed, with *heya* ("stables"; literally, "rooms") of wrestlers under the direction of hereditary masters, with a pyramid of ranks through which the most successful wrestlers moved until the champion was determined. In the eighteenth and nineteenth centuries, sumo acquired many ceremonies now perceived as "ancient." The awarding of a bow to the winner of a match, who then performs a dance with it, dates only from 1791, when the shogun presented a bow to the famed wrestler Tanikaze. The ring itself, the *dojo*, can be traced back no farther than the Edo Period. Its purification by strewing salt is an eighteenth-century innovation.[14]

In the late nineteenth and early twentieth centuries, sumo underwent what Eric Hobsbawm has termed "the reinvention of tradition." After decades of intensive Meiji-period modernization, many members of the nation's elite felt the need to emphasize once again traits that they felt to be distinctively Japanese. In 1890, in reaction to the concept of a champion systematically determined on the basis of tournament victories and defeats, the elders in charge of the sport added a final layer to the *banzuke* or pyramid of ranks. The *yokozuna* or grand champion was not to be determined objectively on the basis of his quantified won/lost record in the annual round of tournaments but was instead to be chosen on the basis of the objective record *and* the personal characteristics that made him a suitable symbol of the Japanese people. In sociological terms, eligibility on the basis of achievement was modified by an element of ascription. The *yokozuna* was and is quite special. Ordinary wrestlers who lose a series of matches drop to a lower rank, rather like major-league baseball players sent back to the minors after a bad season, but the *yokozuna* is exempted from demotion. Once a wrestler becomes a *yokozuna*, it is impossible for him to lose that status, no matter how many times he is defeated by aspiring younger wrestlers. (The dignified thing for a fading *yokozuna* to do is to retire.)

Early in the twentieth century, additional Shinto elements were introduced into sumo wrestling. The referee's black hat, for instance, which looks like those worn by the Shinto priests depicted in Heian art, was adopted in 1909. The same is true of the referee's colorful kimono. The roof which traditionally covered the sumo ring had been modeled on the Japanese farmhouse. It was redesigned in 1931 to imitate the roof of the Ise Shrine, the most sacred site of Japanese Shinto.[15] All in all, sumo seems to provide evidence for Johann P. Arnason's contention that "globalization strengthens or reactivates national identities, communities and projections."[16]

The result of these cross-currents of modernization and what we might refer to as "traditionalization" was the hybrid sport that we see today. The mighty wrestlers, wearing a belt of rope symbolizing the sacred cords that hang from the gates of Shinto shrines, stride into the *dojo*, stamp their bare feet on the ground to expel evil spirits from the ring, scatter salt on the earth in an ancient ritual of purification, and glare at each other for a period of minutes strictly determined by the exigencies of modern television. The higher the rank, the more sustained the glare. Gone are the four pillars supporting the roof and representing the gods of summer, autumn, winter, and spring. In order to provide the spectators (and the television cameras) unimpeded views, the *dojo*'s symbolic roof and reminders of its pillars have been suspended from the rafters of the arena. No matter. Sumo, like the imperial line that traces its origins back to the goddess of the sun, is authentically Japanese. No traditional sport—with the possible exception of Spanish bullfighting—has more successfully "naturalized" its concessions to modernity.

Although speculation has linked the bullfight with prehistoric fertility rites and with the ancient religion of Mithraism, brought to Spain by Roman legions that had been stationed in the East,[17] the sport as we know it took form in the eighteenth century. The traditional elements of the *corrida de toros* are so obvious that it is easy to overlook the fact that the *matador* now performs his fancy footwork in a highly rationalized ludic environment. "The history of bullfighting," concludes Timothy Mitchell, "is the history of the development of ever more efficient techniques for controlling the animal raw material." The traditional elements of the sport that excite, and sometimes horrify, the tourist are also what the ethnographically inclined observer first notices. How can one not focus, when introduced to the *corrida de toros*, upon the colorful entrances and exits, the capes and costumes, the repertory of stylized motions, everything, in short, that makes bullfighting a symbol of Spanish culture for writers like Ernest Hemingway (and for the designers of travel posters)? Bullfighting is unquestionably an "archaic folk ritual," but it is also the consequence of "the slow but steady rationalization of the various ways that the peoples of Spain have played with bulls."[18]

Unlike the traditional elements that make the *corrida* a colorful spectacle superficially intelligible even to the tourist, the modernization of the sport is visible only to the informed eye. If one looks carefully, however, evidence of rationalization is plentiful. The matadors are registered nationally in the *Sector Taurino del Sindicato Nacional de Espectáculo*. Although the procession of matadors, picadors, *banderilleros*, and others enters the arena in the traditionally prescribed order, the *matadores* now compete in an order of seniority determined by the date of their official promotion from *matador de novillos* to *matador de toros*. They are supported by two *picadores* whose horses have been given tranquilizers to suppress their understandable nervousness. Each bull is supposed to have thirty minutes in the arena before the kill. Once the matador has entered the arena, he has exactly fifteen minutes to dispatch the bull. The arena must be no more than seventy and no fewer than forty-five meters in diameter. It is ringed by a barrier that is supposed to be precisely 1.7 meters high. The wall that separates the arena from the seats is 2.2

meters high. The *corrida* itself, which includes a repertory of traditional movements, has resisted quantification.

The achievements of a matador are best described not by the statistics that have been employed to quantify baseball but rather by the lyricism of an Ernest Hemingway or Henry de Montherlant. Brilliant performances are rewarded by the presentation of one ear, two ears, or two ears and a tail. The crowd decides whether or not the first ear should be granted. The *Presidente*, who is the Director General of Security when the *corrida* takes place in Madrid and the Civil Governor when the event occurs in the provinces, determines whether or not to award greater honors. Their judgments are, quite obviously, subjective (and frequently met by jeers from those who judged differently). As the ritualized contest comes to an end, the medical experts who examined the bulls before they were allotted to the matadors return to inspect them once again to certify that no one had tampered with them. To the average *aficionado*, the weave of traditional and modern threads is seamless.

Sumo's successful adaptation was managed under the direction and control of the elders whose families have, for generations, decided what was sumo and what was not. Bullfighting, too, has survived without the direct support of the state. The Arab governments of North Africa have, however, made it a matter of public policy that *their* traditional games survive as "resistance and alternatives to the new colonialism."[19] Although they have demonstrated no desire to withdraw from the "world system" of modern sports, ministers of sports in Morocco, Algeria, and Tunisia have encouraged their people simultaneously to preserve traditional sports like *al kora* (a ballgame) and *haih a deux* (similar to prisoner's base). Some regimes have gone further. The *Comité Militaire du Salut National* that ruled the Islamic Republic of Mauritania decreed in 1980 that it was "indispensable . . . to rehabilitate and develop traditional sportive activities: foot races, horse races, camel races, target archery, and wrestling." Spokesmen for the regime condemned the International Olympic Committee for its false claim "to represent the world of sports."[20]

The intransigence of Libya and Mauritania, however, seem to be the exception that proves the rule. In the Islamic world as throughout sub-Saharan Africa, historians and journalists who begin by expressing pride in traditional sports almost invariably conclude by boasting of medals won at the Olympic Games or the *Jeux Africains*. Although the economic means of Third World states are more limited than were those of the USSR at the peak of its power and influence, developing nations seem determined, when it comes to sports, to follow the route taken by the Soviet Union, which published lyrical accounts of traditional Russian games and invested billions of rubles in a systematic (and successful) effort to identify, support, equip, and train athletes whose primary mission in life was to surpass the Americans at the Olympic Games and thus to demonstrate to the world the superiority of "new socialist man."[21]

The picture, viewed from the traditionalist's perspective, is not entirely grim. Henning Eichberg, who has published numerous books and articles condemning the artificiality of modern sports and praising the spontaneity and vitality of traditional pastimes,[22] writes enthusiastically of the Inuit peoples of the Arctic. Typical of their "culture of laughter" is the drum-dance, a combination of sports, grotesque physical contortions, laughter, music, dance, poetry, shamanism, magic, and collective ecstasy. In the era of Danish colonization, however, Greenland's "culture of laughter" was threatened with extinction.

> One of the first measures of the Danish and German-pietist missionaries was to forbid the drum-dance as something heathen. The drums were gathered and burned or delivered to museums. In the place of the dancing body other forms of physical culture were introduced: sitting, separated by sex, in rows and columns, on the benches of eighteenth-century Christian churches; the disciplined practice, after

1900, in rows and columns, of Danish-Swedish gymnastics; training for sports; the consumption of Western popular music in newly constructed hotels.[23]

The colonizers failed, however, to extinguish the "culture of laughter." In the era of decolonization, the Inuit Circumpolar Conference revived the drum-dance and other indigenous folkways of Greenland, Canada, Alaska, and Siberia.

Renewed commitment to traditional ways does not mean that the Inuit have repudiated all aspects of modernity. As early as 1970, the Inuit of northern Canada demanded and received a television station to be used, among other things, for showing documentaries of their native dances and games. Since this station allows interactive television, it is a "challenge to the transmitter-receiver model." According to Geneviève Rail, an eloquent defender of traditional culture, this mode of communication encourages democratic discourse and allows a hitherto suppressed culture to recover at least a modicum of control over its own destiny.[24]

Other scholars, alarmed at the "collective amnesia that some have called modernity,"[25] have joined together to found the *Vlaamse Volkssport Centrale* (1980) and a number of other organizations dedicated to the preservation and revival of traditional sports. Conferences like the one held at Berrien in Brittany in the spring of 1990 have opened up lines of communication among those who work actively for a *"renaissance des jeux populaires."*

Enthusiasts for traditional sports have not been content merely to publish newsletters like the *Nieuwsbrief van het Sportmuseum Vlaanderen* or to read papers at academic symposia. In May of 1985, the *Jeux des Petits États d'Europe* were celebrated in San Marino by athletes from San Marino, Monaco, Lichtenstein, Andorra, Iceland, Malta, Luxembourg, and Cyprus. A month later, the First Inter-Island Games took place on the Isle of Man, with competitors from islands as distant one from another as Guernsey, Iceland, and St. Helena. That same year, athletes from Brittany, Cornwall, and other areas of suppressed ethnicity came together in the First European Olympiade of the Minorities.[26] Eichberg, who is unquestionably one of the most prolific and eloquent advocates of the preservation of traditional sports, may be right about a "subversive tendency toward multiplicity."[27] He has optimistically predicted that the "age of Western colonial dominance is coming to an end—and with it the predominance of Olympic sports." Eichberg believes that modern sports will become less popular, that they will linger as "a sort of circus, show business, and media attraction" while "the masses in different cultures, nations, and regions will have their own festivals revealing their own patterns, their own traditions."[28] Perhaps. The eddies swirl and time will tell which way the currents flow.

III

ASSESSMENT

9

CULTURAL IMPERIALISM?

How can the process of diffusion be explained? It is certain that the adoption by one group of a sport popular among another involves a recognition of the intrinsic properties of the sport. These properties, more or less determined by the rulebook, are unquestionably a factor in the collective as well as in the individual response to a hitherto unknown sport. In the contest for popularity, some sports are doomed from the start. It is reasonably certain that whiffleball will never replace soccer football as the world's most widely played game. It is equally certain that Fiji Islanders are unlikely to become bobsledders and that very few Uzbeks own surfboards, but in such cases as these geography—not some intrinsic lack of appeal—is the obvious explanation. If any lesson is to be learned from the study of ludic diffusion, it is that intrinsic properties alone cannot determine a sport's popularity.

Slightly more sophisticated, but equally futile, is the effort to account for the process of global ludic diffusion on the basis of some kind of congruence between the intrinsic characteristics of a sport and the collective psychological disposition of its enthusiasts. Charles Peverelly, writing in 1866, may have been the first and was certainly not the last to assert that baseball "is a game which is peculiarly suited to the American temperament and disposition."[1] A German authority, writing in 1989, observed that Africans have taken to soccer football because they are "fascinated by everything that is round and can bounce."[2] This kind of simple-minded ethnocentric psychological explanation will not do. One problem is that modern games are ubiquitous; can baseball be "peculiarly suited to the American temperament" and also to the Mexican and to the Japanese? Another problem is that popularity waxes and wanes. Did the Japanese undergo a psychic transformation when they took up baseball and relegated to obscurity the sport of *inukyûdô* (a form of archery in which dogs were used as targets)? As Maarten van Bottenburg rightly remarked in a study of the "differential popularization" of sports in contemporary Europe, fluctuations in the preference for this or that specific sport cannot be explained in terms of "innate taste differences."[3]

If neither the intrinsic properties of a sport nor the match between those properties and some alleged collective psychological disposition is sufficient to account for the rapidity or the slowness of ludic diffusion from one nation to another, what does? Among the factors determing the process, the most important is the relative political, economic, and cultural power of the nations involved. In the words of Ruud Stokvis, a Dutch sociologist who has specialized in the study of ludic diffusion, the popularity of any given sport in any given country "depends upon the development of the positions of economic and political power among the nations of the world system."[4] We can be sure that, in general, the sports characteristic of wealthy and powerful nations "will be adopted by the populations of other lands who fall within the spheres of influence of the mighty." Stokvis goes a step further and argues that England and the United States are the *only* countries "where the most important modern sports were not developed under the influence of foreigners."[5]

In pursuing this line of argument, one must distinguish more precisely than Stokvis has among the various forms of power— political, economic, cultural. The distinctions among them are not arcane and there is no need to define them here. What is important is to recognize that the power vectors are usually but by no means invariably aligned. A nation that exercises political or economic power most often, although not always, exercises cultural power as well. The cultural vector sometimes points in a different direction from the political and economic vectors and, to stay with the mathematical analogy a moment longer, each of the vectors can represent the resolution of forces that may well be in opposition. Another way to express this fact is to say, as Arjun Appadurai does, that "people, machinery, money, images, and ideas now follow increasingly non-isomorphic paths."[6]

Each path, moreover, allows for two-way traffic (even when the volume in one direction is greater than in the other). Canadians, for instance, have taken to a version of gridiron football and their football teams have imported a number of American players, but at least a few Americans have discovered the excitement of Canadian lacrosse. In fact, instances of this kind of back-and-forth diffusion of sports between the politically or economically weaker power and the politically or economically stronger one abound. Polo provides another example. It was introduced into Britain from India by repatriated military men at approximately the same time that British missionary educators imposed cricket upon the recalcitrant sons of the native Indian elite.[7] Decades after baseball became Cuba's national game and decades before the exodus of anti-Communist Cubans to the United States, jai-lai—a Cuban version of Basque pelota—had thousands of Floridian fans. Judo is an even more striking example of reverse diffusion because it took hold in Europe and the United States at a time when Japan, defeated on the battlefield and subjected to military occupation, had barely begun to recover from the material ravages of war.[8] As a rule, however, receptivity to "exotic" sports has been limited to the more affluent and better educated sectors of the population.

If it is essential to distinguish among the aspects of power and to avoid facile assumptions about unidirectionality, it is no less essential to remind ourselves that the motivations involved in the diffusion of sports have been diverse. Political motives have certainly been important. In British India and elsewhere, there were many occasions where the colonizers forced modern sports upon the colonized, quite intentionally, as part of a program of political domination, as "a useful instrument of colonial purpose."[9] It is, however, a reductionist mistake to suggest, as Peter Rummelt does, that European missionaries, military men, and civil administrators propagated modern sports simply as a convenient form of social control.[10] Worthier motives—such as the desire to improve the health, to encourage the fortitude, and to diminish the religious animosities of the native population—cannot be ignored or condescendingly discounted as mere colonialist camouflage.

If a purely political model of ludic diffusion is woefully inadequate to the historical complexity of the process, then a purely economic model is no more satisfactory. One economic model of ludic diffusion is drawn from André Gunder Frank's theories of the "development of dependency." What most clearly distinguishes Frank's model from older conceptions of economic imperialism and from liberal-pluralist models of development (like W. W. Rostow's) is the insistence that modernization is impossible unless the "peripheral" society breaks away from the capitalist "world-system":

> My thesis is that . . . capitalist contradictions and the historical development of the capitalist system have generated underdevelopment in the peripheral satellites whose economic surplus was expropriated, while generating economic development in the metropolitan centers which appropriate that surplus. . . . [No] country which has been firmly tied to the metropolis as a satellite through incorporation into the world capitalist system has achieved the rank of an economically developed country, except by finally abandoning the capitalist system.[11]

The economic successes of Japan, South Korea, Taiwan, and Singapore, and the miserable plight of what was once the Union of Soviet Socialist Republics, may or may not disprove Frank's assertions about economic dependence and the only way to overcome it; there can be no doubt that the history of modern sports has conclusively demonstrated the ability of "satellites" to surpass the "metropolis" (a phenomenon to which I shall return in a moment).

Joseph Maguire's economic analysis of ludic diffusion is much more persuasive than arguments based on Frank's dogmatic theories. Citing the recent invasion of the European market by the National Baskeball Association and the National Football League, Maguire has drawn attention to the parallel between ludic diffusion and modern multinational corporate expansion.[12] In both cases, the parent organization controls the subsidiary and repatriates the profits. The London Monarchs are, therefore, as legitimate an illustration of international capitalist enterprise as the branch offices of IBM, British Petroleum, and SONY.

Economic factors also explain the diffusion of professional ice hockey from Canada to the United States. Bruce Kidd correctly observes that Canadian sports, like the Canadian economy, are largely dependent on the United States.[13] His most telling examples are Canadian baseball and football. Baseball and football, however, are by no means the whole story. Consider the National Hockey League.

> During the first seven years of its existence, the NHL was purely a Canadian league, operating with only three or four teams. . . .Beginning in 1924, the NHL added a second team in Montreal . . . and expanded into the United States, adding the Boston Bruins and moving the Hamilton Tigers to New York as the New York Americans. The New York Rangers, Detroit Cougars (later Red Wings), Chicago Blackhawks, and Pittsburgh Pirates were added in 1926.[14]

In 1991, when fifteen of the league's twenty-two franchises were located south of the border, Canadian stars like Wayne Gretzky and Mario Lemieux were still likely to outshine their American-born teammates and Canadian teams were far more likely than American-based teams to carry off the Stanley Cup (which Montreal did, yet again, in 1993).

If the diffusion of American football and Canadian hockey were typical, one might well explain the diffusion of all modern sports with a simple economic model of profit-driven expansion, but the diffusion of football and hockey is *not* typical. It may be that the kind of expansion exemplified by the NFL in Europe and the NHL in the United States will *become* the dominant mode as the process of globalization continues into the twenty-first century, but the historical record provides relatively few examples of pre-World War II economic motivation in the international diffusion of modern sports. (The qualification—"international"—is important. Ludic diffusion *within* a nation is an altogether different matter.)

Many of the scholars engaged in the debate over ludic diffusion describe themselves as Marxists and nearly all of them prefer materialist to idealist explanations for social phenomena. When they broaden their theoretical horizons to encompass more than politics and economics, which most of them do, they are likely to speak of *cultural* imperialism. Acknowledging that many proselytizers for modern sports felt a conventional *religious* vocation is, however, harder for them. Mangan is one of the few historians who has given adequate emphasis to this motive. In fact, the historical record is replete with instances of ludic diffusion motivated by religious zeal. Cecil Earle Tyndale-Biscoe's fanatic behavior at his school in Kashmir is merely the most dramatic instance of "muscular Christianity" in the colonies. One can fault Tyndale-Biscoe and his brethren for their arrogance but not for insincerity or a reluctance to encounter personal hardship and danger. At the same time that British missionary educators resorted to cricket or soccer football in their tireless efforts to Christianize the native peoples of Asia and Africa, the YMCA was the principal force behind the diffusion of basketball and volleyball. Although devout believers in historical materialism may resist the notion, it is nonetheless true that the urge to bring the heathen to Christ can motivate as powerfully as the desire to sell them Coca-Cola.

Religion, of course, is only one aspect of culture (succinctly defined as "those practices by which collectivities make sense of their lives").[15] Ludic diffusion has also been driven by a myriad of impulses as diverse as the desire of anglophile Indians to adopt the costumes and the mannerisms of the elegant, self-assured cricketers they had known while at Oxford or Cambridge, the rush of thuggish soccer fans in Cologne to ape the violent behavior of Liverpudlian "football hooligans," the urge of Trinidadian basketball players to mimic the moves of Michael Jordan, and the eagerness of young Parisians to imitate the insouciance of Californian surfers. Such motives seem amply to justify the use of the concept of cultural imperialism, but it is now time to take another step and to return to the question of the adequacy—in reference to the process of ludic diffusion—of this familiar and useful concept.

Sports, like other fields investigated by scholars committed to "cultural studies,"[16] are contested terrain in theory as well as practice. In fact, the contestation that has accompanied ludic diffusion has been lively enough to persuade me that "cultural imperialism" is not, when all is said and done, the most accurate term to characterize what happens during the process of ludic diffusion. "Cultural hegemony" comes closer.

At its margins, hegemony begins to resemble pluralism, but the concept's genealogy reassures its users, understandably anxious not to be accused of liberalism, that their radical credentials are in order. Despite this ironic remark about academic fashion, I concede that the concept of cultural hegemony provides more than a merely cosmetic improvement over the concept of cultural imperialism because Gramscian theory correctly stresses the fact that the cultural interaction is something more complex than the domination by the totally powerful of the entirely powerless.

Media specialists have, for some time now, made good use of Gramscian insights. While acknowledging that a relatively small number of multinational corporations exercise enormous control over the world's mass media, scholars who have checked their hypotheses against the empirical data are no longer quick to assume that corporate executives are "captains of consciousness" with the power to manipulate at will the reader and the viewer. "The orthodox view of audiences in the West," wrote J. O. Boyd-Barrett more than a decade ago, "is now one that stresses the individual's capacity for active selection and selective retention."[17] In fact, Boyd-Barrett's qualification about "the West," is no longer necessary because most researchers in the field of media studies have learned to reject the ethnocentric assumption that non-Western audiences simply accept, without selection or interpretation, whatever explicit or implicit messages the Western media transmit.[18] In the analysis of ludic diffusion, we should seek the same degree of sophistication as that obtained in media studies, neither crediting the "colonialists" with diabolical powers nor denying all agency to the "colonized."

In reference to the process of ludic diffusion, however, the followers of Gramsci have failed to avoid a problem confronted by more orthodox Marxist scholars. Like cultural imperialism, cultural hegemony implies intentionality, which is unfortunate because those who adopt a sport are often the eager initiators of a transaction of which the "donors" are scarcely aware.

This last fact persuades me to introduce still another concept into the discussion. If we wish to understand, in all of its complexity, the process of diffusion that has taken modern sports from England and the United States to the entire world, Thorstein Veblen on emulation is as applicable as Gramsci on hegemony. Veblen, of course, wrote ironically of emulation in order to satirize the absurdly, pathetically imitative behavior of men and women frantic to rise in the hierarchy of social prestige, but Veblen put his finger on an important psychological truth: emulation *is* a powerful motivator. Culturally dominated groups have often had sports imposed upon them; they have also—perhaps just as often—forced their unwelcome way into sports from which the dominant group desired to exclude them. To dismiss this kind of emulation as "false consciousness" or "colonization of the mind" is not persuasive. Dismissal requires us to imagine a quite unimaginable (at least for me) degree of psychological manipulation.

There are, then, many reasons to reconsider conventional views of the diffusion of modern sports. We can begin our reconsideration with a simple but nonetheless important observation. In sports, more often probably than in any other domain, the initially dominated have turned the tables on their erstwhile dominators. Once successful emulation has shattered the ludic monopoly, the literal or metaphorical colonials have a splendid opportunity to enhance their self-esteem, for what can be more delightful than "beating them at their own game"?

Simultaneously, one signals allegiance ("It's your game!") and superiority ("We're better at it than you are!"). For an Australian cricket team to have defeated the English at Lord's, the grounds of the august Marylebone Cricket Club, which is exactly what happened in 1878, "was to have [Australian] confidence re-established. It was also to be restored to the bosom of the mother country."[19]

It was but one in a series of memorable moments. As we saw (in chapter 3), the Japanese who were tormented by feelings of inferiority vis-à-vis the West received an enormous psychological boost in 1896 when their schoolboy team, whose initial challenges had been rudely spurned, severely trounced the baseball team fielded by the Americans of the Yokohama Athletic Club.[20] The triumphant rugby tour of 1905–06, during which New Zealand's "All Blacks" outscored the British by a ten-to-one margin, became part of New Zealand's folklore.[21] The defeat of the East Yorkshire regiment by a Bengali team in Calcutta's 1911 soccer tournament was another occasion for frenzied ethnic jubilation. The Indian press exulted: "It fills every Indian with joy and pride to know that rice-eating, malaria-ridden, barefooted Bengalis have got the better of beef-eating, Herculean, booted John Bull in that peculiarly English sport."[22] It was an additional source of keen satisfaction that the game was played on "the vast expanse of green just in front of Fort William which, since the days of Robert Clive, had symbolised the British military presence in Calcutta."[23] Since cricket was even more fraught with significance, Indians were ecstatic when their national team finally managed, in 1971, to defeat the English side at Lord's. "Radios were garlanded. Crowds poured out on to the streets of Bombay, shouting, gesticulating, blowing horns, not in anger as they often did, but in joy."[24]

The cultural impact of Brazilian victories in the World Cup and of West Indian triumphs in cricket has been studied by a number of scholars.[25] Norwegians were ecstatic in 1981 when

the English team succumbed to them in the World Cup quali-
fications. Bjørge Lillelien's exultant radio commentary was a
classic expression of what sports sociologists refer to as the
"90-minute nationalism" of the stadium: "Maggie Thatcher,
I've got a message for you," shouted Lillelien in perfect British
English, "Your boys took a helluva beating!"[26] The tendency to
gloat over turned tables appeared with equal crassness in the
recent contribution of an Australian journalist to London's
Daily Telegraph:

> Let's go over a few little home truths. . . . First the good news. In the
> history of sport, no one has been more inventive than you Brits. Prac-
> tically every international sport worth speaking of...was invented
> on your once secluded shore. . . . But now the bad news. . . . You can't
> win them any more can you?[27]

"Even the Cubans," writes Joseph L. Arbena, "for all their
nationalistic and ideological rhetoric, prove the success of their
Revolution, if only to themselves, by playing Anglo sport better
than the Anglos."[28]

A turnabout in the balance of ludic power can be the prelude
to more significant shifts in political and economic power.[29]
Modern sports have sometimes functioned to crystalize anticolonialist sentiments and even to provide an organizational
framework for a movement of national liberation. Arbena, sur-
veying the diffusion of European sports throughout Latin
America, concludes "that imported sports had a partially impe-
rialistic impact in that they helped to shape local elites and their
values in ways at least initially beneficial to the Europeans," but
he goes on to admit that these same sports became, in time,
"the agent of anti-colonialism and anti-imperialism."[30] Emilio
Sabourín, the Cuban baseball player and political insurgent, is
a perfect illustration of Arbena's point. I have also referred in
the course of my narrative to the emancipatory impulses institutionalized in the soccer clubs of French-ruled North Africa,
in the *Conseil Supérieur du Sport en Afrique*, and in the South

African Non-Racial Olympic Committee. A profusion of further examples comes to mind. In Spain, for instance, during General Francisco Franco's long dictatorship, when political power was centralized in Madrid, Barcelona's premier soccer club— known familiarly as *Barça*—was an important focus for Catalan nationalism.[31] To speak of modern sports as if they were merely a mechanism for political and economic repression badly distorts the historical record.

If one keeps in mind this emancipatory potential as well as the undeniable role of modern sports as a means of social control and imperial rule, one is less inclined to condemn—as many have—efforts to assist the nations of Africa and Asia in the development of their sports programs. This financial and technical aid, most of which is provided by the International Olympic Committee and by various European governments[32], has been submitted to severe scrutiny by scholars wary of the ideological implications of soccer stadia and running shoes. The Germans, who have been in the forefront of such assistance programs, have agonized over the ethical implications of their endeavor. Karlheinz Gieseler, a thoughtful official of the *Deutscher Sportbund*, warned in 1977 that sports should not become the vehicle of a "secularized missionary ideology."[33] In 1985 an entire issue of the journal *Sportwissenschaft* was devoted to the debate over "sport and development aid in the Third World." The six authors agreed that modern sports are a Western phenomenon whose characteristics are on the whole incompatible with those of traditional forms of physical culture, but none of the six seemed very clear about just what to *do* about the fact that traditional sports are in jeopardy. Klaus Heinemann's unhappy conclusion was that modern sports are largely irrelevant to the needs of the Third World while traditional sports robbed of their original cultural functions have become anachronisms.[34]

Heinemann's conclusion seems too negative. The Third

World governments that request and welcome European and American coaches, trainers, equipment, and technical assistance understand very well that an enthusiasm for modern sports can be shared by ethnically and religiously diverse populations that have very little else in common. Janet Lever's comment, based on her studies of Brazilian soccer, seems almost a truism: "Sport contributes to national integration by giving people of different social classes, ethnicities, races, and religions something to share."[35] Arbena, generalizing about the role of modern sports throughout Latin America, also notes their ability to create "a psychic identity to coincide with somewhat artificially delineated political borders."[36] What is true of Latin America is equally true of Africa, where sports are "seen to have a nation-building role."[37] The term "nation-building," once popular among social scientists, has fallen out of favor because of its associations with an ethnocentric conception of modernization, but the term is nonetheless apt for one (not the only) role of modern sports in countries like Brazil, India, or Nigeria. If nations are what Benedict Anderson's influential theory claims them to be, imagined communities, then modern sports are an important and popularly accessible aid to this politically indispensable form of imagining.[38]

That modern sports can be divisive, too, that they can exacerbate conflict and demolish the social structures, no one doubts. It is nonetheless probable that the integrative consequences of modern sports are stronger than the divisive effects. One reason for this is that *international* sports encounters have a salience and importance for most countries that they simply do not have for the United States (where not even the Olympic Games can arouse passions as intense as those enflamed by our national championships in professional baseball, basketball, and football). National teams are often truly representative of ethnic, religious, and racial diversity. For a moment at least, while the smiling athletes ascend the victors' platform, barriers can be surmounted. (Whether the international sports encounters psychologically unifying a nation tend to promote or undermine peaceful relations *between* nations is another question.)

International sports events are, moreover, opportunities for newly independent states to make known their presence to a world that customarily pays them little attention (except to report their natural or man-made disasters). A nation like Costa Rica or Malaysia can enjoy, if not its place in the sun, at least an occasional appearance on the television screen. "While generally strengthening black self-confidence everywhere," writes Richard Mandell, Kenyans like Kipchoge Keino "boosted their country's international prestige, diplomatic standing, and very likely its political stability as well."[39]

Traditionalists insist, however, that talk of the possible contribution of sports to "nation-building" misses the point. For them, modern sports are a form of cultural domination and ludic diffusion is tantamount to the imperialist or hegemonic destruction of authentic native cultural forms. The traditionalist argument has an initial plausibility, but it is seriously flawed. The notion—dare I call it "politically correct"?—that the adoption of another culture's sports is *ipso facto* a sign of lost authenticity ignores the fact that cultures are never static. As Joseph Maguire has noted, "cultures and peoples are responsive and active in the interpretation of the global flow of people, ideas, images and technologies."[40] Edward Said, the last person anyone can call an apologist for cultural imperialism, has made the same point with epigrammatic forcefulness (and with a sly allusion to Marx and Engels): "the history of all cultures is the history of cultural borrowings."[41] His point is, as even white Americans have learned to say, "right on."

Two almost comically obvious but nonetheless frequently overlooked examples from outside the domain of sports should be enough to persuade the most skeptical historian that "cultural imperialism" has *never* been the simple unidirectional phenomenon some of its critics have made it out to be. The introduction of the tomato, in the sixteenth century, significantly altered Italian cuisine. What Florentine or Sicilian gourmet now shuns the tomato as an alien ingredient? The introduction of the horse utterly transformed the culture of the Plains Indians of North America. What Sioux or Pawnee activist rails now against the horse as an unwelcome intrusion of the white man's culture? While it is certainly true that a culture can be annihilated, it is also true that cultures can be resiliant, adaptive, and transformative—in sports as in every other domain.

When Leni Riefenstahl returned to the African tribes that she had made famous in *The Last of the Nuba* (1973), she was horrified to discover that the mighty wrestlers were no longer the naked, white-ash-covered, calabash-ornamented "primitives" she had filmed and photographed only a few years earlier. The wrestlers wore ragged shorts and decorated their bodies with tin cans and plastic bottles. Some wore sun-glasses. The ritual elements of the match had declined in importance. Riefenstahl was glum. "Where the seamy side of civilization spreads itself," she concluded, "human happiness vanishes."[42] Ethnographers have painted the transformation of Nuba wrestling in more cheerful colors. Although it is now a partially modernized sport organized by a federation of clubs and performed on a regular schedule at fixed sites for paying spectators, wrestling nonetheless allows the urban Nuba to maintain a sense of ethnic identity and tribal solidarity. Paradoxically, the urban wrestlers have divested themselves of the cans and bottles that offended Riefenstahl in order to present a more "authentic" spectacle. "Here," write Rolf Husmann and Christoph Meier, "we have a domain where migrants [to Khartoum] can reach back to traditional and familiar patterns of behavior the better to master their new urban lives."[43]

Writing about the anthropological film *Trobriand Cricket* (1974), Richard Cashman has made an important point about the "indigenous subversion" of externally imposed ludic forms. His remarks deserve full quotation:

> The film . . . provides proof, if proof were necessary, that the view "from above" and colonial salesmanship do not tell us the full story. Cricket in the Trobriand Islands was introduced from above, by missionaries. The film shows in a quite remarkable way how this British colonial team game, which emphasized competition, discipline, and various public-school and imperial values, was totally transformed to reflect tribal values: so that everyone could play on each side (each team had about 40 players), not just the best eleven, the home side was the one which should always win (but by a modest margin), and there were appropriate tribal dances at the fall of each wicket.[44]

No one who has seen the film—with its scenes of ritual adepts fashioning the implements of the contest, with its scenes of players dancing and chanting their entries and exits, with its scenes of players collectively celebrating the catching of a ball or the taking of a wicket, with its scenes of the entire village enjoying the postgame feast—no one who sees all this can doubt that Cashman has a point. Trobriand *cricket* has become *Trobriand* cricket.

A similar process of cultural adaptation has been described by Maarten van Bottenburg in his account of the Dutch game of *korfball*. In the summer of 1902, Nico Broekhuysen, a schoolteacher, enrolled in a summer course that introduced him to the game of basketball. Intrigued but not completely satisfied, Broekhuysen decided to modify the game and to teach it to his students at the *Amsterdamse Nieuwe Schoolvereniging*. As in James Naismith's original rules, body contact was strictly forbidden. As in Senda Berenson's rules for girls' basketball, the court was divided into three zones whose boundaries the players were not to cross. Unlike Naismith's and Berenson's games, *korfball* was coeducational. Girls guarded girls and boys guarded boys, but either could pass the ball to the other and neither was allowed to dribble. An English teacher, J. C. G. Grase, encouraged Broekhuysen to publish the rules of *korfball* and their students formed the first clubs. The sport is still played in Dutch schools and clubs, where it is considered to be a "non-sexist" alternative to basketball.[45]

Conclusions akin to those of Husmann, Cashman, and Bottenburg have been reached by others who have analyzed—rather than simply bewailed—the global diffusion of modern sports. Jay R. and Joan D. Mandle, having closely studied the cultural transformation of basketball on the islands of Trinidad and Tobago, rejected the simplistic notion that the popularity of the NBA game is in itself proof of cultural imperialism: "In light of the profundity of the grass roots commitment to basketball, it seems clearly inaccurate to see the sport primarily as an external imposition or as testimony to some other society's virtues. . . . . What is important is not where a cultural form originated but what happens to it upon its arrival."[46] Wise words.

In place of jeremiads about the loss of "authenticity," we do well to acknowledge that modern sports have—for better *and* for worse—become the heritage of humankind. The traditional sports that they ousted from the varied cultures of non-Western societies will doubtless survive and continue to contribute to human diversity, but it is a romantic illusion to imagine—for instance—that the indigenous Mexican game *ulama* is any more culturally "authentic" than a Mexican bull-fight or a Mexican baseball game. To maintain the contrary is to deny agency and to essentialize culture.

If it is ethnocentrically arrogant to assume—as many nineteenth-century missionaries did and as many twentieth-century "development experts" still do—that premodern sports are primitive vestiges of culturally inferior modes of social organization, it is no less arrogant for Western critics to insist that non-Western peoples are wrong to prefer modern sports to traditional ones. The young Moroccan women who have discovered in sports a way to overcome "the shame of their bodies" imposed upon them by Islamic tradition have as much right to play basketball as the critics of "cultural imperialism" have to urge them to govern their behavior by the dictates of the Koran.[47] The standardized universality of modern sports does, unquestionably, represent a loss of diversity when contrasted with the bewildering variety of traditional sports, but referring to the displacement of older ludic forms as "cultural genocide," as a prominent French writer does, is ideological jargon rather than critical discourse.[48] Standardized universality does replace diversity, but, when accompanied by the other characteristics of modern sports, it enables everyone to play the game—whatever game it is. As Ommo Grupe noted at a recent international symposium, modern sports are—despite their many abuses— inherently cosmopolitan; their "language, symbols, and rules, unlike those in many other social and cultural fields, are universally understood."[49] Throughout the world, in Northern Ireland as in Burkina Faso[50], modern sports are one of the frail institutions that leaders of religiously and ethnically divided societies call upon to resist the factionalism that threatens always to devolve into fratricidal conflict. If sports are an occasion for the expression of *communitas*, which they can be, let them express the human community as well as the tribal one.

NOTES

ABBREVIATIONS USED IN THE NOTES

CJHS Canadian Journal of the History of Sport
GL   Geschichte der Leibesübungen, ed. Horst Überhorst, 6 vols. (Berlin: Bartels & Wernitz, 1971–1989)
IJHS Internation Journal of the History of Sport
IRSS International Review of Sport Sociology
SSJ   Sociology of Sport Journal

INTRODUCTION

1. On the question of the British origins of modern sports, see Herbert Schöffler, *England, das Land des Sportes* (Leipzig: Tauchnitz, 1935); Christian von Krockow, *Sport und Zivilisation* (Munich: Piper, 1972); Henning Eichberg, *Der Weg des Sports in die industrielle Gesellschaft*, 2nd ed.

(Baden-Baden: Nomos, 1979); Allen Guttmann, *From Ritual to Record* (New York: Columbia University Press, 1978), pp. 15–55; Richard Mandell, *Sport: A Cultural History* (New York: Columbia University Press, 1984), pp. 132–57. For a variety of challenges to this interpretation, see Arnd Krüger and John McClelland, eds., *Die Anfänge des modernen Sports in der Renaissance* (London: Arena, 1984); John Marshall Carter and Arnd Krüger, eds., *Ritual and Record* (Westport: Greenwood Press, 1990).

2. The British were the pioneers in cycling too, but the French overtook them by the end of the century when they led in founding the *Union Cycliste Internationale*; see Maarten van Bottenburg, "The Differential Popularization of Sports in Continental Europe," *The Netherlands Journal of Social Sciences*, 28:1 (April 1992): 7. The leader of the *Tour* wears a yellow jersey because *L'Auto* was printed on yellow paper. See Ronald Hubscher, Jean Durry and Bernard Jeu, *l'Histoire en mouvements* (Paris: Armand Colin, 1992), p. 444.

3. In addition to *From Ritual to Record*, see *A Whole New Ball Game: An Interpretation of American Sports* (Chapel Hill: University of North Carolina Press, 1988), pp. 1–12.

4. Buzkashi and its modernization are discussed in Chapter 8.

5. Andrzej Wohl, *Die gesellschaftlich-historischen Grundlagen des bürgerlichen Sports* (Cologne: Pahl-Rugenstein, 1973).

6. Eichberg, *Der Weg des Sports in die industrielle Zivilisation*; Krockow, *Sport und Industriegesellschaft*.

7. Melvin L. Adelman, *A Sporting Time* (Urbana: University of Illinois Press, 1986); Steven A. Riess, *City Games* (Urbana: University of Illinois Press, 1989).

8. Guttmann, *From Ritual to Record*, pp. 57–89.

9. From the Latin *ludus* = "play," "game."

10. Claude Hurtebize, "Géopolitique de la genèse, de la diffusion et des interactions culturelles dans la culture corporelle et le sport," *Géopolitique du sport*, eds. Borhane Errais, Daniel Mathieu, and Jean Praicheux (Besançon: Université de Franche-Comté, 1990), p. 87.

11. Johan Galtung, "The Sport System as a Metaphor for the World System," *Sport: The Third Millennium*, eds. Fernand Landry, Marc Landry, and Magdeleine Yerlès (Sainte-Foye: Presses de l'Université Laval, 1991), p. 150.

12. *Cambridge University Magazine*: quoted in J. A. Mangan, "Prologue," *The Cultural Bond: Sport, Empire and Society*, ed. J. A. Mangan (London: Frank Cass, 1992), p. 5.

13. Welldon: quoted in J. A. Mangan, *The Games Ethic and Imperialism* (New York: Viking Press, 1986), p. 36.

14. Peter Rummelt, Sport im Kolonialismus, Kolonialismus im Sport (Cologne: Pahl-Rugenstein, 1986); Rummelt, "Das sportpolitische Erbe im Kolonialismus...," *Beiträge zur Zusammenarbeit im Sport mit der Dritten Welt*, eds. Rolf Andresen, Hermann Rieder, and Gerhard Trosien (Schorndorf: Karl Hofmann, 1989), pp. 18–33.

15. André Gunder Frank, *Capitalism and Underdevelopment in Latin America* (New York: Monthly Review Press, 1967); Fernando Henrique Cardoso and Enzo Faletto, *Dependency and Development in Latin America*, trans. Marjory Mattingly Urquidi (1971; Berkeley: University of California Press, 1979); James D. Cockcroft, André Gunder Frank, and Dale L. Johnson, eds., *Dependence and Underdevelopment* (Garden City: Doubleday-Anchor Books, 1972).

16. Immanuel Wallerstein, *The Modern World System*, 3 vols. (New York: Academic Press, 1974–89).

17. Alan Klein, "Baseball as Underdevelopment: The Political Economy of Sport in the Dominican Republic," *SSJ*, 6:2 (June 1989): 95–112.

18. Borhane Errais, "La planète sportive," *Sport: The Third Millennium*, p. 582; Minseok An and George H. Sage, "The Golf Boom in South Korea: Serving Hegemonic Interests," *SSJ*, 9:4 (December 1992): 372–84.

19. Antonio Gramsci, *Selections from the Prison Notebooks*, trans. and ed. by Quinton Hoare and Geoffrey Nowell Smith (New York: International Publishers, 1971). In 1993, Columbia University Press issued the first of a projected six-volume edition of these notebooks.

20. John Tomlinson, *Cultural Imperialism* (Baltimore: Johns Hopkins University Press, 1991), p. 7.

21. Ralph Waldo Emerson, *Works*, 14 vols. (Boston: Houghton Mifflin, 1883–1893): 1:9, 113.

22. Edward W. Said, *Culture and Imperialism* (New York: Knopf, 1993), p. 213.

23. For an introduction to this debate, see Janet A. Walker, "On the Applicability of the Term 'Novel' to Modern Non-Western Long Fiction," *Yearbook of Comparative and General Literature* 37 (1988): 47–68.

24. See, for instance, Herbert I. Schiller, *Communication and Cultural Domination* (White Plains: M. E. Sharpe, 1976; Jeremy Tunstall, *The Media Are American* (New York: Columbia University Press, 1977); Anthony Smith, *The Geopolitics of Information* (New York: Oxford Uni-

versity Press, 1981); Armand Mattelart, *L'Internationale publicitaire* (Paris: Editions la Découverte, 1989).

25. Smith, *Geopolitics of Information*, pp. 68–110.

26. Ibid., p. 43.

27. Tapio Varis, "Global Traffic in Television," *Journal of Communication*, 24 (1974): 102–9; Michael Tracey, "The Poisoned Chalice? International Television and the Idea of Dominance," *Daedalus*, 114:4 (1985): 17–56.

28. See Mustapha Masmoudi, "The New World Information Order," *Journal of Communication*, 29:2 (Spring 1979): 172–85; for details on the protracted UNESCO debate over cultural imperialism and the mass media, see Thomas L. McPhail, *Electronic Colonialism*, 2nd ed. (Newbury Park: Sage Publications, 1987).

29. Schiller, *Communication and Cultural Domination*, p. 1.

30. Smith, *Geopolitics of Information*, p. 147.

31. Ariel Dorfman and Armand Mattelart, *How to Read Donald Duck: Imperialist Ideology in the Disney Comic* (New York: International General, 1984).

32. Julianne Burton, "Don (Juanito) Duck and the Imperial-Patriarchal Unconscious: Disney Studies, the Good Neighbor Policy, and the Packing of Latin America," *Nationalisms and Sexualities*, eds. Andrew Parker, Mary Russo, Doris Sommer, and Patricia Yaeger (New York: Routledge, 1992), pp. 21–41.

33. N. A. Scotch, "Magic, Sorcery, and Football among Urban Zulu," *Journal of Conflict Resolution*, 5 (1961): 70–74; James Gissua and Michael Hess, "Icing on the Cake? Colonialism, Institutional Transfer and Sport in Papua New Guinea," *Sporting Traditions*, 10:1 (November 1993): 78–91.

1. CRICKET

1. Rowland Bowen, *Cricket* (London: Eyre and Spottiswoode, 1970), pp. 28–30.

2. Derrick: quoted in H. S. Altham, *A History of Cricket* (1926; London: George Allen & Unwin, 1962), p. 21.

3. Ibid., p. 22.

4. Christopher Brookes, *English Cricket* (London: Weidenfeld and Nicolson, 1978), p. 24.

5. Bowen, *Cricket*, pp. 49–52.

6. Nyren: quoted in Brookes, *English Cricket*, p. 57.

7. Tomothey J. L. Chandler, "Games at Oxbridge and the Public Schools, 1830–80: The Diffusion of an Innovation," *IJHS*, 18:2 (September 1991): 175.

8. Nancy Joy, *Maiden Over* (London: Sporting Handbooks, 1950), pp. 14–16; Rachel Heyhoe Flint and Netta Rheinberg, *Fair Play: The Story of Women's Cricket* (London: Angus and Robertson, 1976), pp. 14–18; Kathleen E. McCrone, *Playing the Game: Sport and the Physical Emancipation of English Women, 1870–1914* (Lexington: University Press of Kentucky, 1988), pp. 143–48.

9. Quoted in James Bradley, "The MCC, Society and Empire," *IJHS*, 7:1 (May 1990): 15.

10. William Byrd, *Secret Diary*, eds. Louis B. Wright and Marion Tinling (Richmond: Dietz Press, 1941), p. 144.

11. Foster Rhea Dulles, *America Learns to Play* (New York: D. Appleton-Century, 1940), p. 52.

12. George B. Kirsch, *The Creation of American Team Sports: Baseball and Cricket, 1838–72* (Urbana: University of Illinois Press, 1989), pp. 21–49; George B. Kirsch, "The Rise of Modern Sports: New Jersey Cricketers, Baseball Players, and Clubs, 1845–60," *New Jersey History*, 101 (Spring-Summer 1983): 57; Robert M. Lewis, "Cricket and the Beginnings of Organized Baseball in New York City," *IJHS*, 4:3 (December 1987): 315–32.

13. Waller: quoted in J. Thomas Jable, "Latter-Day Cultural Imperialists: British Influence on the Establishment of Cricket in Philadelphia, 1842–1872," *Pleasure, Profit, Proselytism*, ed. J. A. Mangan (London: Frank Cass, 1988), p. 175.

14. Ibid., p. 178.

15. Lillywhite: quoted in ibid., p. 179.

16. Ibid., p. 184.

17. Ibid., pp 187–188; Tom Melville, "The Passing of Philadelphia Cricket," *IJHS*, 10:1 (April 1993): 87–92.

18. Alan Metcalfe, *Canada Learns to Play* (Toronto: McClelland and Stewart, 1987), p. 83.

19. Ibid., p. 22.

20. Paul R. Dauphinais, "A Class Act: French-Canadians in Organized Sport, 1840–1910," *IJHS*, 7:3 (December 1990): 432–42. French Canadians are still statistically underrepresented in modern sports; see Philip

G. White and James E. Curtis, "Participation in Competitive Sport among Anglophones and Francophones in Canada," *IRSS*, 25:2 (1990): 125–38.

21. Quoted in David W. Brown, "Imperialism and Games on the Playing Fields of Canada's Private Schools," *Olympic Scientific Congress 1984: Official Report: Sport History*, eds. Norbert Müller and Joachim K. Rühl (Niedernhausen: Schors Verlag, 1985), p. 129.

22. Nancy Howell and Maxwell L. Howell, *Sports and Games in Canadian Life* (Toronto: Macmillan of Canada, 1969), pp. 42–43.

23. Thring: quoted in David W. Brown, "Canadian Imperialism and Sporting Exchanges: The Nineteenth-Century Cultural Experience of Cricket and Lacrosse," *CJHS*, 18:1 (May 1987): 57.

24. Beers: quoted in Don Morrow et al., *A Concise History of Sport in Canada* (Toronto: Oxford University Press, 1989), p. 49.

25. Howell and Howell, *Sports and Games*, p. 73.

26. Metcalfe, *Canada Learns to Play*, p. 26.

27. Howell and Howell, *Sports and Games*, p. 82.

28. Morrow et al., *Concise History*, p. 128

29. On the governors-general, see Gerald Redmond, "Imperial Viceregal Patronage: The Governors-General of Canada and Sport in the Dominion, 1867–1909," *IJHS*, 6:2 (September 1989): 193–217.

30. Morrow et al., *Concise History*, p. 126.

31. Brian Stoddart, *Saturday Afternoon Fever: Sport in the Australian Culture* (North Ryde, New South Wales: Angus & Robertson, 1986), pp. 15–55.

32. R. S. Whitington, *An Illustrated History of Australian Cricket* (London: Pelham Books, 1974), p. 18.

33. Ibid.; John A. Daly, *Elysian Fields: Sport, Class and Community in Colonial South Australia, 1836–1890* (Adelaide: John A. Daly, 1982), p. 38.

34. Dutton: quoted in John A. Daly, "A New Britannia in the Antipodes: Sport, Class and Community in Colonial South Australia," *Pleasure, Profit and Proselytism*, ed. James. A. Mangan (London: Frank Cass, 1988), p. 165.

35. Ibid., p. 166.

36. David W. Brown, "Muscular Christianity in the Antipodes," *Sporting Traditions*, 3:2 (May 1987): 173–87; Marion K. Stell, *Half the Race: A History of Australian Women in Sport* (North Ryde: Angus & Robertson, 1991), pp. 14–16, 33–34; Ray Crawford, "Sport for Young Ladies: The

Victorian Independent Schools, 1875–1925," *Sporting Traditions*, 1:1 (November 1984): 67–68.

37. Richard Cashman and Amanda Weaver, *Wicket Women: Cricket and Women in Australia* (Kensington: New South Wales University Press, 1991), pp. 1–5.

38. Eric Midwinter, *W. G. Grace* (London: George Allen & Unwin, 1981), pp. 41–75; Bowen, *Cricket*, p. 286; Maxwell L. and Reet A. Howell, "Sport in Australia," *GL*, 6:111–12.

39. Ibid., p. 128; Daly, "A New Britannia," p. 170.

40. John Arlott, *The Ashes* (London: Pelham Books, 1972).

41. William F. Mandle, "Cricket and Australian Nationalism in the 19th Century," *Journal of the Royal Australian Historical Society*, 59:4 (December 1973): 225–46.

42. Richard Cashman, "Symbols of Unity: Anglo-Australian Cricketers, 1877–1900," *IJHS*, 7:1 (May 1990): 97–110.

43. Rockley Wilson: quoted in Ric Sissons and Brian Stoddart, *Cricket and Empire: The 1932–33 Bodyline Tour of Australia* (London: George Allen and Unwin, 1984), p. 10.

44. Laurence LeQuesne, *The Bodyline Controversy* (London: Secker and Warburg, 1983), p. 34.

45. Sissons and Stoddart, *Cricket and Empire,*. p. 60.

46. Ibid., p. 109.

47. Although culturally as well as geographically quite close to Australia, New Zealand was colonized enough later for rugby—a product of the late nineteenth century—to become the national sport rather than cricket. See Scott A. G. M. Crawford, "Sport at the End of the World," *GL*, 6:174–96; Crawford, "Patterns of Leisure in Early Otago—New Zealand," *Stadion*, 5:1 (1979): 42–67; Crawford, "'We Have Rough Labour, But We Can Afford a Day for Recreation Too,'" *Stadion*, 10 (1984): 95–133; Crawford, "'Muscles and Character Are There the First Object of Necessity,'" *British Journal of Sport History*, 2:2 (September 1985): 109–26; Crawford, "Rugby in Contemporary New Zealand," *Journal of Sport and Social Issues*, 12:2 (Fall 1988): 108–21.

48. Maurice St. Pierre, "West Indian Cricket: Cultural Contradiction?" *Arena Review*, 14:1 (May 1990): 14.

49. Brian Stoddart, "Cricket, Social Formation and Cultural Continuity in Barbados," *Journal of Sport History*, 14:3 (Winter 1987): 318.

50. Keith A. P. Sandiford and Brian Stoddart, "The Elite Schools and Cricket in Barbados," *IJHS*, 4:3 (December 1987): 347.

51. Jeffrey Hill, "Cricket and the Imperial Connection," *The Global Sports Arena*, eds. John Bale and Joseph Maguire (London: Frank Cass, 1993), p. 57.

52. C. L. R. James, "Cricket in West Indian Culture," *New Society*, 1 (June 6, 1963): 8–9.

53. John Bunyan, *Grace Abounding to the Chief of Sinners* (1666; Oxford: Oxford University Press, 1962), p. 10.

54. C. L. R. James, *Beyond a Boundary* (1963; New York: Pantheon Books, 1983), pp. 17, 33, 35, 51, 53.

55. Ibid., pp. 56, 252. Thomas Hughes was the author of the immensely popular novel of life at Rugby School, *Tom Brown's Schooldays* (1857).

56. Brian Stoddart, "Caribbean Cricket," *International Journal*, 43:4 (Autumn 1988): 618–42; Christine Cummings, "The Ideology of West Indian Cricket," *Arena Review*, 14:1 (May 1990): 25–32.

57. Orlando Patterson, "The Cricket Ritual in the West Indies," *New Society*, 23 (June 26, 1969): 988–89.

58. Kevin A. Yelvington, "Ethnicity 'Not Out': The Indian Cricket Tour of the West Indies and the 1976 Elections in Trinidad and Tobago," *Arena Review*, 14:1 (May 1990): 1.

59. Stoddart, "Caribbean Cricket," p. 639. South African cricket developed in a manner similar to the evolution of the game in the BWI except that racial discrimination became a matter of law rather than custom; see André Odendaal, "South Africa's Black Victorians: Sport and Society in South Africa in the Nineteenth Century," *Pleasure, Profit, Proselytism*, pp. 193–214.

60. Jay R. and Joan D. Mandle, "Basketball, Civil Society and the Post Colonial State in the Commonwealth Caribbean," *Journal of Sport and Social Issues*, 14:2 (Fall 1990): 59–75.

61. Jay R. and Joan D. Mandle, *Grass Roots Commitment: Basketball and Society in Trinidad and Tobago* (Parkersburg, Iowa: Caribbean Books, 1988), p. 66.

62. Richard Cashman, *Patrons, Players and the Crowd: The Phenomenon of Indian Cricket* (New Delhi: Longman Orient, 1980), pp. 1–3.

63. Joseph S. Alter, *The Wrestler's Body: Identity and Ideology in North India* (Berkeley: University of California Press, 1992); Jeevanandam P.

Thomas, "A Brief Historical Survey of Physical Education and Sports in India," *GL*, 6:199–214.

64. Mihir Bose, *A History of Indian Cricket* (London: Andre Deutsch, 1990), p. 24.

65. Ibid., pp. 27–33.

66. Harris: quoted in Cashman, *Patrons, Players and the Crowd*, p. 11.

67. Ibid., pp. 13–18.

68. Sherring: quoted in Mangan, *The Games Ethic and Imperialism*, p. 135.

69. Pennell: quoted in J. A. Mangan, "Christ and the Imperial Games Fields," *British Journal of Sports History*, 1:2 (September 1984): 188.

70. Mangan, *The Games Ethic and Imperialism*, p. 178.

71. Tyndale-Biscoe: quoted in ibid., p. 183.

72. Tyndale-Biscoe: quoted in ibid., p. 185.

73. Ibid., p. 186.

74. Wickham, quoted in Cashman, *Patrons, Players and the Crowd*, p. 25.

75. Kincaid: quoted in Simon Wilde, *Ranji* (London: Kingswood Press, 1990), p. 163.

76. Bose, *History of Indian Cricket*, pp. 44, 49.

77. Ibid., pp. 47–52; Cashman, *Patrons, Players and the Crowd*, pp. 27–34. Cashman gives the name as Bhupinder.

78. Cardus: quoted in ibid., p. 35.

79. Ranjitsinhji: quoted in Wilde, *Ranji*, p. 48.

80. Ranjitsinhji: quoted in Cashman, *Patrons, Players and the Crowd*, p. 35.

81. Ibid., p. 26.

2. SOCCER

1. Claude Hurtebize, "Géopolitique de la genèse de la diffusion et des interactions culturelles dans la culture corporelle et le sport," *Géopolitique du sport*, eds. Borhane Errais, Daniel Mathieu, and Jean Praicheux (Besançon: Université de Franche-Comté, 1990), p. 87.

2. Horst Überhorst, "Leibesübungen in Altchina," *GL*, 1:110–27.

3. Overbury: quoted in Francis Peabody Magoun, *History of Football: From the Beginnings to 1871* (Bochum: Pöppinghaus, 1938), p. 38. Magoun remains the best source for the prehistory of modern soccer.

4. Percy M. Young, *A History of British Football*, rev. ed. (London: Arrow Books, 1973), p. 113.

5. Timothy J. L. Chandler, "Games at Oxbridge and the Public Schools, 1830–80," *IJHS*, 8:2 (September 1991): 173.

6. Young, *History of British Football*, p. 132.

7. Eric Dunning and Kenneth Sheard, *Barbarians, Gentlemen and Players* (Oxford: Martin Robertson, 1979), p. 106.

8. James Walvin, *The People's Game* (London: Allen Lane, 1975), pp. 31–68; Tony Mason, *Association Football and English Society, 1863–1915* (Atlantic Highlands, New Jersey: Humanities Press, 1980), pp. 21–68.

9. Nicholas Fishwick, *English Football and Society, 1910–1950* (Manchester: Manchester University Press, 1989), p. 150.

10. Ruud Stokvis, "De populariteit van sporten," *Amsterdams Sociologisch Tijdschrift* 15:4 (March 1989): 679.

11. John Bale, "The Adoption of Football in Europe," *CJHS*, 11:2 (December 1980): 56–66; John Bale, "International Sports History as Innovation Diffusion," *CJHS*, 15:1 (May 1984): 38–63.

12. Eugen Weber, "Gymnastics and Sports in *Fin-de-Siècle* France," *American Historical Review*, 76:1 (February 1971): 84, n. 31.

13. Dubois: quoted by Robert Neirynck, "De Scholen der Jozefieten, Xaverianen en Benediktijnen en de Ontwikkeling van de Voetbalsport in Belgie (1863–1895)" (Catholic University of Louvain, 1985), p. 43.

14. Ibid.

15. Ruud Stokvis, *Strijd over Sport* (Devanter: Van Loghum Slaterus, 1979), pp. 47–48.

16. Ibid.

17. Maarten van Bottenburg, "The Differential Popularization of Sports in Continental Europe," *The Netherlands Journal of Social Sciences*, 28:1 (April 1992): 12.

18. Stokvis, *Strijd over Sport*, p. 73.

19. Wilhelm Hopf, "'Wie Könnte Fussball ein deutsches Spiel werden?'" ed. Wilhelm Hopf, *Fussball* (Bensheim: Pädagogischer Extra Buchverlag, 1979), pp. 66–71. The seniors were exempted.

20. Ulfert Schröder, "Fussball in Deutschland," *Fussball-Weltgeschichte*, ed. Karl-Heinz Huba (Munich: Copress, 1992), pp. 68–70; Sportmuseum Berlin, ed., *Sport in Berlin* (Berlin: Dirk Nishen, 1991), p. 90.

21. Schröder, "Fussball in Deutschland," p. 70.

22. Christiane Eisenberg, "Football in Germany: Beginnings, 1890–1914," *IJHS*, 8:2 (September 1991): 207.

23. Frank Filter, "Fussballsport in der Arbeiter-Turn- und Sportbewegung," *Sozial- und Zeitgeschichte des Sports*, 2:1 (1988): 55–73. Eventually, soccer sections were organized within the ATSB.

24. Siegfried Gehrmann, "Der F. C. Schalke 04," *Fussball*, pp. 117–20.

25. Ibid.

26. Rolf Lindner and Heinrich T. Breuer, *Sind Doch Nicht Alles Beckenbauers* (Frankfurt: Syndikat, 1978).

27. Weber, "Gymnastics and Sports," p. 84; Laurent Coadic, "Implantation et diffusion du football en Bretagne (1890–1925)," *Sport et Histoire*, 1 (1992): 29.

28. Weber, "Gymnastics and Sports," p. 84; Alfred Wahl, *Les Archives du Football: Sport et Société en France (1880–1980)* (Paris: Gallimard/Juillard, 1989), pp.30–31.

29. Ibid., pp. 33–36. Weber, "Gymnastics and Sports," p. 84; Tony Mason, "Some Englishmen and Scotsmen Abroad," *Off the Ball*, eds. Alan Tomlinson and Garry Whannel (London: Pluto Press, 1986), p. 70.

30. Wahl, *Archives du Football*, p. 32; Jacques Georges, "Fédération Française de Football," *Sport de France* (Paris: Service de Presse, 1971), pp. 109–15.

31. Richard Holt, *Sport and Society in Modern France* (London: Macmillan, 1981), p. 67.

32. Wahl, *Archives du Football,*, pp. 32–56; Pierre Lanfranchi, "Apparition et Affirmation du Football en Languedoc, 1900–1935," *La Naissance du Mouvement Sportif Associatif en France*, eds. Pierre Arnaud and J. Camy (Lyon: Presses Universitaires de Lyon, 1986), pp. 259–73; Christian Bromberger, Alain Havot, Jean-Marc Mariottini, "Allez l'O.M.! Forza Juve!" *Terrain*, 8 (April 1987): 15.

33. Wahl, *Archives du Football*, pp. 88–94.

34. Pierre Lanfranchi, "Rugby contro Calcio: La Genesi delle due Pratiche Sportive nella Francia Meridionale," *Ricerche Storiche*, 19:2 (May-August 1989): 1–13.

35. Alain Ehrenberg, *Le cult de la performance* (Paris: Calmann-Lévy, 1991), p. 27; Wahl, *Archives du Football*, pp 80, 82.

36. Pierre Lanfranchi, "The Migration of Footballers: The Case of France," *The Global Sports Arena*, eds. John Bale and Joseph Maguire (London: Cass, 1993), pp. 63–77; Bromberger et al., "Allez l'O.M.!" p. 23.

37. Antonio Papa, "Le Domeniche di Clio: Origini a Storia del Foot-ball in Italia," *Belfagor*, 2 (1988): 134. Exactly the same pattern occurred in Spain, where soccer spread first among the resident British and the sons of the industrial bourgeoisie of Barcelona; see Gabriel Colomé, "Il Barcelona e la società catalana," *Il Calcio e il suo Pubblico*, ed. Pierre Lanfranchi (Naples: Edizioni Scientifiche Italiane, 1992), pp. 59–65.

38. Antonio Ghirelli, *Storia del Calcio in Italia*, rev. ed., (Turin: Giulio Einaudi, 1990), pp. 19–22; Guido Panico, "Le origini del foot-ball in Italia," *Il Calcio e il suo Pubblico*, pp. 49–55; Giovanni Albonago, "Fussball in Italien," *Fussball-Weltgeschichte*, p. 88; Paul Gardner, *The Simplest Game* (Boston: Little, Brown, 1976), pp. 36–37.

39. On the mostly nonexistent relations between the Renaissance game and the modern one, see Stefano Pivato, "Il Pallone prima del Football," *Il Calcio e il suo Pubblico*, pp. 19–30.

40. Ghirelli, *Storia del Calcio in Italia*, pp. 25–48.

41. Stefano Pivato, "Soccer, Religion, Authority: Notes on the Early Evolution of Association Football in Italy," *IJHS*, 8:3 (December 1991): 427.

42. Ghirelli, *Storia del Calcio in Italia*, pp. 41–42; József Vetö, *Sports in Hungary*, trans. István Butykay (Budapest: Corvina Press, 1965), p. 45.

43. Alan Tomlinson, "Going Global: The FIFA Story," *Off the Ball*, p. 85.

44. Wahl, *Archives du Football*, p. 98.

45. Tomlinson, "Going Global," p. 85; Gardner's list of founders does not include Sweden; see *The Simplest Game*, p. 39.

46. Wahl, *Archives du Football*, p. 98; Walvin, *People's Game*, pp. 121–22, 152; Per Olof Holmäng, "International Sports Organizations, 1919–1925," *IJHS*, 9:3 (December 1992): 458–60.

47. Harold Perkin, "Teaching the Nations How to Play," *IJHS*, 6:2 (September 1989): 148; Joseph L. Arbena, "Sport and Social Change in Latin America," *Sport and Social Development*, eds. Alan G. Ingham and John W. Loy (Champaign: Human Kinetics, 1993), pp. 97–117.

48. Enrique C. Romero Brest, Alberto R. Dallo, and Simón Silvestrini, "Los Deportes y la Educación Fisica en la Republica Argentina," *GL*, 6: 847–48; Eduardo A. Olivera, *Origenes de los Deportes Britanicos en el Rió de la Plata* (Buenos Aires: L. J. Rosso, 1932), pp. 11–12, 15.

49. Brest et al, "Los Deportes y la Educación Fisica en la Republica Argentina," pp. 849, 866, 871–72, 876; Olivera, *Origenes*, pp. 61, 99–112

50. Cited in Brest et al., "Los Deportes y la Educación Fisica," p. 866.

51. Olivera, *Origenes*, pp. 30–34; Héctor Alberto Chaponick, *Historia*

del Fútbol Argentino, 3 vols. (Buenos Aires: Editorial Eiffel, 1955), 1: 24–25, 44–46, 49–50; Horacio J. Spinetto, "Ciento Veinte Años de Rugby Argentino," *Todo Es Historia*, 25 (January 1992): 8.

52. Olivera, *Origenes*, pp. 30–34; Chaponick, *Historia*, 1:15, 17, 50, 59; Brest et al., "Los Deportes y la Educación Fisica," pp. 868–69.

53. Walvin, *People's Game*, p. 96.

54. Chaponick, *Historia*, 1:17, 51, 54, 59.

55. Ibid., 1:18, 23–24, 51–52.

56. Ibid., 1:27, 65–92; Brest et al.,"Los Deportes y la Educación Fisica," p. 869; Osvaldo Bayer, *Fútbol Argentino* (Buenos Aires: Editorial Sudamericana, 1990), p. 20.

57. José L. Buzzetti and Eduardo Gutierrez Cortinas, *Historia del Deporte en el Uruguay (1830–1900)* (Montevideo: Talleres Graficos Castro, 1965), p. 118.

58. Franklin Morales, "Historia del Deporte del Uruguay," *GL*, 6: 980.

59. Ibid., pp. 980–83; Glanville, *Soccer*, pp. 58, 71–80; Federico B. Kirbus, "Fussball in Uruguay," *Fussball-Weltgeschichte*, p. 125.

60. Antonio Vera, *El Fútbol en Chile* (Santiago: Editoria Nacional Quimantú, 1973), p. 9.

61. Glanville, *Soccer*, p. 57;

62. Ilan Rachum, "Futebol: The Growth of a Brazilian National Institution," *New Scholar*, 8:1–2 (1978): 185; Ulfert Schröder, "Fussball in Brasilien," *Fussball-Weltgeschichte*, pp. 61, 64.

63. Rachum, "Futebol," pp. 187–89; Glanville, *Soccer*, pp. 57–58.

64. Ibid., p. 58.

65. Janet Lever, *Soccer Madness* (Chicago: University of Chicago, 1983), pp. 75–76.

66. Pelé: quoted by Philip Evanson, "Understanding the People: *Futebol*, Film, Theater and Politics in Present-Day Brazil," *South Atlantic Quarterly*, 81:4 (Autumn 1982): 400. On Pelé, see François Thébaud, *Pelé*, trans. Leo Weinstein (New York: Harper & Row, 1976); Edson Arantes do Nascimento and Robert L. Fish, *My Life and the Beautiful Game* (Garden City: Doubleday, 1977).

67. Anthony Kirk-Greene, "Badge of Office? Sport and His Excellency in the British Empire," *IJHS*, 6:2 (September 1989): 236.

68. Bernadette Deville-Danthu, "La participation des sportifs indigènes à l'Exposition Coloniale Internationale de Paris de 1931," *Sport et Histoire*, n.s., 2 (1992): 14, 19.

69. Welldon: quoted in J. A. Mangan, *The Games Ethic and Imperialism* (New York: Viking Press, 1985), p. 36.

70. Ibid., p. 79.

71. Anthony Kirk-Greene, "Imperial Administration and the Athletic Imperative: The Case of the District Officer in Africa," *Sport in Africa* , eds. William J. Baker and James A. Mangan (New York: Africana Pub. Co., 1987), p. 99.

72. Anthony Kirk-Greene, "The Sudan Political Service," *International Journal of African Historical Studies*, 15:1 (1982): 22.

73. Anthony Kirk-Greene, "Imperial Administration and the Athletic Imperative," *Sport in Africa*, p. 104.

74. George Godia, "Sport in Kenya," *Sport in Asia and Africa* , ed. Eric A. Wagner (Westport: Greenwood Press, 1989), p. 269.

75. Mangan, *Games Ethic and Imperialism*, p. 108.

76. James A. Mangan, "Ethics and Ethnocentricity: Imperial Education in British Tropic Africa," *Sport in Africa*, p. 147.

77. Ibid., p. 148.

78. Sev A. Obura to author, October 29, 1980.

79. Mangan, *Games Ethic and Imperialism*, p. 177.

80. Helen Osayimwen-Oladipo, "The Historical Development of Sport in Nigeria," *GL*, 6:467; E. O. Ojeme, "Sport in Nigeria," *Sport in Asia and Africa* , p. 253; Issac Olu Akindutire, "The Historical Development of Soccer in Nigeria," *CJHS*, 22:1 (May 1991): 20–31.

81. Mangan, "Ethics and Ethnocentricity," p. 152.

82. Godia, "Sport in Kenya," p. 269; Ademola Onifade, "Historical Development of Amateur Sports and their Administrative Agencies in Nigeria," *CJHS*, 16:2 (December 1985): 33–43.

83. Diakabana N'Senga, "Genèse et Développement du Sport en République du Zaïre," *GL*, 6:406; Bangela Lema, "Sport in Zaire," *Sport in Asia and Africa*, pp. 232–33.

84. Alfred Wahl, "Football et Jeux de Ballon," *L'Empire du sport*, ed. Daniel Hick (Aix-en-Provence: Centres des Archives d'Outre-Mer, 1992), pp. 44–45; Phyllis M. Martin, "Colonialism, Youth and Football in French Equatorial Africa," *IJHS*, 8:1 (May 1991): 56–71.

85. Alain Monsellier, "Histoire des activités physiques traditionelles et des sports modernes au Sénégal," *GL*, 6:364; Bernadette Deville-Danthu, "Les premières tentatives d'encadrement des activités physique et sportives de la jeunesse en A.O.F. (1922–1936)," *Les jeunes en*

Afrique, eds. H. D'Almeida-Topor et al. (Paris: Harmattan, 1992), pp. 459–60.

86. Emmanuel Abolo Biwole Siegfried Honga, "Histoire des activités physiques traditionelles et du sport moderne au Cameroun de la période coloniale à nos jours," *GL*, 6:398; Daniel Hick, *L'Empire du sport*, p. 11 (photograph).

87. Ali A. Mazrui, "Africa's Triple Heritage of Play," *Sport in Africa*, p. 219.

88. Peter Rummelt, *Sport im Kolonialismus, Kolonialismus im Sport* (Cologne: Pahl-Rugenstein, 1986), pp. 168–73; Floris J. G. van der Merwe, "History and Development of Sport in Southwest Africa/Namibia," *GL*, 6:532–35.

89. Thomas Q. Reefe, "The Biggest Game of All," *Sport in Africa*, pp. 63–64.

90. Youssef Fates, "Sport en Algérie," *GL*, 6:301; Bernadette Deville-Danthu, "Note sur l'histoire du sport dans l'empire français," *L'Empire du sport*, p. 13.

91. Ben Larbi Mohamed and Borhane Errais, "Un Siècle d'Histoire du Sport en Tunisie, 1881–1981," *GL*, 6:277, 283–84.

92. Harold Perkin, "Teaching the Nations How to Play," p. 148.

93. Everett M. Rogers, *Diffusion of Innovations*, 3rd ed. (New York: Free Press, 1983).

94. Alan M. Klein, "Sport and Colonialism in Latin America and the Caribbean," *Studies in Latin American Popular Culture*, 10 (1991): 265.

3. BASEBALL

1. Albert G. Spalding, *America's National Game* (New York: American Sports Pub. Co., 1911), p. 10. The standard histories of the game are Harold Seymour, *Baseball*, 3 vols. (New York: Oxford University Press, 1960–90); David Quentin Voigt, *American Baseball*, 3 vols. (Norman: University of Oklahoma Press, 1966–83). On the early years of the game, see George B. Kirsch, *The Creation of American Team Sports* (Urbana: University of Illinois Press, 1989), and Warren Goldstein, *Playing for Keeps* (Ithaca: Cornell University Press, 1989). On Spalding's career, see Arthur Bartlett, *Baseball and Mr. Spalding* (New York: Farrar, Straus & Young, 1951); Peter Levine, *A. G. Spalding and the Rise of Baseball* (New York: Oxford University Press, 1985).

2. Harold Peterson, *The Man Who Invented Baseball* (New York: Scribner's, 1973), p. 72. Seymour gives June 19, 1846, as the date of the first official game; see *Baseball*, 1:18.

3. Ibid., p. 15; on the Knickerbockers, see also Benjamin G. Rader, *Baseball: A History of America's Game* (Urbana: University of Illinois Press, 1992), pp. 3–5.

4. "Baseball Fever": quoted in Rader, *Baseball*, p. 5.

5. On the working-class origins of most of the early teams, see Warren Goldstein, *Playing for Keeps*; on the political connections of the teams, see Steven A. Riess, *Touching Base: Professional Baseball and American Culture in the Progressive Era* (Westport: Greenwood Press, 1980).

6. Gai I. Berlage, "Sociocultural History of the Origin of Women's Baseball at the Eastern Women's Colleges during the Victorian Period," *Cooperstown Symposium on Baseball and the American Culture*, ed. Alvin L. Hall (Westport: Meckler Publishing Co., 1991), pp. 108–9. See also Harold Seymour, *Baseball: The People's Game* (New York: Oxford University Press, 1990), pp. 443–511.

7. Dale A. Somers, *The Rise of Sport in New Orleans, 1850–1900* (Baton Rouge: Louisiana State University Press, 1972), p. 119; John A. Lucas and Ronald A. Smith, *Saga of American Sport* (Philadelphia: Lea and Febiger, 1978), pp. 364–66; Barbara Gregorich, *Women at Play: The Story of Women in Baseball* (New York: Harcourt, Brace, 1993); Lois Browne, *The Girls of Summer* (New York: HarperCollins, 1992).

8. Hiraiwa: quoted in Donald Roden, "Baseball and the Quest for National Dignity in Meiji Japan," *American Historical Review*, 85:3 (June 1980): 516.

9. Ibid., 519, n. 31. A slightly different version of events appears in Tohru Watanabe, "The Why of the Japanese Choice of Baseball," *Civilization in Sport History* [sic], ed. Shigeo Shimizu (Kobe: Department of Education-Kobe University, 1987), pp. 113–28.

10. Shinsuke Tanada, "Diffusion into the Orient: The Introduction of Western Sports in Kobe, Japan," *IJHS*, 5:3 (December 1988): 372–76.

11. Roden, "Baseball and the Quest for National Dignity," p. 518.

12. Ibid., p. 519.

13. Anonymous student: quoted in ibid., p. 521.

14. Ibid., p. 524.

15. *Japan Weekly Mail*: quoted in ibid., p. 525.

16. Ibid., pp. 519–25.

17. Norgren: quoted in Robert J. Sinclair, "Baseball's Rising Sun: American Interwar Baseball Diplomacy and Japan," *CJHS*, 16:2 (December 1985): 48.

18. Whiting, *You Gotta Have Wa*, (New York: Macmillan, 1989).

19. Toshio Saeki, "Sport in Japan," *Sport in Asia and Africa*, ed. Eric A. Wagner (Westport: Greenwood Press, 1989), p. 55.

20. *Sporting News*: quoted in Richard C. Crepeau, "Pearl Harbor: A Failure of Baseball?" *Journal of Popular Culture*, 15:4 (Spring 1982): 72; Sinclair, "Baseball's Rising Sun," 51.

21. Roden, "Baseball and the Quest for National Identity," p. 519.

22. Mark Twain, Quoted in Harry C. Palmer, "The 'Around the World' Tour," *Athletic Sports in America, England, and Australia*, ed. Harry Clay Palmer (Philadelphia: Hubbard Bros., 1889), p. 447.

23. Wolf Krämer-Mandeau, "Ocupación, Dominación y Liberación—la Historia del Deporte en Nicaragua," *GL*, 6:1043; see also John Krich, *El Béisbol* (New York: Atlantic Monthly Press, 1989), p. 223.

24. Edel Casas, Jorge Alfonso, and Albert Pestana, *Viva y en Juego* (Havana: Editorial Cientifico Técnica, 1986), pp. 7–10.

25. Angel Torres, *Historia del Béisbol Cubano, 1878–1976* (Los Angeles: Angel Torres, 1976), pp. 11, 37; Wolf Krämer-Mandeau *Sport und Körpererziehung auf Cuba* (Cologne: Pahl-Rugenstein, 1988), p. 24; Rob Ruck, *The Tropic of Baseball: Baseball in the Dominican Republic* (Westport: Meckler, 1991), p. 2.

26. William H. Beezley, *Judas at the Jockey Club* (Lincoln: University of Nebraska Press, 1987), p. 20.

27. Krämer-Mandeau, *Sport und Körpererziehung*, p. 18.

28. Gálvez: quoted in Michael M. and Mary Adams Oleksak, *Béisbol: Latin Americans and the Grand Old Game* (Grand Rapids, Michigan: Masters Press, 1991), pp. 6–7.

29. Gualberto Gómez: quoted in Casas et al., *Viva y Juego*, p. 18.

30. Donn Rogosin, *Invisible Men: Life in Baseball's Negro Leagues* (New York: Atheneum, 1983), p. 61; Krämer-Mandeau, *Sport und Körpererziehung*, p. 25.

31. Rogosin, *Invisible Men*, p. 160.

32. Ibid., pp. 162–63.

33. Julian Barnes, "The Mystery of a Masterpiece," *New York Review*, 40:8 (April 22, 1993): 27.

34. Beezley, *Judas at the Jockey Club*, p. 18

35. Ibid., p. 19.

36. William H. Beezley, "Bicycles, Modernization, and Mexico," *Sport and Society in Latin America: Diffusion, Dependency, and the Rise of Mass Culture*, ed. Joseph L. Arbena (Westport: Greenwood Press, 1988), p. 25.

37. Beezley, *Judas at the Jockey Club*, pp. 20–22.

38. Gilbert M. Joseph, "Forging the Regional Pastime: Baseball and Class in Yucatan," *Sport and Society in Latin America*, pp. 29–61.

39. Oleksak, *Béisbol*, p. 19.

40. Beezley, *Judas at the Jockey Club*, p. 25.

41. Joseph L. Arbena, "Sport, Development, and Mexican Nationalism, 1920–1970," *Journal of Sport History*, 18:3 (Winter 1991): 355.

42. Rogosin, *Invisible Men*, p. 174.

43. Oleksak, *Béisbol*, pp. 50–52.

44. Ruck, *Tropic of Baseball* p. 5.

45. Alan M. Klein, *Sugarball: The American Game, the Dominican Dream* (New Haven: Yale University Press, 1991), p. 17.

46. Sullivan, quoted in ibid, p. 110.

47. Ruck, *Tropic of Baseball*, p. 136.

48. Ibid., pp. 7–8, 14.

49. Krich, *El Béisbol*, p. 111.

50. Rogosin, *Invisible Men*, p. 168.

51. Klein, *Sugarball*, pp. 22–23

52. Ruck, *Tropic of Baseball*, p. 73.

53. Ibid, p. 62.

54. In addition to the cited books by Klein and Ruck, see Gare Joyce, *The Only Ticket Off the Island* (Toronto: Lester and Orpen Dennys, 1990).

55. Klein, *Sugarball*, p. 42.

56. Krich, *El Béisbol*, p. 156.

57. Ruck, *Tropic of Baseball*, p. 28; see also Alan M. Klein, "Sport and Culture as Contested Terrain: Americanization in the Caribbean," *Sociology of Sport Journal*, 8:1 (March 1991): 79–85.

58. Jim McKay and Toby Miller, "From Old Boys to Men and Women of the Corporation: The Americanization and Commodification of Australian Sport," *SSJ*, 8:1 (March 1991): 86–94; Brian Stoddart, "Wide World of Golf: A Research Note on the Interdependence of Sport, Culture, and Economy," *SSJ*, 7:4 (1990): 378–88.

59. Bruce Mitchell, "Baseball in Australia," *Sporting Traditions*, 7:1 (November 1990): 2–24.

60. Palmer, "The 'Around the World' Tour," pp. 151–282.

61. Ibid., p. 260.

62. Referee : quoted in Mitchell, "Baseball in Australia," p. 18.

63. Ibid., pp. 16–21; Bruce Mitchell, "A National Game Goes International," *IJHS*, 9:2 (August 1992): 288–301.

64. Ray Crawford, "Sport for Young Ladies: The Victorian Independent Schools, 1875–1925," *Sporting Traditions*, 1:1 (November 1984): 75.

65. Richard White, "A Backwater Awash: The Australian Experience of Americanisation," *Theory, Culture, and Society*, 1:3 (1983): 108–22.

66. Mitchell, "A National Games Goes International," p. 296.

67. Braham Dabscheck, "A Long Deep Drive into Centre Field? Australian Baseball Turns Professional," *Australian Society for Sports History Bulletin* (March 1991): 14–19.

68. Jack Sands and Peter Gammons, *Coming Apart at the Seams* (New York: Macmillan, 1993), p. 229.

69. McKay and Miller, "From Old Boys to Men and Women of the Corporation," p. 87.

70. On these innovations, see Richard Cashman, *'Ave a Go, Yer Mug! Australian Cricket Crowds from Larrikin to Ocker* (Sydney: Collins, 1984), pp. 153–67.

71. Mitchell, "A National Game Goes International," p. 298.

72. Ibid.

4. BASKETBALL

1. James Naismith, "Basket-Ball," *American Physical Education Review*, 19:5 (May 1914): 339–40. This and the next three paragraphs are taken, with minor revisions, from Allen Guttmann, *A Whole New Ball Game*, pp. 70–72.

2. Naismith, "Basket-Ball," pp. 339–40.

3. Berenson divided the court into three zones with two players per team in each of them. The players were not allowed to leave their zone, to dribble the ball, or to guard aggressively.

4. Catherine E. D'Urso, "A View of American Attitudes toward Femininity: The Hisory of Physical Education for Women and Collegiate Women's Basketball" (unpublished essay, Amherst College, 1989), pp. 47–48.

5. Lynne Emery, "The First Intercollegiate Contest for Women," *Her Story in Sport*, ed. Reet A. Howell (West Point: Leisure Press, 1982), pp.

417–23; Martha Banta, *Imaging American Women* (New York: Columbia University Press, 1987), p. 90.

6. Jonathan Kolatch, *Sports, Politics, and Ideology in China* (New York: Jonathan David, 1972), p. 9.

7. Ibid.

8. Ibid.

9. Elmer L. Johnson, *The History of YMCA Physical Education* (Chicago: Follett, 1979), p. 160.; Janice A. Beran, "Physical Education and Sport in the Philippines," *Sport in Asia and Africa*, ed. Eric A. Wagner (Westport: Greenwood Press, 1989), pp. 151–52.

10. Joseph Mills Hanson, ed., *The Inter-Allied Games* (Paris: The Games Committee, 1919), p. 11.

11. Ibid., p. 12.

12. James Naismith, *Basketball* (New York: Association Press, 1941), pp. 153–54.

13. According to Rolf von der Laage, there were seventy athletes representing the Philippines, forty from China, and twenty from Japan; see *Sport in China* (Berlin: Bartels & Wernitz, 1977), p. 46; Chinese president cited in Hanson, *Inter-Allied Games*, p. 13.

14. Kolatch, *Sports, Politics, and Ideology in China*, p. 29; McDonald W. Sullivan, Li Bao-jun, Zhu Long-yi, "Philip Beach Sullivan" (Archives, Basketball Hall of Fame).

15. Jürgen Ritterbach, "Die Geschichte des Basketballs in Deutschland von den Anfängen bis 1945" (Köln: Deutsche Sporthochschule, 1988), pp. 6–25.

16. Hajo Bernett, "Die ersten 'olympischen' Wettbewerbe im internationalen Frauensport," *Sozial- und Zeitgeschichte des Sports*, 2:2 (1988): 73.

17. John Bale, *Sport and Place: A Geography of Sport in England, Scotland and Wales* (London: C. Hurst, 1982), p. 137; Joseph Maguire, "The Commercialization of English Elite Basketball 1972–1988," *IRSS*, 23:4 (1988): 310–11.

18. Maarten van Bottenburg, "The Differential Popularization of Sports in Continental Europe," *The Netherlands Journal of Social Sciences*, 28:1 (April 1992): 20.

19. Hanson, *Inter-Allied Games*, pp. 14–20.

20. Ibid., pp. 88, 201–2; Johnson, *YMCA Physical Education*, p. 90; William J. Baker, *Sports in the Western World* (Totowa, New Jersey: Rowman and Littlefield, 1982), p. 213.

21. In addition to Switzerland and Italy, the founding members represented Argentina, Portugal, Greece, Rumania, Czechoslovakia, and Latvia.

22. Ritterbach, "Geschichte des Basketballs," p. 44.

23. Ibid., pp. 31–35.

24. Ibid., pp. 28, 33–34, 38–42, 66–68.

25. Maguire, "Commercialization of English Elite Basketball," pp. 305–22; Joseph Maguire, "American Labour Migrants, Globalisation and the Making of English Basketball," *The Global Sports Arena*, ed. John Bale and Joseph Maguire (London: Frank Cass, 1993), pp. 226–55.

26. John Bale, *The Brawn Drain* (Urbana: University of Illinois Press, 1991); Bale and Maguire, eds, *The Global Sports Arena*.

27. Maguire, "Commercialization of English Elite Basketball," p. 238.

28. Jack McCallum, "Tomorrow the World," *Sports Illustrated*, 69:20 (November 7, 1988): 62; Curry Kirkpatrick, "Sitting Pretty in Rome," *Sports Illustrated*, 71:16 (October 9, 1989): 28. Shaw eventually returned to the Celtics, but *Il Messaggero* got its revenge when Boston's 1990 draft pick, Dino Radja, chose to play for Rome; see Harvy Araton and Filip Bondy, *The Selling of the Green* (New York: Harper/Collins, 1992), pp. 1–10.

29. Bottenburg, "Popularity of Sports," pp. 23–26; Sandro Provvisionato, *Lo Sport in Italia* (Rome: Savelli, 1978), p. 235.

5. AMERICAN FOOTBALL

1. Ronald Hubscher, Jean Durry and Bernard Jeu, *l'Histoire en mouvements* (Paris: Armand Colin, 1992), p. 317; Gisèle Lacroix, "Le look fun et ses enjeux," *Géopolitique du sport*, ed. Borhane Errais, Daniel Mathieu, and Jean Praicheux (Besançon: Université de Franche-Comté, 1990), pp. 61–72.

2. Paul Gardner, *The Simplest Game* (Boston: Little, Brown, 1976), p. 164

3. David Hackett Fischer, *Albion's Seed: Four British Folkways in America* (New York: Oxford University Press, 1989), p. 149.

4. Parke H. Davis, *Football: The American Intercollegiate Game* (New York: Scribner's, 1911), pp. 35–37.

5. The best analyses of the ritual are Edwin Cady's *The Big Game*

(Knoxville: University of Tennessee Press, 1978) and Michael Oriard's *Reading Football* (Chapel Hill: University of North Carolina Press, 1993). There is no good history of American football.

6. Davis, *Football*, pp. 45–50, 62–66.

7. Ibid. p. 69; Eric Dunning and Kenneth Sheard, *Barbarians, Gentlemen and Players* (Oxford: Martin Robertson, 1979), p. 111.

8. David Riesman and Reuel Denney, "Football in America," *Individualism Reconsidered* (Glencoe: Free Press, 1954), p. 250.

9. Harry C. Palmer, "The 'Around the World' Tour," *Athletic Sports in America, England, and Australia*, ed. Harry C. Palmer (Philadelphia: Hubbard Bros., 1889), pp. 404–41.

10. Joseph Durso, *The Days of Mr. McGraw* (Englewood Cliffs: Prentice-Hall, 1969), p. 187.

11. Joseph Maguire, "American Football, British Society, and Global Sport Development," *The Sports Process*, ed. Eric G. Dunning, Joseph A. Maguire, and Robert E. Pearton (Champaign: Human Kinetics, 1993), pp. 207–15; Garry Whannel, *Fields in Vision: Television Sport and Cultural Transformation* (London: Routledge, 1992), p. 102.

12. Joseph Maguire, "More Than a Sporting Touchdown: The Making of American Football in England, 1982–1990," *SSJ*, 7:3 (September 1990): 213–37; Maguire, "American Football, British Society, and Global Sport Development," pp. 209–13; Steven Barnett, *Games and Sets: The Changing Face of Sport on Television* (London: British Film Institute, 1990), pp. 68, 101.

13. Maguire, "More Than a Sporting Touchdown," pp. 222–33; Maguire, "American Football," pp. 213–14.

14. Ibid., p. 224.

15. Ibid., pp. 216–17.

16. Table 5.1 is adapted from Joseph Maguire, "The Media-Sport Production Complex: The Case of American Football in Western European Societies," *European Journal of Communication*, 6 (1991): 320.

17. Ibid., p. 321.

18. Goodell: quoted in Steve Rushin, "On the Road Again," *Sports Illustrated*, 79:7 (August 16, 1993): 20.

19. Rick Reilly, "One to Remember," *Sports Illustrated*, 74:23 (June 17, 1991): 44–50; Christopher Davies, "A Jolly Good Show," *Sports Illustrated*, 74:23 (June 17, 1991): 50; Peter King, "World Beater," *Sports Illustrated*, 76:20 (May 25, 1992): 42–44.

20. Maguire, "More Than a Sporting Touchdown," p. 234.

21. Goodell: quoted in Rushin, "On the Road Again," p. 20.

6. THE OLYMPIC GAMES

1. On the *quiditas* of modern sports, see Allen Guttmann, *From Ritual to Record: The Nature of Modern Sports* (New York: Columbia University Press, 1978), pp. 15–55.

2. Christopher R. Hill, *Olympic Politics* (Manchester: University of Manchester Press, 1992), pp. 9–15.

3. David C. Young, *The Olympic Myth of Greek Amateur Athletics* (Chicago: Ares, 1984).

4. Katharine Moore, "The Pan-Britannic Festival," *Pleasure, Profit, Proselytism*, ed. J. A. Mangan (London: Frank Cass, 1988), pp. 144–62.

5. Pierre de Coubertin, *Une Campagne de vingt-et-un ans (1887–1908)* (Paris: Librairie de l'éducation physique, 1909); Coubertin, *Mémoires olympiques* (Lausanne: Bureau international de pédagogie sportive, 1931); Marie-Thérèse Eyquem, *Pierre de Coubertin* (Paris: Calmann-Lévy, 1966); Louis Callebat, *Pierre de Coubertin* (Paris: Fayard, 1988).

6. Richard D. Mandell, *The First Modern Olympics* (Berkeley: University of California Press, 1976); John J. MacAloon, *This Great Symbol: Pierre de Coubertin and the Origins of the Modern Olympic Games* (Chicago: University of Chicago Press, 1981).

7. Gunter Gebauer and Christoph Wulf, "Die Spiele der Gewalt," *Körper und Einbildungskraft: Inszenierungen des Helden im Sport*, ed. Gunter Gebauer (Berlin: Dietrich Reimer, 1988), pp. 11–30; Thomas Alkemeyer, "Gewalt und Opfer im Ritual der Olympischen Spiele 1936," *Körper und Einbildungskraft*, pp. 44–79.

8. Leni Riefenstahl, *Memoiren*, 2 vols. (Frankfurt: Ullstein, 1990–1992), 1: 254–85; Glenn B. Infield, *Leni Riefenstahl* (New York: Crowell, 1976); Cooper C. Graham, *Leni Riefenstahl and Olympia* (Metuchen: Scarecrow Press, 1986).

9. Coubertin: quoted in Bernadette Deville-Danthu, "Les jeux d'outre mer," *L'empire du sport*, ed. Daniel Hick (Aix-en-Provence: 1992), p. 61; see also Otto Mayer, *A Travers les anneaux olympiques* (Geneva: Cailler, 1960), pp. 103–4.

10. Deville-Danthu, "Les Jeux d'outre-mer," p. 66.

11. Jean-Claude Ganga, *Combats pour un sport africain* (Paris: L'Har-

mattan, 1979), pp. 147–52; see also Achôt Mélik-Chakhnazarov, *Le sport en afrique* (Paris: Présence Africaine, 1970), pp. 27–29, 34–46, 141–74.

12. John J. MacAloon, "The Turn of Two Centuries: Sport and the Politics of Intercultural Relations," *Sport: The Third Millennium*, ed. Fernand Landry, Marc Landry, and Magdeleine Yerlès (Sainte-Foy: Presses de l'Université Laval, 1991), p. 42.

13. J. L. Chappelet, *Le système olympique* (Grenoble: Presses universitaires de Grenoble, 1991), p. 99.

14. James W. Riordan, "Tsarist Russia and International Sport," *Stadion*, 14:2 (1988): 228.

15. Walter Abmayr, "Afrika und Leichtathletik," *Beiträge zur Zusammenarbeit im Sport mit der Dritten Welt*, ed. Rolf Andresen, Hermann Rieder, and Gerhard Trosien (Schorndorf: Karl Hofmann, 1989), p. 59. There is disagreement over El Quafi's name.

16. Bernadette Deville-Danthu, "L'AOF pépinière d'athlètes: révélation, illusions et désillusions," *Jeux et Sports dans l'histoire* (Paris: Harmattan, 1992), pp. 255–70; Bernadette Deville-Danthu, "Les premières tentatives d'encadrement des activités physique et sportives de la jeunesse en A.O.F. (1922–1936)," *Les jeunes en Afrique*, eds. H. D'Almeida-Topor et al. (Paris: 1992), pp. 448–462.

17. Peter Rummelt, *Sport im Kolonialismus, Kolonialismus im Sport* (Cologne: Pahl-Rugenstein, 1986), p. 227; Ramadhan Ali, *Africa at the Olympics* (London: Africa Books, 1976), p. 67.

18. Don Anthony, "The North-South and East-West Axes of Development in Sport," *Sport: The Third Millenium*, p. 333.

19. Milton Coffré Iluffi, "Historia del Deporte y la Educación Fisica en Chile," *GL*, 6:944–46; Enrique C. Romero Brest et al., "Los Deportes y la Educación Fisica en la Republica Argentina," *GL*, 6: 873, 885; Wolf Krämer-Mandeau *Sport und Körpererziehung auf Cuba* (Cologne: Pahl-Rugenstein, 1988).

20. William R. May, "Sports,"*The Handbook of Japanese Popular Culture*, eds. Richard Gid Powers and Hidetoshi Kato (Westport: Greenwood Press, 1986), p. 174; Kokusai Bunka Shinkokai [Society for International Cultural Relations], *Sports* (Tokyo: Kokusai Bunka Shinkokai, 1939), p. 8; Allen Guttmann, *The Olympics* (Urbana: University of Illinois Press, 1992), pp. 51–52, 69.

21. Allen Guttmann, *Women's Sports: A History* (New York: Columbia

University Press, 1991), pp. 163–71, 186–88, 199–206, 243–50; Guttmann, *The Olympics*, p. 155.

22. Swanpo Sie, "Sports and Politics: The Case of the Asian Games and the GANEFO," *Sport and International Relations*, eds. Benjamin Lowe, David B. Kanin, Andrew Strenk (Champaign: Stipes, 1978), pp. 279–96; see also Allen Guttmann, *The Games Must Go On: Avery Brundage and the Olympic Movement* (New York: Columbia University Press, 1984), pp. 227–29.

23. Richard E. Lapchick, *The Politics of Race and International Sport: The Case of South Africa* (Westport: Greenwood Press, 1975); Richard Espy, *Politics of the Olympic Games* (Berkeley: University of California Press, 1979), pp. 94–106; Guttmann, *The Games Must Go On*, pp. 232–40.

24. Karl Adolf Scherer, *Der Männerorden* (Frankfurt: Limpert, 1974); Wolf Krämer-Mandeau, "Figuration, Formation, Umbruch und Identität," paper delivered at the "Spiele der Welt-Welt der Spiele" Congress (Berlin, July 1993), pp. 5–6.

25. Jörg Möller, "Der deutsche Arzt Erwin von Bälz und die Entwicklung von Körperkultur und Sport in Japan," *Stadion*, 16:1 (1990): 129–41.

26. *Répertoire du Mouvement Olympique '93* (Lausanne: Comité Olympique International, 1993), pp. 39–48.

27. Brundage to Aldao, October 29, 1945 (Avery Brundage Collection, Box 50, University of Illinois). On Brundage's Olympic career, see Guttmann, *The Games Must Go On*, pp. 62–255.

28. "Plan for Reorganizing the International Olympic Committee...," *Bulletin du CIO*, 67 (August 15, 1959); "Minutes of the 58th Session of the International Olympic Committee, Athens, June 19–21, 1961," *Bulletin du CIO*, 75 (August 15, 1961); see also Guttmann, *The Games Must Go On*, pp. 170–72.

29. CONI (*Comite Nazionale Olimpico d'Italia*) to NOC's, October 3, 1964; Giulio Onesti to Avery Brundage, March 20, 1965; Brundage to Onesti, September 14, 1965 (Avery Brundage Collection, Box 61); "Minutes 66th Session of the International Olympic Committee, February 2–5, 1968" (Avery Brundage Collection, Box 93); Brundage to Vice-Presidents of the IOC, October 8, 1971 (Avery Brundage Collection, Box 58); see also Guttmann, *The Games Must Go On*, pp. 173–86.

30. For these organizational developments, see Michael Morris (Lord Killanin), *My Olympic Years* (London: Secker & Warburg, 1983); David

Miller, *The Olympic Revolution* (New York: Pavilion Books, 1992); J. L. Chappelet, *Le Système olympique* (Grenobles: Presses universitaires de Grenoble, 1991).

31. Guttmann, *The Games Must Go On*, pp. 179–80.

32. *Répertoire du Mouvement Olympique '93*, pp. 81–96.

33. *Bulletin Officiel du CIO*, 5:16 (July 1930): 19.

34. *IOC Newsletter*, Nr. 15 (December 1968).

35. Brundage's notes on meeting, November 21, 1956 (Avery Brundage Collection, Box 78).

36. Kevin Gray Carr, "Making Way: War, Philosophy, and Sport in Japanese Judo" *Journal of Sport History*, 20:2 (Summer 1933): 167–180.

37. Avery Brundage to Otto Mayer, February 4, 1961 (Avery Brundage Collection, Box 48).

38. Michel Brousse, "Du Samouraï à l'athlète: l'essor du judo en France," *Sport/Historie*, 3 (1989): 11, 17, 21; see also B. C. and J. M. Goodger, "Judo in the Light of Theory and Sociological Research,"*IRSS*, 12:2 (1977): 5–34; Goodger and Goodger, "Organisational and Cultural Change in Post-War British Judo," *IRSS*, 15:1 (1980): 21–48, Carr, "Making Way," pp. 180–88.

7. TURNEN

1. The most detailed general account of the *Turnbewegung* is still Edmund Neuendorff's *Geschichte der neueren deutschen Leibesübungen vom Beginn des 18. Jahrhunderts bis zur Gegenwart*, 4 vols. (Dresden: Limpert Verlag, 1934).

2. Hajo Bernett, *Die pädagogische Neugestaltung der bürgerlichen Leibesübung durch die Philanthropen* (Schorndorf: Karl Hofmann, 1960).

3. For Jahn's views, see his *Werke*, ed. Carl Euler, 2 vols. (Hof: Verlag von G. A. Grau, 1884–85). The literature on Jahn is enormous. For a brief and balanced view, see Horst Überhorst, *Zurück zu Jahn?* (Bochum: Universitätsverlag, 1969).

4. Jahn: quoted in Neuendorff, *Geschichte*, 2:122.

5. On the conservative politics of the *Deutsche Turnerschaft*, see Hans-Georg John, *Politik und Turnen: Die Deutsche Turnerschaft als nationale Bewegung im Deutschen Kaiserreich von 1871–1914* (Ahrensburg: Czwalina, 1976); Lorenz Peiffer, *Die Deutsche Turnerschaft* (Ahrensburg: Czwalina, 1976).

6. Hartmut Becker, *Antisemitismus in der Deutschen Turnerschaft* (Sankt Augustin: Hans Richarz, 1980). On the tragic fate of the Zionist clubs, see Hajo Bernett, *Der jüdische Sport im nationalsozialistischen Deutschland, 1933–1938* (Schorndorf: Karl Hofmann, 1978).

7. Neuendorff, *Geschichte*, 3:194.

8. Christa Kleindienst-Cachay, *Die Verschulung des Turnens* (Schorndorf: Karl Hofmann, 1980); Michael Krüger, "'Das Turnen als reaktionäres Mittel': Wilhelm Angerstein und die Disziplinierung des Turnens," *Sportwissenschaft*, 23:1 (1991): 9–34..

9. Neuendorff, *Geschichte*, 4:474.

10. *Zeitschrift*: quoted in Maarten van Bottenburg, "The Differential Popularization of Sports in Continental Europe," *The Netherlands Journal of Social Sciences*, 28:1 (April 1992): 6.

11. Horst Geyer, "Stellvertreter der Nation," *Die vertrimmte Nation*, ed. Jörg Richter (Reinbek: Rowohlt Verlag, 1972), pp. 80–81.

12. Neuendorff, *Geschichte*, 4:486.

13. Krüger, "Turnen als reaktionäres Mittel," p. 32.

14. Neuendorff, *Geschichte*, 4:485.

15. Harro Hagen: quoted in Henning Eichberg, *Weg des Sports in die industrielle Zivilisation* (Baden-Baden: Nomos, 1973), p. 120.

16. Schmidt: quoted in Neuendorff, *Geschichte*, 4:386.

17. Karl Planck, *Fusslümmelei* (Stuttgart: Kohlhammer, 1898), p. 6.

18. Roland Renson, " 'Le corps académique': La genèse de l'éducation physique universitaire en Belgique," *Stadion*, 17:1 (1991): 87–99; Thierry Terret, "À la recherche de l'identité Belge: le Capitaine Docx et la promotion d'éclecticisme," *Sport Histoire*, n.s. 1 (1992): 81–101.

19. Cupérus: quoted in Raymond Barrull, "L'émergence de la gymnastique sportive à la fin du XIXe siècle et au début du XXe siècle," *La Naissance du Mouvement Sportif Associatif en France*, eds. Pierre Arnaud and J. Camy (Lyon: Presses Universitaires de Lyon, 1986), p. 65.

20. Ruud Stokvis, *Strijd over Sport* (Devanter: Van Loghum Slaterus, 1979), pp. 65, 72.

21. Bottenburg, "The Differential Popularization of Sports in Continental Europe," *The Netherlands Journal of Social Sciences*, 28:1 (April 1992): 17.

22. Ronald Hubscher, Jean Durry and Bernard Jeu, *l'Histoire en mouvements* (Paris: Armand Colin, 1992), p. 139; Arnold Wehrle, *500 Jahre Spiel und Sport in Zürich* (Zurich: Verlag Berichthaus, 1960), p. 64; Fritz

Pieth, *Sport in der Schweiz* (Olten: Walter Verlag, 1979), pp. 44–46.

23. Ibid., p. 135.

24. Bottenburg, "Differential Popularization," p. 16.

25. Felice Fabrizio, *Storia dello Sport in Italia* (Rimini: Guaraldi, 1977), pp. 19–20.

26. Michele Di Donato, "Italien, *GL*, 5: 242; Michele Di Donato, "Sport and Physical Education in Italy," *Sport and Physical Education Around the World*, ed .William Johnson (Champaign: Stipes, 1980), pp. 354–70.

27. Jacques Defrance, *L'Excellence corporelle: La formation des activités physiques et sportives modernes, 1770–1914* (Rennes: Presses universitaires de Rennes, 1987); Hubscher et al., *L'Histoire en mouvements*, p. 139.

28. Bottenburg, "Differential Popularization," p. 17.

29. Jacques Thibault, *Sport et éducation physique, 1870–1970*, 2nd ed. (Paris: Vrin, 1979), p. 90.

30. P. Chambat, "Les Fêtes de la discipline: gymnastique et politique en France (1879–1914)," *La Naissance du mouvement sportif associatif en France*, eds. Pierre Arnaud and J. Camy (Lyon: Presses Universitaires de Lyon, 1986), pp.85–86; on the patriotic gymnastics clubs, see also Pierre Arnaud, ed., *Les Athlètes de la République* (Toulouse: Editions Privat, 1987).

31. On Ling and other Scandinavian physical educators, see Peter McIntosh, "Therapeutic Exercise in Scandinavia," *Landmarks in the History of Physical Education*, ed. Peter McIntosh, 3rd ed. (London: Routledge and Kegan Paul, 1981), pp. 85–111.

32. Gilbert Andrieu, "L'Influence de la gymnastique suédoise sur l'éducation physique en France entre 1874 et 1914," *Stadion*, 14:2 (1988): 163–80.

33. On Bergman-Osterberg, see Sheila Fletcher, *Women First: The Female Tradition in English Physical Education* (London: Athlone Press, 1984).

34. Fügner, quoted in Claire Nolte, "'Our Task, Direction and Goal': The Development of the Sokol National Program to World War I, *Die slawische Sokolbewegung*, ed. Diethelm Blecking (Dortmund: Forschungsstelle Ostmitteleuropa, 1991), p. 39. I have corrected Nolte's translation.

35. Diethelm Blecking, "Zum historischen Problem der slawischen Sokolbewegung," *Die slawische Sokolbewegung*, p. 13.

36. Tyrs: quoted in Nolte, "'Our Task, Direction and Goal,'" p. 43.

37. Diethelm Blecking, "Zum historischen Problem der slawischen

Sokolbewegung," pp. 7–22; Michal Terech, "Der 'Sokol' bei den slawischen Nationen," *Die slawische Sokolbewegung*, pp. 23–36.

38. Wolfgang Kessler, "Der Sokol in den jugoslawischen Gebieten," *Die slawische Sokolbewegung*, pp. 198–218.

39. Przemyslaw Matusik, "Der polnische 'Sokol' zur Zeit der Teilungen und in der II. Polnischen Republik," *Die slawische Sokolbewegung*, pp. 104–35.

40. Kessler, "Der Sokol in den jugoslawischen Gebieten," pp. 198–218.

41. Losan Mitev, "Die Entwicklung der Turngesellschaften 'Sokol' und 'Junak' in Bulgarien bis zum Jahr 1914," *Die slawische Sokolbewegung*, pp. 175–81.

42. Teresch, "Der 'Sokol' bei den slawischen Nationen," p. 33.

43. József Vetö, *Sports in Hungary* (Budapest: Corvina Press, 1965), pp. 12–14.

44. Lothar Wiese, "Zur Geschichte des deutschen Turnens in Südamerika mit besonderer Berücksichtigung Brasiliens," *GL*, 6:954–75. The quotation is from p. 961. See also Lothar Wiese, "Zur Sozialgeschichte des Deutschen Turnens in Südamerika," *Sozial- und Zeitgeschichte des Sports*, 2:2 (1988): 7–32; Wolf Krämer-Mandeau, "Gymnastic Systems and Turner Movement [sic] in Latin America," *Turnen and Sport*, ed. Roland Naul (New York: Waxmann, 1991), pp. 21–49.

45. Deobold B. Van Dalen and Bruce L. Bennett, *A World History of Physical Education*, 2nd ed. (Englewood Cliffs: Prentice-Hall, 1971), pp. 558–99.

46. Erich Geldbach, "Die Verpflanzung des Deutschen Turnens nach Amerika: Beck, Follen, Lieber," *Stadion* 1:2 (1975): 331–76. The quotation is from p. 337. See also Bruce L. Bennett, "The Making of Round Hill School," *Quest*, 4 (April 1965): 53–63.

47. Follen: quoted in Geldbach, p. 346.

48. Horst Überhorst, *Turner unterm Sternenbanner* (Munich: Heinz Moos Verlag, 1978), pp. 44–51; Hannes Neumann, *Die deutsche Turnbewegung in der Revolution 1848/49 und in der amerikanischen Emigration* (Schorndorf: Karl Hofmann, 1968), pp. 63–103; Robert Knight Barney, "German Forty-Eighters and Turnvereine in the United States during the Antebellum Period," *CJHS*, 3:2 (December 1982): 62–79; Robert Knight Barney, "German-American Turnvereins and Socio-Politico-Economic

Realities in the Antebellum and Civil War Upper and Lower South," *Stadion*, 10 (1984): 135–81. The quotation is from p. 140.

49. Überhorst, *Turner unterm Sternenbanner*, pp. 73–85; Neumann, *Deutsche Turnbewegung*, pp. 104–17.

50. Überhorst, *Turner unterm Sternenbanner*, pp. 127–32.

51. Quoted in Überhorst, *Turner unterm Sternenbanner*, p. 151.

8. TRADITIONAL SPORTS

1. Sigrid Paul, "The Wrestling Tradition and Its Social Functions," *Sport in Africa*, eds. Willliam J. Baker and James. A. Mangan (New York: Africana Pub. Co., 1987), pp. 23–46.

2. Derek Birley, *Sport and the Making of Britain* (Manchester: University of Manchester Press, 1993), pp. 281–82.

3. Anna Biano Dettori, "Traditonelle Spiele im Aostatal," *Körperkultur und Identität*, eds. Henning Eichberg and J'FE{rn Hansen (Münster: LIT Verlag, 1989), pp. 25–30.

4. Hans-Peter Laqueur, *Zur kulturgeschichtlichen Stellung des türkischen Ringkampfs einst und jetzt* (Frankfurt: Peter Lang, 1979), pp. 26–28.

5. J. Lowell Lewis, *Ring of Liberation: Deceptive Discourse in Brazilian Capoeira* (Chicago: University of Chicago Press, 1992), p. 161.

6. Among the many accounts of the ritual stickball game, the most useful is Kendall Blanchard, *The Mississippi Choctaws at Play* (Urbana: University of Illinois Press, 1981).

7. Allen Guttmann, *A Whole New Ball Game: An Interpretation of American Sports* (Chapel Hill: University of North Carolina Press, 1988), p. 22.

8. G. Whitney Azoy, *Buzkashi: Game and Power in Afghanistan* (Philadelphia: University of Pennsylvania Press, 1982).

9. Many other examples can be found in Carl Diem's classic work, *Asiatische Reiterspiele* (Berlin: Deutscher Archiv Verlag, 1941). Polo is the most familiar modern form of these traditional games..

10. Roger Holmes, "The Survival and Revival of Traditional Sports and Games in Cornwall," *Éclipses et renaissance des jeux populaires* , eds. Jean-Jacques Barreau and Guy Jaouen (Rennes: Fédération Internationale des Luttes Celtiques, 1991), pp. 51–58; Guy Jaouen, "Gouren: Jeu et sport de lutte," *Körperkultur und Identität*, eds. Henning Eichberg and J'FE{rn Hansen (Münster: LIT Verlag, 1989), pp. 15–24; Laqueur, *Zur kulturgeschichtlichen Stellung des türkischen Ringkampfs*; Joseph S. Alter,

The Wrestler's Body: Identity and Ideology in North India (Berkeley: University of California Press, 1992).

11. Laquer, *Zur kulturgeschichtlichen Stellung des türkischen Ringkampfs.*, p. 104.

12. P. L. Cuyler, *Sumo: From Rite to Sport* (New York: Weatherhill, 1979), p. 21.

13. Cuyler, *Sumo*, p. 38.

14. Lee Austin Thompson, "The Modernization of Sumo as a Sport" (Ph. D. dissertation, Osaka University, 1989), pp. 142, 205–6.

15. Ibid.,, pp. 202–6.

16. Johann P. Arnason, "Nationalism, Globalization and Modernity," *Theory, Culture and Society*, 7 (1990): 225.

17. William H. Desmonde, "The Bull-Fight as a Religious Ritual," *American Imago*, 9 (June 1952): 173–95; Timothy Mitchell, *Blood Sport: A Social History of Spanish Bullfighting* (Philadelphia: University of Pennsylvania Press, 1991; Garry Marvin, *Bullfight* (Oxford: Basil Blackwell, 1988).

18. Timothy J. Mitchell, "Bullfighting: The Ritual Origin of Scholarly Myths," *Journal of American Folklore*, 99:394 (October–December 1986): 397, 406.

19. Henning Eichberg and Ali Yehia El Mansouri, "Sport in Libya," *GL*, 6: 267.

20. Michael Hirth, "Éducation physique et sport en République Islamique du Mauritanie," *GL*, 6:352, 354.

21. In the vast literature devoted to "sports under Communism," the most important title is still James Riordan's *Sport in Soviet Society* (London: Cambridge University Press, 1977).

22. Of Eichberg's numerous contributions to this theme, see "Spielverhalten und Relationsgsellschaft in West Sumatra," *Stadion*, 1:1 (1975): 1–48; "Von der grünen Heide zur fensterlosen Halle," *Jahrbuch der Turnkunst*, 76 (1981–82): 73–85; "Leistung zwischen Wänden—die sportive Parzellierung der Körper," *Berliner Historische Studien*, 9 (1983): 119–39; "Zielgraden und Krumme Linien," *Stadion*, 10 (1984): 227–45; "The Enclosure of the Body," *Journal of Contemporary History*, 21 (1986): 99–121; *Leistungsräume Sport als Umweltproblem* (Münster: LIT-Verlag, 1988); "Von Tristram Shandy zu 'Marschall Vorwärts': Zur sozialen Zeit der Körper in Sport, Krieg und Fort-Schritt," *Sportwissenschaft*, 19:3 (1989): 272–96; "Trommeltanz der Inuit," *Körperkultur und Identität*,

eds. Henning Eichberg and Jĺrn Hansen (Münster: LIT-Verlag, 1989), pp 51–64; "Travelling, Comparing, Emigrating: Configurations of Sport Mobility," *The Global Sports Arena*, eds John Bale and Joseph Maguire (London: Cass, 1993), pp. 256–80.

23. Eichberg, "Trommeltanz," p. 59.

24. Geneviève Rail, "Technologie post-moderne et culture," *Sport: The Third Millennium*, eds. Fernand Landry, Marc Landry, and Magdeleine Yerlès (Sainte-Foy: Presses de l'Université Laval, 1991), pp. 731–39.

25. Jean-Jacques Barreau, "Traditions festives, activités ludiques et spectacle sportif," *Eclipses et renaissance des jeux populaires* , eds Jean-Jacques Barreau and Guy Jaouen (Rennes: Fédération Internationale des Luttes Celtiques, 1990), p. 17.

26. Henning Eichberg, "A Revolution of Body Culture: Traditional Games on the Way from Modernisation to 'Postmodernity,' "*Éclipses et renaissance des jeux populaires*, pp. 106–7.

27. Ibid., p. 106.

28. Henning Eichberg, "Olympic Sport—Neocolonization and Alternatives," *IRSS*, 19:1 (1984): 102.

9. CULTURAL IMPERIALISM?

1. Charles A. Peverelly, *The Book of American Pastimes* (New York: C. A. Peverelly, 1866), p. 337.

2. Holger Obermann, "Fussball als Exportartikel," *Beiträge zur Zusammenarbeit im Sport in der Dritten Welt*, ed. Rolf Andresen, Hermann Rieder, and Gerhard Trosien (Schorndorf: Karl Hofmann, 1989), p. 50.

3. Maarten van Bottenburg, "The Differential Popularization of Sports in Continental Europe," *The Netherlands Journal of Social Sciences*, 28:1 (April 1992): 4.

4. Ruud Stokvis, "De populariteit van sporten," *Amsterdams Sociologisch Tijdschrift*, 15:4 (March 1989): 674.

5. Ruud Stokvis, *De Sportwereld* (Alphen aan den Rijn: Samsom Uitgeverij, 1989), pp. 18, 21.

6. Arjun Appadurai, "Disjuncture and Difference in the Global Cultural Economy," *Theory, Culture and Society*, 7 (1990): 301.

7. Robert A. Stebbins, "Stacking in Professional American Football: Implications from the Canadian Game," *IRSS*, 28:1 (1993): 65–71; Alexander M. Weyand and Milton R. Roberts, *The Lacrosse Story* (Balti-

more: Herman, 1965); Richard Holt, *Sport and the British* (Oxford: Clarendon Press, 1989), pp. 209–10.

8. B. C. and J. M. Goodger, "Organization and Cultural Change in Post-War British Judo," *IRSS*, 15:1 (1980): 21–48; Martin J. Rosenblum, "Martial Arts Poetics," *Journal of American Culture*, 4:3 (Fall 1981): 148–53; J. M. Goodger, "Pluralism, Transmission, and Change in Sport," *Quest*, 38 (1986): 135–47; Michel Brousse, "Du Samuraï à l'Athlète," *Sport/Histoire*, 3 (1989): 11–25.

9. Mangan, *The Games Ethic and Imperialism*, (New York: Viking, 1986), p. 18.

10. Peter Rummelt, *Sport im Kolonialismus, Kolonialismus im Sport* (Cologne: Pahl-Rugenstein, 1986).

11. André Gunder Frank, *Capitalism and Underdevelopment in Latin America* (New York: Monthly Review Press, 1967), pp. 3, 11. Not all theorists of "dependency" are as dogmatic as Frank about the utter impossibility of development within the capitalist system; see Fernando Cardoso and Enzo Faletto, *Dependency and Development in Latin America*, trans. Marjory Mattingly Urquidi (Berkeley: University of California Press, 1979), pp. 185–86.

12. Joseph Maguire, "The Commercialization of English Elite Basketball 1972–88," *IRSS*, 23:4 (1988): 305–22; "American Labour Migrants, Globalisation and the Making of English Basketball," *The Global Sports Arena*, eds. John Bale and Joseph Maguire (London: Frank Cass, 1993), pp. 226–55; "More Than a Sporting Touchdown: The Making of American Football in England 1982–1990," *SSJ*, 7:3 (September 1990): 213–37; , "The Media-Sport Production Complex: The Case of American Football in Western European Societies," *European Journal of Communication*, 6 (1991): 315–35; "American Football, British Society, and Global Sport Development," *The Sports Process*, eds. Eric G. Dunning, Joseph A. Maguire, and Robert E. Pearton (Champaign: Human Kinetics, 1993), pp. 207–29.

13. Bruce Kidd, "Sport, Dependency and the Canadian State," *Sport in the Sociocultural Process*, 3rd ed., eds. Marie Hart and Susan Birrell (Dubuque: William C. Brown, 1981), pp. 707–21.

14. James Quirk and Rodney D. Fort, *Pay Dirt: The Business of Professional Team Sports* (Princeton: Princeton University Press, 1992), pp. 35–36.

15. John Tomlinson, *Cultural Imperialism* (Baltimore: Johns Hopkins University Press, 1991), p. 7.

16. For the relevance to sports studies of Stuart Hall and the Birmingham Center for Contemporary Cultural Studies, see Richard Gruneau, "The Critique of Sport in Modernity," *The Sports Process*, pp. 85–109; David L. Andrews and John W. Loy, "British Cultural Studies and Sport," *Quest*, 45:2 (May 1993): 255–76.

17. J. O. Boyd-Barrett, "Cultural Dependency and the Mass Media," *Culture, Society and the Media*, eds. Michael Gurevitch, Tony Bennett, James Curran, and Janet Woollacott (London: Methuen, 1982), p. 193; see also Ien Ang, *Watching "Dallas": Soap Opera and the Melodramatic Imagination* (London: Methuen, 1985); Ellen Seiter, Hans Borchers, Gabriele Kreutzner, Eva-Maria Warth, eds., *Remote Control: Television, Audiences, and Cultural Power* (London: Routledge, 1989).

18. For example, see Irene Penacchioni, "The Reception of Popular Television in Northeast Brazil," *Media, Culture, and Society*, 6:4 (1984): 337–41; Michael Tracey, "The Poisoned Chalice? International Television and the Idea of Dominance," *Daedalus* 114:4 (1985): 17–56; Tamar Liebes and Elihu Katz, "On the Critical Abilities of Television Viewers," *Remote Control*, pp. 204–22.

19. William. Mandle, "Cricket and Australian Nationalism in the Nineteenth Century," *Sport in Australia*, eds. T . D. Jaques and G. R. Pavia (Sydney: McGraw-Hill, 1976), p. 62.

20. Donald Roden, "Baseball and the Quest for National Dignity in Meiji Japan," *American Historical Review*, 85:3 (June 1980): 511–34.

21. John Nauright, "Sport, Manhood, and Empire: British Responses to the New Zealand Rugby Tour of 1905," *IJHS*, 8:2 (September 1991): 239–55.

22. Tony Mason, "Football on the Maidan: Cultural Imperialism in Calcutta," *IJHS*, 7:1 (1990): 85–96.

23. Mihir Bose, *A History of Indian Cricket* (London: Andre Deutsch, 1990), p. 17.

24. Ibid., p. 14.

25. R. M. Levine, "The Burden of Success: *Futebol* and Brazilian Society through the 1970s," *Journal of Popular Culture*, 14 (1980): 453–64; Janet Lever, *Soccer Madness* (Chicago: University of Chicago Press, 1983); C. L. R. James, *Beyond a Boundary* (London: Stanley Paul, 1963); Orlando Patterson, "The Cricket Ritual in the West Indies," *New Society*, 13 (1969): 988–89; Brian Stoddart, "Cricket, Social Formation and Cultural Continuity in Barbados," *Journal of Sport History*, 14:3 (1987): 317–40;

Keith A. P. Sandiford and Brian Stoddart, "The Elite Schools and Cricket in Barbados," *IJHS*, 4 (December 1987): 333–50.

26. A tape of this event and a discussion of it were sent to me by Prof. Matti Goksĭyr (August 6, 1993).

27. *Daily Telegraph* (2/24/93): quoted in Joseph Maguire, "Globalization, Sport and National Identities," Loisir et Société, 16:2 (Autumn 1993): 302.

28. Joseph L. Arbena, "Sport, Development, and Mexican Nationalism, 1920–1970," *Journal of Sport History*, 18:3 (Winter 1991): 362; see also, Joseph L. Arbena, "Sport and Revolution: The Continuing Cuban Experience," *Studies in Latin American Popular Culture*, 9 (1990): 325.

29. This is suggested in Harold Perkin, "Teaching the Nations How to Play: Sport and Society in the British Empire and Commonwealth," *IJHS*, 6:2 (September 1989): 145–55.

30. Joseph L. Arbena, "The Diffusion of Modern European Sport in Latin America: A Case Study of Cultural Imperialism?" *South Eastern Latin Americanist*, 33:4 (March 1990): 6.

31. Gabriel Colomé, "Il Barcelona e la società catalana," *Il Calcio e il suo Pubblico*, ed. Pierre Lanfranchi (Naples: Edizioni Scientifiche Italiane, 1992), pp. 59–65.

32. Washington provided a "minuscule" share of the aid given in the postwar period; see Roy Clumpner, "Federal Involvement in Sport to Promote American Interest or Foreign Policy Objectives, 1950–1973," *Sport and International Relations*, eds. Benjamin Lowe, David B. Kanin, and Andrew Strenk (Champaign: Stipes, 1978), pp. 400–52. On the USSR's extensive program, see Baruch A. Hazan, "Sport as an Instrument of Political Expansion," *Sport in Africa*, eds. William J. Baker and James. A. Mangan (New York: Africana Publishing Co., 1987), pp. 250–271.

33. Karlheinz Gieseler, "Junge Völker—neuer Sport?" *Zeitschrift für Kulturaustausch*, 27:4 (1977): 13.

34. Klaus Heinemann, "Sport und Entwicklungshilfe in Ländern der Dritten Welt," *Sportwissenschaft*, 15: 3 (1985): 239; see also Rolf Andresen, Hermann Rieder, Gerhard Trosien, eds. *Beiträge*.

35. Janet Lever, *Soccer Madness* (Chicago: University of Chicago Press, 1983), p. 19.

36. Joseph L. Arbena, "Sport and Nationalism in Latin America, 1880–1970," *History of European Ideas*, 16:4–6 (1993): 837. Arbena concludes that sports have been "relatively ineffective" (842) in promoting

national unity, but he acknowledges that other scholars are more positive.

37. Anthony Clayton, "Sport and African Soldiers: The Military Diffusion of Western Sport throughout Sub-Saharan Africa," *Sport in Africa*, p. 129; see also James H. Frey, "The Internal and External Role of Sport in National Development," *Journal of National Development*, 1 (Winter 1988): 65–82..

38. Benedict Anderson, *Imagined Communities: Reflections on the Origin and Spread of Nationalism*, rev. ed. (New York: Verso, 1991).

39. Richard D. Mandell, *Sport: A Cultural History* (New York: Columbia University Press, 1984), p. 269.

40. Maguire, "Globalization, Sport and National Identities," pp. 310–11.

41. Edward W. Said, *Culture and Imperialism* (New York: Knopf, 1993), p. 217.

42. Leni Riefenstahl, *Memoiren*, 2 vols. (Frankfurt: Ullstein, 1990–92), 2:344.

43. Rolf Husmann and Christoph Meier, "Nuba-Ringen in Khartum," *Tradition, Migration, Notstand—Themen heutiger Sudanethnographie*, ed. Bernhard Streck (Göttingen: Edition Re, 1990), p. 82; see also Husmann, "'Nuba Wrestling': Von traditionellen Ringkämpfen zur modernen Sportveranstaltung im Sudan," *Unterrichtsmedien im Sport*, eds. Klaus Jäger and Robert Prohl (Erlensee: SFT-Verlag, 1993), pp. 50–63.

44. Richard Cashman, "Cricket and Colonialism: Colonial Hegemony and Indigenous Subversion?" *Pleasure, Profit, Proselytism*, ed. James. A. Mangan (London: Frank Cass, 1988), p. 261. In another context, Arjun Appadurai refers to "indigenization"; see "Disjunction and Difference," p. 295. The film in question is by J. W. Leach and Gary Kildea. See also Joachim K. Rühl, "20th Century Amalgamation of British Games Traditions with Indigenous Social Concepts on the Trobriand Islands," paper delivered at the "Spiele der Welt-Welt der Spiele" Congress, Berlin, July 1993.

45. Maarten van Bottenburg, "Als 'n Man Met een Baard op 'n Bokkewagen," *Vrijetijd en Samenleving*, 9:1 (1991): 5–27; Bart Crum, "A Critical Analysis of Korfball as a 'Non-Sexist Sport,'" *IRSS*, 23:3 (1988): 233–40.

46. Jay R. and Joan D. Mandle, *Grass Roots Commitment: Basektball and Society in Trinidad and Tobago* (Parkersburg, Iowa: Caribbean Books, 1988), pp. 19–20.

47. Sakina Bargach and Alain Moreau, "Les activités physiques et sportives, enjeu de l'émancipation des jeunes au maroc," *Géopolique du sport*, eds. Borhane Errais, Daniel Mathieu, and Jean Praicheux (Besançon: Université de Franche-Comté, 1990), pp. 141–52. On Third World women and the liberating potential of modern sports, see also Janice N. Brownfoot, "Emancipation, Exercise and Imperialism: Girls and the Games Ethic in Colonial Malaya," *IJHS*, 7:1 (May 1990): 61–84.

48. Borhane Errais, "La planète sportive," *Sport: The Third Millennium*, eds. Fernand Landry, Marc Landry, and Magdeleine Yèrles (Sainte-Foye: Presses de l'Université Laval, 1991), p. 582.

49. Ommo Grupe, "The Sport Culture and the Sportization of Culture," *Sport: The Third Millennium*, p. 143.

50. Richard Demak, "Bridge Over Troubled Water," *Sports Illustrated* 75:23 (November 25, 1991): 16–23; Jean-Pierre Augustin and Yaya-Karim Drabo, "La politique sportive menée au Burkina Faso de 1983 à 1988," *Géopolitique du sport*, pp. 171–77.

BIBLIOGRAPHY

Abmayr, Walter. "Afrika und Leichtathletik." In Andresen et al., pp. 58–71.

Adelman, Melvin L. *A Sporting Time*. Urbana: University of Illinois Press, 1986.

Albonago, Giovanni. "Fussball in Italien." In Huba, pp. 88–93.

Ali, Ramadhan. *Africa at the Olympics*. London: Africa Books, 1976.

Alkemeyer, Thomas. "Gewalt und Opfer im Ritual der Olympischen Spiele 1936." In Gebauer, pp. 44–79.

Alter, Joseph S. *The Wrestler's Body: Identity and Ideology in North India*. Berkeley: University of California Press, 1992.

Altham, H. S. *A History of Cricket*. London: George Allen & Unwin, 1962.

An Minseok and George H Sage. "The Golf Boom in South Korea: Serving Hegemonic Interests." *SSJ*, 9:4 (December 1992): 372–84.

Anderson, Benedict. *Imagined Communities: Reflections on the Origin and Spread of Nationalism*. rev. ed. New York: Verso, 1991.

Andresen, Rolf, Hermann Rieder, and Bernhard Trosien, eds. *Beiträge zur Zusammenarbeit im Sport in der Dritten Welt*. Schorndorf: Karl Hofmann, 1989.

Andrews, David L. and John W. Loy. "British Cultural Studies and Sport." *Quest*, 45:2 (May 1993): 255–76.

Andrieu, Gilbert. "L'Influence de la gymnastique suédoise sur l'éducation physique en France entre 1874 et 1914." *Stadion*, 14:2 (1988): 163–80.

Ang, Ien. *Watching "Dallas": Soap Opera and the Melodramatic Imagination*. London: Methuen, 1985.

Anthony, Don. "The North-South and East-West Axes of Development in Sport." In Landry et al., pp. 331–37.

Appadurai, Arjun. "Disjuncture and Difference in the Global Cultural Economy." *Theory, Culture and Society*, 7 (1990): 295–310.

Arantes do Nascimento, Edson and Robert L. Fish. *My Life and the Beautiful Game*. Garden City: Doubleday, 1977.

Araton, Harvey and Filip Bondy. *The Selling of the Green*. New York: HarperCollins, 1992.

Arbena, Joseph L. "The Diffusion of Modern European Sport in Latin America: A Case Study of Cultural Imperialism?" *South Eastern Latin Americanist*, 33:4 (March 1990): 1–8.

Arbena, Joseph L. "Sport and Nationalism in Latin America, 1880–1970." *History of European Ideas* 16:4–6 (1993): 837–44.

Arbena, Joseph L. "Sport and Revolution: The Continuing Cuban Experience." *Studies in Latin American Popular Culture*, 9 (1990): 319–28.

Arbena, Joseph L. "Sport and Social Change in Latin America." In Ingham and Loy, pp. 97–117.

Arbena, Joseph L., ed. *Sport and Society in Latin America: Diffusion, Dependency, and the Rise of Mass Culture*. Westport: Greenwood Press, 1988.

Arbena, Joseph L. "Sport, Development, and Mexican Nationalism, 1920–1970." *Journal of Sport History*, 18:3 (Winter 1991): 350–64.

Arlott, John. *The Ashes*. London: Pelham Books, 1972.

Arnason, Johann P. "Nationalism, Globalization and Modernity." *Theory, Culture and Society*, 7 (1990): 207–36.

Arnaud, Pierre. *Les Athlètes de la République*. Toulouse: Éditions Privat, 1987.

Arnaud, Pierre and Camy, J., eds. *La Naissance du mouvement sportif associatif en France.* Lyon: Presses Universitaires de Lyon, 1986.

Augustin, Jean-Pierre and Yaya-Karim Drabo. "La Politique sportive menée au Burkina Faso de 1983 à 1988." In Errais et al., pp. 171–77.

Avery Brundage Collection. University of Illinois Archives.

Azoy, G. Whitney. *Buzkashi: Game and Power in Afghanistan.* Philadelphia: University of Pennsylvania Press, 1982.

Baker, William J. *Sports in the Western World.* Totowa: Rowman and Littlefield, 1982.

Baker, William J. and J. A. Mangan, eds. *Sport in Africa.* New York: Africana, 1987.

Bale, John. *The Brawn Drain.* Urbana: University of Illinois Press, 1991.

Bale, John. "International Sports History as Innovation Diffusion." *CJHS,* 15:1 (May 1984): 36–63.

Bale, John. *Sport and Place: A Geography of Sport in England, Scotland and Wales.* London: C. Hurst, 1982.

Bale, John. "The Adoption of Football in Europe." *CJHS,* 11:2 (December 1980): 56–66.

Bale, John and Joseph Maguire, eds. *The Global Sports Arena.* London: Frank Cass, 1993.

Banta, Martha. *Imaging American Women.* New York: Columbia University Press, 1987.

Bargach, Sakina and Alain Moreau. "Les activités physiques et sportives, enjeu de l'émancipation des jeunes au Maroc." In Errais et al., pp. 141–52.

Barnes, Julian. "The Mystery of a Masterpiece." *New York Review,* 40:8 (April 22, 1993): 27–29.

Barnett, Steven. *Games and Sets: The Changing Face of Sport on Televison.* London: British Film Institute, 1990.

Barney, Robert Knight. "German Forty-Eighters and Turnvereine in the United States during the Antebellum Period." *CJHS,* 3:2 (December 1982): 62–79.

Barney, Robert Knight. "German-American Turnvereins and Socio-Politico-Economic Realities in the Antebellum and Civil War Upper and Lower South." *Stadion,* 10 (1984): 135–81.

Barreau, Jacques. "Traditions festives, activités ludiques et spectacle sportif." In Barreau and Jaouen, pp. 17–26.

Barreau, Jean-Jacques and Guy Jaouen, eds. *Éclipses et renaissance des jeux populaires*. Rennes: Fédération Internationale des Luttes Celtiques, 1990.

Barrull, Raymond. "L'Émergence de la gymnastique sportive à la fin du XIXe siècle en France." In Arnaud and Camy, pp. 55–84.

Bartlett, Arthur. *Baseball and Mr. Spalding*. New York: Farrar, Straus & Young, 1951.

Bayer, Osvaldo. *Fútbol Argentino*. Buenos Aires: Editorial Sudamericana, 1990.

Becker, Hartmut. *Antisemitismus in der Deutschen Turnerschaft*. Sankt Augustin: Hans Richarz, 1980.

Beezley, William H. "Bicycles, Modernization, and Mexico." In Arbena, pp. 15–28.

Beezley, William H. *Judas at the Jockey Club*. Lincoln: University of Nebraska Press, 1987.

Bennett, Bruce L. "The Making of Round Hill School." *Quest*, 4 (April 1965): 53–63.

Beran, Janice A. "Physical Education and Sport in the Philippines." In Wagner, pp. 147–64.

Berlage, Gai I. "Sociocultural History of the Origin of Women's Baseball at the Eastern Women's Colleges during the Victorian Period." In Hall, pp. 100–22.

Bernett, Hajo. "Die ersten 'olympischen' Wettbewerbe im internationalen Frauensport." *Sozial- und Zeitgeschichte des Sports*, 2:2 (1988): 66–86.

Bernett, Hajo. *Der jüdische Sport im nationalsozialistischen Deutschland, 1933–38*. Schorndorf: Karl Hofmann, 1978.

Bernett, Hajo. *Die pädagogische Neugestaltung der bürgerlichen Leibesübung durch die Philanthropen*. Schorndorf: Karl Hofmann, 1960.

Birley, Derek. *Sport and the Making of Britain*. Manchester: Manchester University Press, 1993.

Blanchard, Kendall. *The Mississippi Choctaws at Play*. Urbana: University of Illinois Press, 1981.

Blecking, Diethelm, ed. *Die slawische Sokolbewegung*. Dortmund: Forschungsstelle Ostmitteleuropa, 1991.

Blecking, Diethelm. "Zum historischen Problem der slawischen Sokolbewegung." In Blecking, pp. 7–22.

Bose, Mihir. *A History of Indian Cricket*. London: André Deutsch, 1990.

Bottenburg, Maarten van. "Als 'n Man Met een Baard op 'n Bokkewagen." *Vrijetijd en Samenleving*, 9:1 (1991): 5–27.

Bottenburg, Maarten van. "The Differential Popularization of Sports in Continental Europe." *The Netherlands Journal of Social Sciences*, 28:1 (April 1992): 3–30

Bowen, Rowland. *Cricket*. London: Eyre & Spottiswoode, 1970.

Boyd-Barrett, J. O. "Cultural Dependency and the Mass Media." In Gurevitch et al., pp. 174–95.

Bradley, James. "The MCC, Society and Empire." *IJHS*, 7:1 (May 1990): 3–22.

Brest, Enrique Romero, Alberto R. Dallo, and Simón Silvestrini. "Los Deportes y la Educación Fisica en la Republica Argentina." In Überhorst, *Geschichte*, 6:846–86.

Bromberger, Christian, Alain Havot, and Jean-Marc Mariottini. "Allez L'O.M.! Forza Juve!" *Terrain* 8 (April 1987): 8–41.

Brookes, Christopher. *English Cricket*. London: Weidenfeld & Nicolson, 1978.

Brousse, Michel. "Du Samouraï à l'athlète: l'essor du judo en France." *Sport et Histoire*, 3 (1989): 11–25.

Brown, David W. "Canadian Imperialism and Sporting Exchanges: The Nineteenth-Century Cultural Experience of Cricket and Lacrosse." *CJHS*, 18:1 (May 1987): 55–66.

Brown, David W. "Imperialism and Games on the Playing Fields of Canada's Private Schools." In Müller and Rühl, pp. 127–34.

Brown, David W. "Muscular Christianity in the Antipodes." *Sporting Traditions*, 3:2 (May 1987): 173–87.

Browne, Lois. *Girls of Summer*. New York: HarperCollins, 1993.

Brownfoot, Janice N.. "Emancipation, Exercise and Imperialism: Girls and the Games Ethic in Colonial Malaya." *IJHS*, 7:1 (May 1990): 61–84.

Burton, Julianne. "Don (Juanito) Duck and the Imperial-Patriarchal Unconscious: Disney Studies, the Good Neighbor Policy, and the Packing of Latin America". In Parker et al., pp. 21–41.

Buzzetti, José and Eduardo Gutierrez Cortinas. *Historia del Deporte en el Uruguay (1830–1900)*. Montivideo: Talleres Graficos Castro, 1965.

Byrd, William. *Secret Diary*, eds. Louis B. Wright and Marion Tinling. Richmond: Dietz Press, 1941.

Cady, Edwin. *The Big Game*. Knoxville: University of Tennessee Press, 1978.

Callebat, Louis. *Pierre de Coubertin*. Paris: Fayard, 1988.

Cardoso, Fernando Henrique and Enzo Faletto. *Dependency and Development in Latin America*. Trans. Marjory Mattingly Urquidi. Berkeley: University of California Press, 1979.

Carr, Kevin Gray. "Making Way: War, Philosophy, and Sport in Japanese Judo." *Journal of Sport History*, 20:2 (Summer 1993): 167–88.

Carter, John Marshall and Arnd Krüger, eds. *Ritual and Record*. Westport: Greenwood Press, 1990.

Casas, Edel, Jorge Alfonso and Alberto Pestna. *Viva y en Juego*. Havana: Editorial Cientifico Técnica, 1986.

Cashman, Richard. *'Ave a Go, yer Mug! Australian Cricket Crowds from Larrikin to Ocker*. Sydney: Collins, 1984.

Cashman, Richard. "Cricket and Colonialism: Colonial Hegemony and Indigenous Subversion." In Mangan, *Pleasure, Profit, Proselytism*, pp. 258–72.

Cashman, Richard. *Patrons, Players and the Crowd: The Phenomenon of Indian Cricket*. New Delhi: Longman Orient, 1980.

Cashman, Richard. "Symbols of Unity: Anglo-Australian Cricketers, 1877–1900." *IJHS*, 7:1 (May 1990): 97–110.

Cashman, Richard and Amanda Weaver. *Wicket Women: Cricket and Women in Australia*. Kensington: New South Wales University Press, 1991.

Chambat, P. "Les Fêtes de la discipline: gymnastique et politique en France (1879–1914)." In Arnaud and Camy, pp. 85–96.

Chandler, Timothy J. L. "Games at Oxbridge and the Public Schools, 1830–80: The Diffusion of an Innovation." *IJHS*, 18: 2 (September 1991): 171–204.

Chaponick, Héctor Alberto. *Historia del Fútbol Argentino*. 3 vols. Buenos Aires: Editorial Eiffel, 1955.

Chappelet, J. L. *Le Système olympique*. Grenoble: Presses universitaires de Grenoble, 1991.

Clayton, Anthony. "Sport and African Soldiers: The Military Diffusion of Western Sport throughout Sub-Saharan Africa." In Baker and Mangan, pp. 114–37.

Clumpner, Roy. "Federal Involvement in Sport to Promote American Interest of Foreign Policy Objectives, 1950–1973." In Lowe, Kanin and Strenk, pp. 400–52.

Coadic, Laurent. "Implantation et diffusion du football en Bretagne (1890–1925)." *Sport et Histoire*, n.s., 1 (1992): 27–50.

Cockcroft, James D., André Gunder Frank, and Dale L. Johnson, eds. *Dependence and Underdevelopment.* Garden City: Doubleday-Anchor Books, 1972.

Colomé, Gabriel. "Il Barcelona e la società catalana." In Lanfranchi, pp. 59–65.

Coubertin, Pierre de. *Mémoires olympiques.* Lausanne: Bureau international de pédagogie sportive, 1931.

Coubertin, Pierre de. *Une Campagne de vingt-et-un ans (1887–1908).* Paris: Librairie de l'Éducation physique, 1909.

Crawford, Ray. "Sport for Young Ladies: The Victorian Independent Schools, 1875–1925." *Sporting Traditions*, 1:1 (November 1984): 61–82.

Crawford, Scott A. G. M. "Muscles and Charactrer Are There the First Object of Necessity." *British Journal of Sports History*, 2:2 (September 1985): 109–26.

Crawford, Scott. A. G. M. "Patterns of Leisure in Early Otago-New Zealand." *Stadion*, 5:1 (1979): 42–67.

Crawford, Scott A. G. M. "Rugby in Contemporary New Zealand." *Journal of Sport and Social Issues*, 12:2 (Fall 1988): 108–21.

Crawford, Scott A. G. M. "Sport at the End of the World." In Überhorst, *Geschichte*, 6: 174–96.

Crawford, Scott A. G. M. "We Have Rough Labour But We Can Afford a Day for Recreation Too." *Stadion*, 10 (1984): 95–133.

Crepeau, Richard C. "Pearl Harbor: A Failure of Baseball?" *Journal of Popular Culture*, 15:4 (Spring 1982): 67–74.

Crum, Bart. "A Critical Analysis of Korfball as a 'Non-Sexist Sport,'" *IRSS*, 23:3 (1988): 233–40.

Cummings, Christine. "The Ideology of West Indian Cricket." *Arena Review*, 14:1 (May 1990): 25–32.

Cuyler, P. L. *Sumo: From Rite to Sport.* New York: Weatherhill, 1979.

D'Almeida-Topor, Hélène, Odile Goerg, Catherine Coquery-Vidrovitch, and Françoise Guitart, eds. *Les Jeunes en afrique.* Paris: Harmattan, 1992.

Dabscheck, Braham. "A Long Deep Drive into Centre Field? Australian Baseball Turns Professional." *Australian Society for Sports History Bulletin* (March 1991): 14–19.

Daly, John A. *Elysian Fields: Sport, Class and Community in Colonial South Australia, 1836–1890*. Adelaide: John A. Daly, 1982.

Daly, John A. "A New Britannia in the Antipodes: Sport, Class and Community in Colonial South Australia." In Mangan, *Pleasure, Profit, Proselytism*, pp. 163–74.

Dauphinais, Paul R. "A Class Act: French-Canadians in Organized Sport, 1840–1910." *IJHS*, 7:3 (December 1990): 432–42.

Davies, Christopher. "A Jolly Good Show." *Sports Illustrated*, 74:23 (June 17, 1991): 50.

Davis, Parke H. *Football: The American Intrercollegiate Game*. New York: Scribner's, 1911.

Defrance, Jacques. *L'Excellence corporelle: la formation des activités physiques et sportives modernes, 1770–1914*. Rennes: Presses universitaires de Rennes, 1987.

Demak, Richard. "Bridge Over Troubled Water." *Sports Illustrated*, 75:23 (November 25, 1991): 16–23.

Desmonde, William H. "The Bull-Fight as a Religious Ritual." *American Imago*, 9 (June 1952): 173–95.

Dettori, Anna Biano. "Traditionelle Spiele im Aostatal." In Eichberg and Hansen, pp. 25–30.

Deville-Danthu, Bernadette. "L'AOF pépinière d'athlètes: révelation, illusions et désillusions." In *Jeux et sports dans l'histoire*, pp. 255–70.

Deville-Danthu, Bernadette. "Les Jeux d'outre mer." In Hick, pp. 61–68.

Deville-Danthu, Bernadette. "Note sur l'histoire du sport dans l'empire français." In Hick, pp. 10–13.

Deville-Danthu, Bernadette. "La Participation des sportifs indigènes à l'Exposition Coloniale Internationale de Paris de 1931." *Sport et Histoire*, n.s., 2 (1992): 9–26.

Deville-Danthu, Bernadette. "Les Premières tentatives d'encadrement des activités physiques et sportives de la jeunesse en A.O.F. (1922–1936)." In D'Almeida-Topor et al., pp. 448–62.

DiDonato, Michele. :"Italien." In Überhorst, *Geschichte*, 5:239–64.

DiDonato, Michele. "Sport and Physical Education in Italy." In William Johnson, pp. 354–65.

Diem, Carl. *Asiatische Reiterspiele*. Berlin: Deutscher Archiv Verlag, 1941.

Dorfman, Ariel and Mattelart, Armand. *How to Read Donald Duck: Imperialist Ideology in the Disney Comic*. New York: International General, 1984.

Dulles, Foster Rhea. *America Learns to Play*. New York: D. Appleton-Century, 1940.

Dunning, Eric and Kenneth Sheard. *Barbarians, Gentlemen and Players*. Oxford: Martin Robertson, 1979.

Dunning, Eric G., Joseph A. Maguire, and Robert E. Pearton, eds. *The Sports Process*. Champaign: Human Kinetics, 1993.

D'Urso, Catherine E. "A View of American Attitudes toward Femininity: The History of Physical Education for Women and Collegiate Women's Basketball." Amherst: Amherst College, 1989.

Durso, Joseph. *The Days of Mr. McGraw*. Englewood Cliffs: Prentice-Hall, 1969.

Ehrenberg, Alain. *Le Culte de la performance*. Paris: Calmann-Lévy, 1991.

Eichberg, Henning. "The Enclosure of the Body." *Journal of Contemporary History*, 21 (1986): 100–18.

Eichberg, Henning. "Leistung zwischen Wänden—die sportive Parzellierung der Körper." *Berliner Historische Studien*, 9 (1983): 119–39.

Eichberg, Henning. *Leistungsräume: Sport als Umweltproblem*. Münster: LIT-Verlag, 1988.

Eichberg, Henning. "Olympic Sport—Neocolonization and Alternatives." *IRSS*, 19:1 (1984): 97–105.

Eichberg, Henning. "A Revolution of Body Culture: Traditional Games on the Way from Modernisation to 'Postmodernity'." In Barreau and Jaouen, pp. 101–29.

Eichberg, Henning. "Spielverhalten und Relationsgesellschaft in West Sumatra." *Stadion* 1:1 (1975): 1–48.

Eichberg, Henning. "Travelling, Comparing, Emigrating: Configurations of Sport Mobility." In Bale and Maguire, pp. 256–80.

Eichberg, Henning. "Trommeltanz der Inuit." In Eichberg and Hansen, pp. 51–64.

Eichberg, Henning. "Vom Tristram Shandy zu 'Marschall Vorwärts': Zur sozialen Zeit der Körper in Sport, Krieg und Fort-Schritt." *Sportwissenschaft*, 19:3 (1989): 272–96.

Eichberg, Henning. "Von der grünen Heide zur fensterlosen Halle." *Jahrbuch der Turnkunst*, 76 (1981–82): 73–85.

Eichberg, Henning. *Der Weg des Sports in die industrielle Zivilisation*. 2nd ed. Baden-Baden: Nomos, 1979.

Eichberg, Henning. "Zielgraden und Krumme Linien." *Stadion*, 10 (1984): 227–45.

Eichberg, Henning and Jörn Hansen, eds. *Körperkultur und Identität.* Münster: LIT Verlag, 1989.

Eichberg, Henning and Ali Yehia El Mansouri. "Sport in Libya." In Überhorst, *Geschichte,* 6:261–73.

Eisenberg, Christiane. "Football in Germany: Beginnings, 1890–1914." *IJHS,* 8:2 (September 1991): 205–20.

Emery, Lynn. "The First Intercollegiate Contest for Women." In Howell, *Her Story in Sport,* pp. 417–23.

Errais, Borhane, Daniel Mathieu, and Jean Praicheux, eds. *Géopolitique du sport.* Besançon: Université de Franche-Comté, 1990.

Errais, Borhane. "La Planète sportive." In Landry et al., pp. 579–85.

Espy, Richard. *The Politics of the Olympic Games.* Berkeley: University of California Press, 1979.

Evanson, Philip. "Understanding the People: *Fútbol,* Film, Theater and Politics in Present-Day Brazil." *South Atlantic Quarterly,* 81:4 (Autumn 1982): 399–412.

Eyquem, Marie-Thérèse. *Pierre de Coubertin.* Paris: Calmann-Lévy, 1966.

Fabrizio, Felice. *Storia dello Sport in Italia..* Rimini: Guaraldi, 1977.

Fates, Yossef. "Sport en Algérie." In Überhorst, 6:297–318

Filter, Frank. "Fussballsport in der Arbeiter Turn- und Sportbewegung." *Sozial- und Zeitgeschichte des Sports,* 2:1 (1988): 55–73.

Fischer, David Hackett. *Albion's Seed: Four British Folkways in America.* New York: Oxford University Press, 1989.

Fishwick, Nicholas. *English Football and Society, 1910–1950.* Manchester: Manchester University Press, 1989.

Fletcher, Sheila. *Women First: The Female Tradition in English Physical Education.* London: Athlone Press, 1984.

Flint, Rachel Heyhoe and Netta Rheinberg. *Fair Play: The Story of Women's Cricket.* London: Angus & Robertson, 1976.

Frank, André Gunder. *Capitalism and Underdevelopment in Latin America.* New York: Monthly Review Press, 1967.

Frey, James H. "The Internal and External Role of Sport in National Development." *Journal of National Development,* 1 (Winter 1988): 65–82.

Galtung, Johan. "The Sport System as a Metaphor for the World System." In Landry et al., pp. 147–55.

Ganga, Jean-Claude. *Combats pour un sport africain.* Paris: L'Harmattan, 1979.

Gardner, Paul. *The Simplest Game*. Boston: Little, Brown, 1976.

Gebauer, Gunter, ed. *Körper und Einbildungskraft: Inszenierungen des Helden im Sport*. Berlin: Dietrich Reimer, 1988.

Gebauer, Gunter and Wulf, Christoph. "Die Spiele der Gewalt." In Gebauer, pp. 11–30.

Gehrmann, Siegfried. "Der F. C. Schalke 04." In Hopf, pp. 117–20.

Geldbach, Erich. "Die Verpflanzung des Deutschen Turnens nach Ameria: Beck, Follen, Lieber." *Stadion*, 1:2 (1975): 331–76.

Georges, Jacques. "Fédération Française de Football." In *Sport de France*, pp. 109–15.

Geyer, Horst. "Stellvertreter der Nation." In Richter, pp. 75–87.

Ghirelli, Antonio. *Storia del Calcio in Italia*. rev. ed. Turin: Giulio Einaudi, 1990.

Gieseler, Karlheinz. "Junge Völker—neuer Sport?" *Zeitschrift für Kulturaustausch*, 27:4 (1977): 12–19.

Gissua, James and Michael Hess. "Icing the Cake? Colonialism, Institutional Transfer and Sport in Papua New Guinea." *Sporting Traditions*, 10:1 (November 1993): 78–91.

Glanville, Brian. *Soccer*. London: Eyre & Spottiswoode, 1969.

Godia, George. "Sport in Kenya." In Wagner, pp. 267–81.

Goldstein, Warren. *Playing for Keeps*. Ithaca: Cornell University Press, 1989.

Goodger, B. C. and J. M. Goodger. "Judo in the Light of Theory and Sociological Research." *IRSS*, 12:1 (1977): 5–34.

Goodger, B. C. and J. M. Goodger. "Organisational and Cultural Change in Post-War British Judo." *IRSS*, 15:1 (1980): 21–48.

Goodger, J. M. "Pluralism, Transmission and Change in Sport." *Quest*, 38 (1986): 135–47.

Graham, Cooper C. *Leni Riefenstahl and Olympia*. Metuchen: Scarecrow Press, 1986.

Gramsci, Antonio. *Selections from the Prison Notebooks*. Trans. Quinton Hoare and Geoffrey Nowell Smith. New York: International Publishers, 1971.

Gregorich, Barbara. *Women at Play: The Story of Women in Baseball*. New York: Harcourt, Brace, 1993.

Gruneau, Richard. "The Critique of Sport in Modernity." In Dunning, Maguire and Pearton, pp. 85–109.

Grupe, Ommo. "The Sport Culture and the Sportization of Culture." In Landry et al., pp. 135–45.

Gurevitch, Michael, Tony Bennett, James Curran, and Janet Woollacott, eds. *Culture, Society and the Media*. London: Methuen, 1982.

Guttmann, Allen. *From Ritual to Record*. New York: Columbia University Press, 1978.

Guttmann, Allen. *The Games Must Go On: Avery Brundage and the Olympic Movement*. New York: Columbia University Press, 1984.

Guttmann, Allen. *The Olympics*. Urbana: University of Illinois Press, 1992.

Guttmann, Allen. *A Whole New Ball Game*. Chapel Hill: University of North Carolina Press, 1988.

Guttmann, Allen. *Women's Sports: A History*. New York: Columbia University Press, 1991.

Hanson, Joseph Mills, ed. *The Inter-Allied Games*. Paris: The Games Committee, 1919.

Hart, Marie and Susan Birrell, eds. *Sport in the Sociolcultural Process*. 3rd ed. Dubuque: William C. Brown, 1981.

Hazan, Baruch. "Sport as an Instrument of Political Expansion." In Baker and Mangan, pp. 250–71.

Heinemann, Klaus. "Sport und Entwicklungshilfe in Ländern der Dritten Welt." *Sportwissenschaft*, 15:3 (1985): 227–44.

Hick, Daniel, ed. *L'Empire du sport*. Aix-en-Provence: Centre des Archives d'Outre-Mer, 1992.

Hill, Christopher R. *Olympic Politics*. Manchester: University of Manchester Press, 1992.

Hill, Jeffrey. "Cricket and the Imperial Connection." In Bale and Maguire, pp. 49–61.

Hirth, Michael. "Éducation physique et sport en République Islamique du Mauritanie." In Überhorst, *Geschichte*, 6:335–55.

Holmäng, Per Olof. "International Sports Organizations, 1919–1925." *IJHS*, 9:3 (December 1991): 458–60.

Holmes, Roger. "The Survival and Revival of Traditional Sports and Games in Cornwall." In Barreau and Jaouen, pp. 51–58.

Holt, Richard. *Sport and Society in Modern France*. London: Macmillan, 1981.

Holt, Richard. *Sport and the British*. Oxford: Clarendon Press, 1989.

Honga, Emmanuel Abolo Biwole Siegfried. "Histoire des activités physiques traditionelles et du sport moderne au Cameroun de la période coloniale à nos jours." In Überhorst, *Geschichte*, 6:391–401.

Hopf, Wilhelm, ed. *Fussball*. Bensheim: Pädagogischer Extra Buchverlag, 1979.

Hopf, Wilhelm. "Wie könnte Fussball ein deutsches Spiel werden?." In Hopf, pp. 54–80.

Howell, Maxwell L. and Reet A. Howell, "Sport in Australia". In Überhorst, *Geschichte*, 6:107–67.

Howell, Nancy and Maxwell L Howell. *Sports and Games in Canadian Life*. Toronto: Macmillan of Canada, 1969.

Huba, Karl Heinz, ed. *Fussball Weltgeschichte*. Munich: Copress, 1988.

Hubscher, Ronald, Jean Durry, and Bernard Jeu. *L'Histoire en mouvements: le sport dans la société française*. Paris: Armand Collin, 1992.

Hurtebize, Claude. "Géopolitique de la genèse, de la diffusion et des interactions culturelles dans la culture corporelle et le sport." In Errais et al., pp. 87–114.

Husmann, Rolf. "'Nuba Wrestling': Von traditionellen Ringkämpfen zur modernen Sportveranstaltung im Sudan." In Jäger and Prohl, pp. 50–63.

Husmann, Rolf and Meier, Christoph. "Nuba-Ringen in Khartum." In Streck, pp. 69–84.

Iluffi, Milton Coffré. "Historia del Deporte y la Educación Fisica en Chile." In Überhorst *Geschichte*, 6:721–51.

Infield, Glenn B. *Leni Riefenstahl*. New York: Crowell, 1976.

Ingham, Alan G. and John W. Loy, eds. *Sport and Social Development*. Champaign: Human Kinetics, 1993.

Jable, J. Thomas. "Latter-Day Cultural Imperialists: British Influence on the Establishment of Cricket in Philadelphia, 1842–1872." In Mangan, *Pleasure, Profit, Proselytism*, pp. 175–92.

Jäger, Klaus and Robert Prohl, eds. *Unterrichtsmedien im Sport—gesamtdeutsch*. Erlensee: SFT-Verlag, 1993.

Jahn, Friedrich Ludwig. *Werke*, ed. Carl Euler. 2 vols. Hof: Verlag von G. A. Grau, 1884–85.

James, C. L. R. *Beyond a Boundary*. 2nd ed. New York: Pantheon Books, 1983.

James, C. L. R. "Cricket in West Indian Culture." *New Society*, 1 (June 6, 1963): 8–9.

Jaouen, Guy. "Gouren: Jeu et sport de lutte." In Eichberg and Hansen, pp. 15–24.

Jaques, T. D. and G. R. Pavia, eds. *Sport in Australia*. Sydney: McGraw-Hill, 1976.

Jeux et sports dans l'histoire. Paris: Comité des travaux historiques et scientifiques, 1992.

John, Hans-Georg. *Politik und Turnen: Die Deutsche Turnerschaft als nationale Bewegung im Deutschen Kaiserreich von 1871–1914*. Ahrensburg: Czwalina, 1976.

Johnson, Elmer L. *The History of YMCA Physical Education*. Chicago: Follett, 1979.

Johnson, William, ed. *Sport and Physical Education around the World*. Champaign: Stipes, 1980.

Joseph, Gilbert M. "Forging the Regional Pastime: Baseball and Class in Yucatán." In Arbena, pp. 29–61.

Joy, Nancy. *Maiden Over*. London: Sporting Handbooks, 1950.

Joyce, Gare. *The Only Ticket Off the Island*. Toronto: Lester and Orpen Dennys, 1990.

Kessler, Wolfgang. "Der Sokol in den jugoslawischen Gebieten." In Blecking, pp. 198–218.

Kidd, Bruce. "Sport, Dependency, and the Canadian State." In Hart and Birrell, pp. 707–21.

King, Peter. "World Beater." *Sports Illustrated*, 76:20 (May 25, 1992): 42–44.

Kirbus, Federico B. "Fussball in Uruguay." In Huba, pp. 125–28.

Kirk-Greene, Anthony. "Badge of Office? Sport and His Excellency in the British Empire." *IJHS*, 6:2 (September 1989): 218–41.

Kirk-Greene, Anthony. "Imperial Adminstration and the Athletic Imperative: The Case of the District Officer in Africa." In Baker and Mangan, pp. 81–113.

Kirkpatrick, Curry. "Sitting Pretty in Rome." *Sports Illustrated*, 71:16 (October 9, 1989): 27–34.

Kirsch, George B. *The Creation of American Team Sports: Baseball and Cricket, 1838–72*. Urbana: University of Illinois Press, 1989.

Kirsch, George B. "New Jersey and the Rise of American Sports, 1820–1870." *Journal of Regional Cultures*, 4–5 (1984–85): 41–57.

Kirsch, George B. "The Rise of Modern Sports: New Jersey Cricketers, Baseball Players, and Clubs, 1845–60." *New Jersey History*, 101 (Spring–Summer 1983): 53–83.

Klein, Alan M. "Sport and Colonialism in Latin America and the Caribbean." *Studies in Latin American Popular Culture*, 10 (1991): 257–71.

Klein, Alan M. "Sport and Culture as Contested Terrain: Americanization in the Caribbean." *SSJ*, 8:1 (March 1991): 79–85.

Klein, Alan M. *Sugarball: The American Game, the Dominican Dream*. New Haven: Yale University Press, 1991.

Klein, Alan. "Baseball as Underdevelopment: The Political-Economy of Sport in the Dominican Republic." *SSJ*, 6:2 (June 1989): 95–112.

Kleindienst-Cachay, Christa. *Die Verschulung des Turnens*. Schorndorf: Karl Hofmann, 1980.

Kokusai Bunka Shinkokai. *Sports*. Tokyo: Kokusai Bunka Shinkokai, 1939.

Kolatch, Jonathan. *Sports, Politics, and Ideology in China*. New York: Jonathan David, 1972.

Krämer-Mandeau, Wolf. "Figuration, Formation, Umbruch und Identität." Berlin: "Spiele der Welt-Welt der Spiele" Congress, 1993.

Krämer-Mandeau, Wolf. "Gymnastic Systems and Turner Movement [sic]." In Naul, pp. 21–49.

Krämer-Mandeau, Wolf. "Ocupación, Dominación y Liberación—La Historia del Deporte en Nicaragua." In Überhorst, 6:1039–67.

Krämer-Mandeau, Wolf. *Sport und Körpererziehung auf Cuba*. Cologne: Pahl-Rugenstein, 1988.

Krich, John. *El Béisbol*. New York: Atlantic Monthly Press, 1989.

Krockow, Christian von. *Sport und Industriegesellschaft*. Munich: Piper, 1972.

Krüger, Arnd and John McClelland, eds. *Die Anfänge des modernen Sports in der Renaissance*. London: Arena, 1984.

Krüger, Michael. "Das Turnen als reaktionäres Mittel: Wilhelm Angerstein und die Disziplinierung des Turnens." *Sportwissenschaft*, 23:1 (1991): 9–34.

Laage, Rolf von der. *Sport in China*. Berlin: Bartels & Wernitz, 1977.

Lacroix, Gisèle. "Le look fun et ses enjeux." In Errais et al., pp. 61–72.

Landry, Fernand, Marc Landry, and Magdeleine Yerlès, eds. *Sport: The Third Millennium*. Sainte-Foy: Presses de l'Université Laval, 1991.

Lanfranchi, Pierre, ed. *Il Calcio e il suo Pubblico*. Naples: Edizioni Scientifiche Italiane, 1992.

Lanfranchi, Pierre. "Apparition et affirmation du football en Languedoc 1900–1935." In Arnaud and Camy, pp. 259–73.

Lanfranchi, Pierre. "The Migration of Footballers: The Case of France." In Bale and Maguire, pp. 63–77.

Lanfranchi, Pierre. "Rugby contro Calcio: La Genesi delle due Pratiche

Sportive nella Francia Meridionale." *Ricerche Storiche*, 19:2 (May–August 1989): 1–13.

Lapchick, Richard E. *The Politics of Race and International Sport: The Case of South Africa*. Westport: Greenwood Press, 1975.

Laqueur, Hans-Peter. *Zur kulturgeschichtlichen Stellung des türkischen Ringkampfs einst und jetzt*. Frankfurt: Peter Lang, 1979.

Lema, Bangela. "Sport in Zaire." In Wagner, pp. 229–47.

LeQuesne, Laurence. *The Bodyline Controversy*. London: Secker & Warburg, 1983.

Lever, Janet. *Soccer Madness*. Chicago: University of Chicago Press, 1983.

Levine, Peter. *A. G. Spalding and the Rise of Baseball*. New York: Oxford University Press, 1985.

Levine, R. M. "The Burden of Success: *Futebol* and Brazilian Society through the 1970s." *Journal of Popular Culture*, 14 (1980: 453–64.

Lewis, Robert M. "Cricket and the Beginnings of Organized Baseball in New York City." *IJHS*, 4:3 (December 1987): 315–32.

Lewis, J. Lowell. *Ring of Liberation: Deceptive Discourse in Brazilian Capoeira*. Chicago: University of Chicago Press, 1992.

Liebes, Tamar and Elihu Katz. "On the Critical Abilities of Television Viewers." In Seiter et al., pp. 204–22.

Lindner, Rolf and Heinrich T. Breuer. *Sind Doch Nicht Alles Beckenbauers*. Frankfurt: Syndikat, 1978.

Lowe, Benjamin, David B. Kanin, and Andrew Strenk, eds. *Sport and International Relations*. Champaign: Stipes, 1978.

Lucas, John A. and Ronald A. Smith. *Saga of American Sport*. Philadelphia: Lea & Febiger, 1978.

MacAloon, John J. *This Great Symbol: Pierre de Coubertin and the Origins of the Modern Olympic Games*. Chicago: University of Chicago Press, 1981.

MacAloon, John J. "The Turn of Two Centuries: Sport and the Politics of Intercultural Relations." In Landry et al., pp. 31–44.

Magoun, Francis Peabody. *History of Football: From the Beginnings to 1871*. Bochum: Pöppinghaus, 1938.

Maguire, Joseph. "American Football, British Society, and Global Sport Development." In Dunning, Maguire and Pearton, pp. 207–15.

Maguire, Joseph. "American Labour Migrants, Globalisation and the Making of English Basketball." In Bale and Maguire, pp. 226–55.

Maguire, Joseph. "The Commercialization of English Elite Basketball, 1972–1988." *IRSS*, 23:4 (1988): 305–22.

Maguire, Joseph. "Globalization, Sport and National Identities: 'The Empires Strike Back,'" *Loisir et Société*, 16:2 (Autumn 1993): 293–322.

Maguire, Joseph. "The Media-Sport Production Complex: The Case of American Football in Western European Societies." *European Journal of Communication*, 6 (1991): 315–36.

Maguire, Joseph. "More Than a Sporting Touchdown: The Making of American Football in England 1982–1990." *SSJ*, 7:3 (September 1990): 213–37.

Mandell, Richard D. *Sport: A Cultural History*. New York: Columbia University Press, 1984.

Mandell, Richard D. *The First Modern Olympics*. Berkeley: University of California Press, 1976.

Mandle, Jay R. and Joan D. Mandle. "Basketball, Civil Society and the Post Colonial State in the Commonwealth Caribbean." *Journal of Sport and Social Issues*, 14:2 (Fall 1990): 59–75.

Mandle, Jay R. and Joan D. Mandle. *Grass Roots Commitment: Basketball and Society in Trinidad and Tobago*. Parkersburg: Caribbean Books, 1988.

Mandle, William F. "Cricket and Australian Nationalism in the 19th Century." *Journal of the Royal Australian Historical Society*, 59:4 (December 1973): 225–46.

Mangan, J. A., ed. *The Cultural Bond: Sport, Empire and Society* (London: Frank Cass, 1992).

Mangan, J. A. "Christ and the Imperial Games Fields." *British Journal of Sports History*, 1:2 (September 1984): 184–201.

Mangan, J. A. "Ethics and Ethnocentricity: Imperial Education in British Tropical Africa." In Baker and Mangan, pp. 31–44.

Mangan, J. A., ed.. *The Games Ethic and Imperialism*. New York: Viking Press, 1986.

Mangan, J. A., ed. *Pleasure, Profit, Proselytism*. London: Frank Cass, 1988.

Martin, Phyllis M. "Colonialism, Youth and Football in French Equatorial Africa." *IJHS*, 8:1 (May 1991): 56–71.

Marvin, Garry. *Bullfight*. Oxford: Basil Blackwell, 1988.

Masmoudi, Mustapha. "The New World Information Order." *Journal of Communication*, 29:2 (Spring 1979): 172–85.

Mason, Tony. *Association Football and English Society, 1863–1915*. Atlantic Highlands: Humanities Press, 1980.

Mason, Tony. "Football on the Maidan: Cultural Imperialism in Calcutta." *IJHS*, 7:1 (1990): 85–96.

Mason, Tony. "Some Englishmen and Scotsmen Abroad." In Tomlinson and Whannel, pp. 67–82.

Mattelart, Armand. *L'Internationale publicitaire*. Paris: Éditions la Découverte, 1989.

Matusik, Przemyslaw. "Der polnische 'Sokol' zur Zeit der Teilungen und in der II. Polnischen Republik." In Blecking, pp. 104–35.

May, William R. "Sports." In Powers and Kato, pp. 167–95.

Mayer, Otto. *A travers les anneaux olympiques*. Geneva: Cailler, 1960.

Mazrui, Ali A. "Africa's Triple Heritage of Play." In Baker and Mangan, pp. 217–28.

McCallum, Jack. "Tomorrow the World." *Sports Illustrated*, 69:20 (November 7, 1988): 58–63.

McCrone, Kathleen E. *Playing the Game: Sport and the Physical Emancipation of English Women, 1870–1914*. Lexington: University Press of Kentucky, 1988.

McIntosh, Peter, J. G. Dixon, A. D. Munrow, and R. F. Willetts. *Landmarks in the History of Physical Education*. 3rd ed. London: Routledge & Kegan Paul, 1981.

McKay, Jim and Toby Miller. "From Old Boys to Men and Women of the Corporation: The Americanization and Commodification of Australian Sport." *SSJ*, 18:1 (March 1991): 89–91.

McPhail, Thomas L. *Electronic Colonialism*. 2nd ed. Newbury Park: Sage Publications, 1987.

Melik-Chaknazarov, Achot. *Le Sport en afrique*. Paris: Présence africaine, 1970.

Melville, Tom. "The Passing of Philadelphia Cricket." *IJHS*, 10:1 (April 1993): 87–92.

Merwe, Floris J. G. van der. "History and Development of Sport in Southwest Africa and Namibia." In Überhorst, *Geschichte*, 6:71–101.

Metcalfe, Alan. *Canada Learns to Play*. Toronto: McClelland & Stewart, 1987.

Midwinter, Eric. *W. G. Grace*. London: George Allen & Unwin, 1981.

Miller, David. *The Olympic Revolution*. New York: Pavilion Books, 1992.

Mitchell, Bruce. "Baseball in Australia." *Sporting Traditions*, 7:1 (November 1990): 2–24.

Mitchell, Bruce. "A National Game Goes International." *IJHS*, 9:2 (August 1992): 288–301.

Mitchell, Timothy. *Blood Sport: A Social History of Spanish Bullfighting*.

Philadelphia: University of Pennsylvania Press, 1991.

Mitchell, Timothy. "Bullfighting: The Ritual Origin of Scholarly Myths." *Journal of American Folklore*, 99 (October-December 1986): 394–414.

Mitev, Losan. "Die Entwicklung der Turngesellschaften 'Sokol' und 'Junak' in Bulgarien bis zum Jahr 1914." In Blecking, pp. 175–81.

Mohamed, Ben Larbi and Borhane Errais. "Un Siècle d'histoire du sport en Tunisie, 1881–1981." In Überhorst, *Geschichte*, 6:276–92.

Moore, Katharine. "The Pan-Britannic Festival." In Mangan, *Pleasure, Profit, Proselytism*, pp. 144–62.

Morales, Franklin. "Historia del Deporte del Uruguay." In Überhorst, *Geschichte*, pp. 978–85.

Morris, Michael (Lord Killanin). *My Olympic Years*. London: Secker & Warburg, 1983.

Morrow, Don, Mary Keyes, Wayne Simpson, Frank Cosentino, and Ron Lappage. *A Concise History of Sport in Canada*. Toronto: Oxford University Press, 1989.

Möller, Jörg. "Der deutsche Azt Erwin von Bälz und die Entwicklung von Körperkultur und Sport in Japan." *Stadion*, 16:1 (1990): 129–41.

Müller, Norbert and Joachim K. Rühl, eds. *Olympic Scientific Congress 1984: Official Report: Sport History*. Niedernhausen: Schors Verlag, 1985).

N'Senga, Diakabana. "Genèse et développement du sport en République du Zaïre." In Überhorst, *Geschichte*, 6:404–17.

Naismith, James. "Basket-Ball." *American Physical Education Review*, 19:5 (May 1914): 339–51.

Naismith, James. *Basketball*. New York: Association Press, 1941.

Naul, Roland, ed. *Turnen and Sport*. New York: Waxmann, 1991.

Nauright, John. "Sport, Manhood and Empire: British Responses to the New Zealand Rugby Tour of 1905." *IJHS*, 8:2 (September 1991): 239–55.

Neirynck, Robert. "De Scholen der Jozefieten, Xaverianen en Benediktijnen en de Ontwikkeling van de Voetbalsport in Belgie (1863–1895)." Louvain: Catholic University of Louvain, 1985.

Neuendorff, Edmund. *Geschichte der neueren deutschen Leibesübungen vom Beginn des 18. Jahrhunderts bis zur Gegenwart*. 4 vols. Dresden: Limpert, 1934.

Neumann, Hannes. *Die deutsche Turnbewegung in der Revolution 1948/49 und in der amerikanischen Emigration*. Schorndorf: Karl Hofmann, 1968.

Nolte, Claire. "'Our Task, Direction and Goal': The Development of the

Sokol National Program to World War I." In Blecking, pp. 37–52.

Obermann, Holger. "Fussball als Exportartikel." In Andresen et al., pp. 249–66.

Odendaal, André. "South Africa's Black Victorians: Sport and Society in South Africa in the Nineteenth Century." In Mangan, *Pleasure, Profit, Proselytism*, pp. 193–214.

Ojeme, E. O. "Sport in Nigeria." In Wagner, pp. 249–66.

Okindutire, Olu. "The Historical Development of Soccer in Nigeria." *CJHS*, 22:1 (May 1991): 20–31.

Oleksak, Michael M. and Mary Adams Oleksak. *Béisbol: Latin Americans and the Grand Old Game*. Grand Rapids: Masters Press, 1991.

Olivera, Eduardo A. *Origenes de los Deportes Britanicos en el Río de la Plata*. Buenos Aires: L. J. Rosso, 1932.

Onifade, Ademola. "Historical Development of Amateur Sports and Their Administrative Agencies in Nigeria." *CJHS*, 16:2 (December 1985): 33–43.

Oriard, Michael. *Reading Football*. Chapel Hill: University of North Carolina Press, 1993.

Osayimwen-Oladipo, Helen. "The Historical Development of Sport in Nigeria." In Überhorst, *Geschichte*, 6:466–76.

Palmer, Harry Clay, ed. *Athletic Sports in America, England, and Australia*. Philadelphia: Hubbard Bros., 1889.

Panico, Guido. "Le Origini del foot-ball in Italia." In Lanfranchi, *Il Calcio* . . . pp. 49–55.

Papa, Antonio. "Le Domeniche di Clio: Origini e Storia del Football in Italia." *Belfagor* 2 (1988): 129–43.

Parker, Andrew, Mary Russo, Doris Sommer, and Patricia Yaeger, eds. *Nationalisms and Sexualities*. New York: Routledge, 1992.

Patterson, Orlando. "The Cricket Ritual in the West Indies." *New Society*, 23 (June 26, 1969): 988–89.

Paul, Sigrid. "The Wrestling Tradition and Its Social Functions." In Baker and Mangan, pp. 23–46

Peiffer, Lorenz. *Die Deutsche Turnerschaft*. Ahrensburg: Czwalina, 1976.

Penacchioni, Irene. "The Reception of Popular Television in Northeast Brazil." *Media, Culture, and Society*, 6:4 (1984): 337–41.

Perkin, Harold. "Teaching the Nations How to Play: Sport and Society in the British Empire and Commonwealth." *IJHS*, 6:2 (September 1989): 145–55.

Peterson, Harold. *The Man Who Invented Baseball*. New York: Scribner's, 1973.

Peverelly, Charles A. *The Book of American Pastimes*. New York: C. A. Peverelly, 1866.

Pieth, Fritz. *Sport in der Schweiz*. Olten: Walter Verlag, 1979.

Pivato, Stefano. "Il Pallone prima del Football." In Lanfranchi, pp. 19–30.

Pivato, Stefano. "Soccer, Religion, Authority: Notes on the Early Evolution of Association Football in Italy." *IJHS*, 8:3 (December 1991): 426–28.

Planck, Karl. *Fusslümmelei*. Stuttgart: Kohlhammer, 1898.

Provvisionato, Sandro. *La Sport in Italia*. Rome: Savelli, 1978.

Quirk, James and Rodney D. Fort. *Pay Dirt: The Business of Professional Team Sports*. Princeton: Princeton University Press, 1992.

Rachum, Ilan. "Futebol: The Growth of a Brazilian National Institution." *New Scholar*, 8:1–2 (1978): 183–200.

Rader, Benjamin G. *Baseball: A History of America's Game*. Urbana: University of Illinois Press, 1992.

Rail, Geneviève. "Technologie post-moderne et culture." In Landry et al., pp. 731–39.

Redmond, Gerald. "Imperial Viceregal Patronage: The Governors-General of Canada and Sport in the Dominion, 1867–1909." *IJHS*, 6:2 (September 1989): 193–217.

Reefe, Thomas Q. "The Biggest Game of All." In Baker and Mangan, pp. 47–78.

Reilly, Rick. "One to Remember." *Sports Illustrated*, 74:23 (June 17, 1991): 44–50.

Renson, Roland. "Le corps académique: la genèse de l'éducation physique universitaire en Belgique." *Stadion*, 17;1 (1991): 87–99.

Répertoire du mouvement olympique '93. Lausanne: Comité Olympique International, 1993.

Richter, Jörg, ed. *Die vertrimmte Nation*. Reinbek: Rowohlt, 1972.

Riefenstahl, Leni. *Memoiren*. 2 vols. Frankfurt: Ullstein, 1990–92.

Riesman, David. *Individualism Reconsidered*. Glencoe: Free Press, 1954.

Riess, Steven A. *City Games*. Urbana: University of Illinois Press, 1989.

Riess, Steven A. *Touching Base: Professional Baseball and American Culture in the Progressive Era*. Westport: Greenwood Press, 1980.

Riordan, James W. *Sport in Soviet Society*. London: Cambridge University Press, 1977.

Riordan, James W. "Tsarist Russia and International Sport." *Stadion*, 14:2 (1988): 221–31.

Ritterbach, Jürgen. "Die Geschichte des Basketballs in Deutschland von den Anfängen bis 1945." Cologne: Deutsche Sporthochschule, 1988.

Roden, Donald. "Baseball and the Quest for National Dignity in Meiji Japan." *American Historical Review*, 85:3 (June 1980): 511–34.

Rogers, Everett M. *Diffusion of Innovations*. 3rd ed. New York: Free Press, 1983.

Rogosin, Donn. *Invisible Men: Life in Baseball's Negro Leagues*. New York: Atheneum, 1983.

Rosenblum, Martin J. "Martial Arts Poetics." *Journal of American Culture*, 4:3 (Fall 1981): 148–53.

Ruck, Rob. *The Tropic of Baseball: Baseball in the Dominican Republic*. Westport: Meckler, 1991.

Rühl, Joachim K. "20th Century Amalgamation of British Games Traditions with Indigenous Social Concepts on the Trobriand Islands." Berlin: "Spiele der Welt-Welt der Spiele" Congress, 1993.

Rummelt, Peter. *Sport im Kolonialismus, Kolonialismus im Sport*. Cologne: Pahl-Rugenstein, 1986.

Rummelt, Peter. "Das sportpolitisches Erbe in Kolonialismus." In Andresen et al., pp. 18–33.

Rushin, Steve. "On the Road Again." *Sports Illustrated*, 79:7 (August 16, 1993): 18–27.

Saeki, Toshio. "Sport in Japan." In Wagner, pp. 51–82.

Said, Edward W. *Culture and Imperialism*. New York: Knopf, 1993.

Sandiford, Keith A. P. and Brian Stoddart. "The Elite Schools and Cricket in Barbados." *IJHS*, 4:3 (December 1987): 333–50.

Sands, Jack and Peter Gammons. *Coming Apart at the Seams*. New York: Macmillan, 1993.

Scherer, Karl Adolf. *Der Männerorden*. Frankfurt: Limpert, 1974.

Schiller, Herbert I. *Communication and Cultural Domination*. White Plains: M. E. Sharpe, 1976.

Schöffler, Herbert. *England, das Land des Sportes*. Leipzig: Tauchnitz, 1935.

Schröder, Ulfert. "Fussball in Brasilien." In Huba, pp. 57–64.

Schröder, Ulfert. "Fussball in Deutschland." In Huba, pp. 65–77.

Scotch, N. A. "Magic, Sorcery, and Football among Urban Zulu." *Journal of Conflict Resolution*, 5 (1961): 70–74.

Seiter, Ellen, Hans Borchers, Gabriele Kreutzner, and Eva-Maria Warth, eds. *Remote Control: Television, Audiences, and Cultural Power*. London: Routledge, 1989.

Seymour, Harold. *Baseball*. 3 vols. New York: Oxford University Press, 1960–90.

Shimizu, Shigeo, ed. *Civilization in Sport History* [sic]. Kobe: Department of Education-Kobe University, 1987.

Sie, Swanpo. "Sports and Politics: The Case of the Asian Games and the GANEFO." In Lowe, Kanin and Strenk, pp. 279–96.

Sinclair, Robert J. "Baseball's Rising Sun: American Interwar Baseball Diplomacy and Japan." *CJHS*, 16:2 (December 1985): 44–53.

Sissons, Ric and Brian Stoddart. *Cricket and Empire: The 1932–33 Bodyline Tour of Australia*. London: George Allen & Unwin, 1984.

Smith, Anthony. *The Geopolitics of Information*. New York: Oxford University Press, 1981.

Somers, Dale A. *The Rise of Sport in New Orleans, 1850–1900*. Baton Rouge: Louisiana State University Press, 1972.

Spalding, Albert G. *America's National Game*. New York: American Sports Publishing Co., 1911.

Spinetto, Horacio J. "Ciento Veinte Años de Rugby Argentino." *Todo Es Historia*, 25 (January 1992): 8–36.

Sport de France. Paris: Service de Presse, 1971.

Sportmuseum Berlin, ed. *Sport in Berlin* Berlin: Dirk Nishen, 1991.

St. Pierre, Maurice. "West Indian Cricket: Cultural Contradiction?" *Arena Review*, 14:1 (May 1990): 13–24.

Stebbins, Robert A. "Stacking in Professional American Football: Implications from the Canadian Game." *IRSS*, 28:1 (1993): 65–71.

Stell, Marion K. *Half the Race: A History of Australian Women in Sport*. North Ryde: Angus & Robertson, 1991.

Stoddart, Brian. "Caribbean Cricket." *International Journal*, 43:4 (Autumn 1988): 618–42.

Stoddart, Brian. "Cricket, Social Formation and Cultural Continuity in Barbados." *Journal of Sport History*, 14:3 (Winter 1987): 316–40.

Stoddart, Brian. *Saturday Afternoon Fever: Sport in the Australian Culture*. North Ryde: Angus & Robertson, 1986.

Stoddart, Brian. "Wide World of Golf: A Research Note on the Interdependence of Sport, Culture, and Economy." *SSJ*, 7:4 (1990): 378–88.

Stokvis, Ruud. "De Populariteit van Sporten." *Amsterdams Sociologisch Tijdschrift*, 15:4 (March 1989): 673–96.

Stokvis, Ruud. *De Sportwereld*. Alphen aan den Rijn: Samsom Uitgeverij, 1989.

Stokvis, Ruud. *Strijd over Sport*. Devanter: Van Loghum Slaterus, 1979.

Streck, Bernhard, ed. *Tradition, Migration, Notstand—Themen heutiger Sudanethnographie*. Göttingen: Edition Re, 1990.

Tanada, Shinsuke. "Diffusion into the Orient: The Introduction of Western Sports in Kobe, Japan." *IJHS*, 5:3 (December 1988): 372–76.

Terech, Michal. "Der 'Sokol' bei den slawischen Nationen." In Blecking, pp. 23–36.

Terret, Thierry. "A la recherche de l'identité Belge: le Capitaine Docx et la promotion d'éclecticisme." *Sport et Histoire*, 3 (1992): 81–101.

Thébaud, François. *Pelé*. Trans. Leo Weinstein. New York: Harper & Row, 1976.

Thibault, Jacques. *Sport et éducation physique, 1870–1970*. 2nd ed. Paris: Vrin, 1979.

Thomas, Jeevanandam P. "A Brief Historical Survey of Physical Education and Sports in India." In Überhorst, *Geschichte*, 6:199–214.

Thompson, Lee Austin. "The Modernization of Sumo as a Sport." Osaka: Osaka University, 1989.

Tomlinson, Alan and Garry Whannel, eds. *Off the Ball*. London: Pluto Press, 1986.

Tomlinson, Alan. "Going Global: The FIFA Story." In Tomlinson and Whannel, pp. 83–98.

Tomlinson, John. *Cultural Imperialism*. Baltimore: Johns Hopkins University Press, 1991.

Torres, Angel. *Historia del Béisbol Cubana, 1878–1976*. Los Angeles: Angel Torres, 1976.

Tracey, Michael. "The Poisoned Chalice? International Television and the Idea of Dominance." *Daedalus*, 114:4 (1985): 17–56.

Tunstall, Jeremy. *The Media Are American*. New York: Columbia University Press, 1977.

Überhorst, Horst. *Geschichte der Leibesübungen*. 6 vols. Berlin: Bartels & Wernitz, 1971–89.

Überhorst, Horst. "Leibesübungen in Altchina." In Überhorst, 1:110–27.

Überhorst, Horst. *Turner unterm Sternenbanner*. Munich: Heinz Moos Verlag, 1978.

Überhorst, Horst. *Zurück zu Jahn?* Bochum: Universitätsverlag, 1969.

Van Dalen, Deobold B. and Bruce L. Bennett, *A World History of Physical*

Education. 2nd ed. Englewood Cliffs: Prentice-Hall, 1971.

Varis, Tapio. "Global Traffic in Television." *Journal of Communication*, 24 (1974): 102–9.

Vera, Antonio. *El Fútbol en Chile*. Santiago: Editoria Nacional Quinmantú, 1973.

Vetö, Józef. *Sports in Hungary*. Trans. István Butykay. Budapest: Corvina Press, 1965.

Voigt, David Quentin. *American Baseball*. 3 vols. Norman: Univeristy of Oklahoma Press, 1966–1983.

Wagner, Eric A., ed. *Sport in Asia and Africa*. Westport: Greenwood Press, 1989.

Wahl, Alfred. *Les Archives du football*. Paris: Gallimard-Juillard, 1989.

Wahl, Alfred. *La Balle au pied: Histoire du football*. Paris: Gallimard, 1990.

Walker, Janet A. "On the Applicability of the Term 'Novel' to Modern Non-Western Long Fiction." *Yearbook of Comparative and General Literature*, 37 (1988): 47–68.

Wallerstein, Immanuel. *The Modern World System*. 3 vols. New York: Academic Press, 1974–89.

Walvin, James. *The People's Game*. London: Allen Lane, 1975.

Watanabe, Tohru. "The Why of the Japanese Choice of Baseball." In Shimizu, pp. 113–28.

Weber, Eugen. "Gymnastics and Sports in *Fin-de-Siècle* France." *American Historical Review*, 76:1 (February 1971): 70–98.

Wehrle, Arnold. *500 Jahre Spiel und Sport in Zürich*. Zurich: Verlag Berichthaus, 1960.

Weyand, A. M. and M. R. Roberts. *The Lacrosse Story*. Baltimore: Herman, 1965.

Whannel, Garry. *Fields in Vision: Television Sport and Cultural Transformation*. London: Routledge, 1992.

White, Philip G. and James E. Curtis. "Participation in Competitive Sport Among Anglophones and Francophones in Canada." *IRSS*, 25:2 (1990): 125–38.

White, Richard. "A Backwater Awash: The Australian Experience of Americanization." *Theory, Culture, and Society*, 1:3 (1983): 108–22.

Whiting, Robert. *You Gotta Have Wa*. New York: Macmillan, 1989.

Whitington, R. S. *An Illustrated History of Australian Cricket*. London: Pelham Books, 1974.

Wiese, Lothar. "Zur Geschichte des deutschen Turnens in Südamerika mit besonderer Berücksichtigung Brasiliens." In Überhorst, *Geschichte*, 6:954–75.

Wiese, Lothar. "Zur Sozialgeschichte des Deutschen Turnens in Südamerika." *Sozial- und Zeitgeschichte des Sports*, 2:2 (1988: 7–32.

Wilde, Simon. *Ranji*. London: Kingswood Press, 1990.

Williams, Raymond. *Marxism and Literature*. Oxford: Oxford University Press, 1977.

Wohl, Andrzej. *Die gesellschaftlich-historischen Grundlagen des bürgerlichen Sports*. Cologne: Pahl-Rugenstein, 1973.

Yelvington, Kevin A. "Ethnicity Not Out: The Indian Cricket Tour of the West Indies and the 1976 Elections in Trinidad and Tobago." *Arena Review*, 14:1 (May 1990): 1–12.

Young, David C. *The Olympic Myth of Greek Amateur Athletics*. Chicago: Ares, 1984.

Young, Percy M. *A History of British Football*. rev. ed. London: Arrow Books, 1973.

INDEX

Canada: *see* sports, modern: in Canada; sports, traditional: in Canada

Canadian Association of Baseball Players, 22

Canal Plus, 118

canoeing, 137

capitalism, 4, 175

capoeira, 159

Cardoso, Fernando Henrique, 5

Cardus, Neville, 38

Carey, Francis, 66

Caribbean World Series, 90-91

Carrasquel, Chico, 80

Cartwright, Alexander Joy, 72, 80

Cashman, Richard, 32, 39, 186-87

casting, 158

Castro, Fidel, 80

Castro, José Rafael de, 81

Cauto, El (baseball club), 87

Central Institute of Physical Education (Stockholm), 148

Central League (Japan), 79

Central Uruguay Railway Cricket Club, 60

Cervecería (baseball club), 87

Chandler, Albert, 86

Channel 4, 114, 116

Channel Nine, 95

Character-Building in Kashmir, 35

Charles University, 149

Chatelaine, La (football club), 44

Cheerleader Productions, 115

Chicago Bears, 116

Chicago Blackhawks, 176

Chicago Cubs, 74, 85, 94

Chicago White Sox, 85, 92

Chicago, University of, 78. 99

Chile: *see* sports, modern: in Chile

China: *see* sports, traditional: in China

Christianity, 24, 30, 34-36, 55, 67-68, 177; *see also* Young Men's Christian Association

Church Missionary Society Grammar School, 66

Cincinnati Reds, 82, 94

Cincinnati *Turngemeinde*, 154

Cinco Estrelles (baseball team), 80

Ciudad Trujillo (baseball club), 88-89

class: *see* social class, as a factor in sports participation

Clemente, Roberto, 80

Club Athlétique Brazzavillois, 67

Club de Gimnasia y Esgrima (Buenos Aires), 57

Club de Habana, El (baseball club), 81

Club Licey, El (baseball club), 87

Club Nacional, 60

Club Nuevo, El (baseball club), 87

cockfighting, 81

Cogswell, Joseph, 153

Colégio Militar (Mexico City), 84

Colegio Nacional, 59

Collège Chaptal, 51

Collège de Saint-Stansilaus, 45

Collège Saint-Bernard, 45

Collège Saint-Matherne, 45

colonialism: *see* imperialism, political and economic

Colón, María Cardidad, 129

Columbia University, 99, 113

Nigeria: *see* sports, modern: in Nigeria

NOC: *see* National Olympic Committees

Nordamerikanischer Turnerbund, 155-56

Norgren, Nels, 78

Northern Ireland: *see* sports, modern: in Northern Ireland

Nuevo Basket (Barcelona), 108

Nyren, John, 16

Obermann, Rodolfo, 147

Official Baseball Guide, 72

Old Caledonians (football club), 59

Olympia (film), 123

Olympiades Féminins, 104

Olympian Games, 121

Olympic Solidarity, 125

Olympics: ancient, 3, 122-23; modern: 3, 10, 62, 63 107, 120-38, 166, 183

Onesti, Giulio, 134-35

Orient Cricket Club, 32

Overbury, Thomas, 42

Owens, Jesse, 127

Oxford University, 17, 42, 50, 64, 113, 177

Pacific League (Japan), 79

Packer, Kerry, 95

Pagano, Ignazio, 54

Paige, Satchel, 88

Pais, El (Buenos Aires), 60

Palmer, Bruce, 105

Palmer, Gladys, 10

Palmer, Harry, 92

Pan-Britannic and Anglo-Saxon Festival, 121

Papa, Antonio, 53

Paramatta Patriots (baseball club), 94

Parsees, 32-33, 37

Paris Football Association Club, 50

Paris Football Club, 50

Parkin, George, 22

Parsons, Talcott, 120

Partido Nacional Revolutionario, 85

Pasquel, Jorge, 86

Patriote, Le (gymnastics club), 147

Patterson, Orlando, 31

Pelé: *see* Arantes do Nascimento, Edson

pelota, 137

Pennell, T. L. 34

Permanent General Assembly of National Olympic Committees, 136

Perry, Matthew, 75

Pershing, John, 105

Perth Heat (baseball club), 94

Peverelly, Charles, 172

PGA: *see* Permanent General Assembly of the National Olympic Committees

Philadelphia Athletics, 81

Philadelphia Cricket Club, 19

Philanthropen, 142, 153

Philippines: *see* sport, modern: in the Philippines

Phillips, Berge, 136

physical education: *see* education, physical

Designer: Andrea Ratazzi
Text: Berkeley
Compositor: CUP
Printer: Maple-Vail
Binder: Maple-Vail